D1523752

SOURCES OF SELF-EVALUATION

Murray Webster, Jr.
Barbara Sobieszek

SOURCES OF SELF-EVALUATION
A FORMAL THEORY OF SIGNIFICANT OTHERS AND SOCIAL INFLUENCE

A WILEY-INTERSCIENCE PUBLICATION

JOHN WILEY & SONS, New York • London • Sydney • Toronto

Library of Congress Cataloging in Publication Data:

Webster, Murray, 1941-
    Sources of Self-evaluation.

    "A Wiley-Interscience publication."
    Bibliography: p. 181
    1. Self-evaluation.   2. Interpersonal relations.
3. Influence (Psychology) I. Sobieszek, Barbara,
joint author. II. Title.

BF697.W36   155.2'5   74-5066
ISBN 0-471-92440-7

Printed in the United States of America

10 9 8 7 6 5 4 3 2 1

FOR JOSEPH BERGER

FOREWORD

A profitable scientific inquiry combines four qualities: a precise, systematic investigation is made of fruitfully conceptualized, fundamental processes. If the inquiry is imprecise, it will be unprofitable because its hypotheses are untestable. If it is unsystematic, it will be unprofitable because its results are isolated, fragmentary. If it is not fruitfully conceived, it leads not only to dead ends but wrong conclusions. If its process is not fundamental, if it is concerned only with the appearances of things, it explains very little. But the necessary combination is a delicate achievement; just how delicate is evident in the literature on the social self. The process of forming the self is fundamental. It has diverse and important consequences in diverse settings; it is crucial in many theories. But, although there is an abundant vein of speculation about the process, much of it fruitful, much of it is too vague to be empirically tested. The few attempts to render these formulations precisely have been important, but the resulting investigations have been mostly unsystematic. The even smaller number of investigations that have been both precise and systematic happen to think of the self in a way that is natural to common sense, but unfruitful. The literature, in fact, shows almost no example of a successful combination of all four qualities of profitable scientific inquiry.

It is for this reason that Webster and Sobieszek's *Sources of Self-Evaluation* must be regarded as an important contribution to the literature on the social self. It successfully combines the four qualities necessary to a profitable scientific inquiry. It is a precise, systematic investigation of the interactionist conception of the self.

The interactionist conception of the self, as everyone knows, makes the self social in origin: the self arises in social interaction. But the conception says a good deal more than this. It also makes the self relational and specific. (See particularly James, 1890, Ch. 10.) That is, self-evaluation is relative to the structure of the social situation. It matters both who the other is and what the situation requires. This is not, as a matter of fact, how common sense regards the matter, nor even how many sociologists regard it. The commonsense view is that the self, whether or not social in origin, becomes a trait of the individual personality. It therefore functions to produce the same behavior consistently in any situation, no matter who the other is or what the situation requires. This is not only the commonsense view of the self, it is also the view of many psychologists, even of many sociologists. Despite widespread obeisance to the memory of Mead and acceptance of the view that the self is somehow social, many students of the self regard it as reasonable to investigate self-esteem as a global personality trait. This conception is employed, for example, by Rosenberg in *Society and the Adolescent Self-Image* and Coopersmith in *Antecendents of Self Esteem*, the two most precise and sustained investigations yet to appear in the literature on the social self. This conception turns out to be unfruitful: It implies, for example, that individuals regarded as inferior by the larger society should in general regard themselves as inferior in any social situation. Blacks should have lower self-esteem than whites; lower class youth should have lower self-esteem than middle class youth. But the data consistently refute this hypothesis. (Cf. Coopersmith, 1967, Ch. 5; Heiss and Owens, 1972; McCarthy and Yancey, 1971; Rosenberg, 1965, Ch. 3; Yancey et al., 1972.) What exactly is it that the data refute? Rosenberg, Coopersmith, Yancey, McCarthy, all assume that inferiority in the larger society has little determining effect on self-evaluation. But from an interactionist point of view the data assume a quite different significance. The data imply not that inferiority in the larger society has no effect, but rather that it is meaningless to say a black or a lower class youth, or anyone else, feels inferior or superior no matter what the situation. Nor is this objection sheer speculation. There is empirical support for the view that blacks, for example, behave as if they felt inferior in biracial work groups requiring intellectual performance. (Cohen, 1972; Katz et al., 1958; Katz et al., 1964.) Furthermore, the effect depends on the fact that the whites in these situations believe the blacks to be inferior (Cohen and Roper, 1972). What the data imply, therefore, is not that status in society has no effect on self-esteem but that investigators have been putting the wrong question to the data. The wrong question was put to the data because an unfruitful conception of the self determined what questions were put. What one more reasonably concludes, I think, is that the interactionist conception of the self is a more fruitful conception.

The interactionist conception of the self is the real subject of Webster and Sobieszek's book. Their "self" is specific and relational; the central problem of the work is how others affect formation of this self, the whole sequence of experiments is concerned with what makes another significant. But many inter-actionists will not recognize the interactionism in this monograph because of its method. The method depends on the fact that fruitfulness is not enough. However fruitful, a rich vagueness permits one to think anything one likes whatever the evidence.

There are two reasons for this. First, if no precise meaning is given to its terms, a formulation readily equivocates. For example, a common hypothesis in the interactionist tradition is that individuals maximize self-evaluation. (See, among others, Goffman, 1959.) In the present book, this hypothesis is tested in several possible ways and is consistently disconfirmed. But the evidence is easily disregarded if one really wants to, for in the face of each disconfirmation the meaning of the hypothesis easily shifts to new ground untouched by the data. A sufficiently vague hypothesis can in fact always dismiss unfavorable evidence as irrelevant. Second, a vague formulation provides vague standards of relevance. In fact, usually everything is relevant. What this means, in practice, is that one is free to pick and choose what is relevant without constraint. But if one is free to pick and choose, one ought to eventually find something favorable to any hypothesis, if only by chance. For example, a quite common procedure is to search for some differences between populations that differ in self-esteem. Such differences are then regarded as consequences of differences in self-esteem. Having discovered such differences, they are readily claimed as support for the hypothesis that self-esteem has diverse and important consequences. But if nothing is said about what it is that should be different, if the consequences are sufficiently vaguely formulated, there is no doubt that this hypothesis will be confirmed. Not only is one free to disregard unfavorable evidence as irrelevant, one is also free to regard any evidence that agrees with (quite vague) expectations as relevant. Unfortunately, the same protection extends to all competing formulations. Hence, if all of them are sufficiently vague, all of them survive, and there is no discoverable way of choosing among them.

An explication of the interactionist conception of the self is therefore the starting point of Webster and Sobieszek's investigation. The self is made precise in terms of the evaluation of attributes; the other, in terms of capacities to evaluate; the consequences, in terms of the formation of performance expectations for self and other that, once formed, determine independence from influence. This explication is guided largely by Berger's theory of expectation processes (Berger et al., 1974). This is justified by findings such as Coopersmith's (1967, Ch. 3) which show that subjects who differ in self-esteem also differ markedly in confidence of success, faith in their judgment, participation in discussions, novelty and independence of judgment, and ease in forming social relationships. All but the last are differences in just those variables organized into a single, systematic conception by the Berger theory of expectation processes. Obviously, an explication of these lines omits a good deal; any explication does. Nothing is said about how opinions, as distinct from attributes, come to be evaluated; nothing is said about how cognitions, as distinct from evaluations, come to be formed; nothing is said about the consequences of affectual relations with the other, as distinct from the other's capacity to evaluate; nothing is said about consequences for the formation of social relations. Some interactionists may feel the price is too high. But the advantages are considerable. It becomes possible, given this explication, to capitalize on what is potentially one of the more fruitful aspects of the interactionist conception by making precise what it is that matters about the other. In the Cooley-Mead hypothesis the other matters, but what it is that matters about the other is suggested only vaguely. As a consequence, differences among others cannot be formulated. This is a serious shortcoming, for it forces one to suppose that all individuals care equally about the evaluations of all other individuals, which surely is false. Of course, one knows that somehow some individuals are significant and others are not. But in incorporating the Cooley-Mead hypothesis into theories in which self-evaluation is an important process, for example Zetterberg's theory of compliant actions (Zetterberg, 1957), the importance of differences in others, because one cannot formulate them, are necessarily neglected. One consequence is that the theory permits one to deduce that professors are as much influenced by what students think of them as students are by what professors think of them and professors conform more to the norms of students than students do to the norms of professors. That these hypotheses are refuted by the data (see, for example, Camilleri and Berger, 1967, or Berger and Conner, 1969) does not prove that others are not significant; it proves only the importance of knowing what it is that makes the other significant. That Webster and Sobieszek are able to provide some answers to this question is due to their particular way of explicating the interactionist theory.

Of course, this is not the first explication of the interactionist conception of the self. Miyamoto and Dornbusch (1956) gave one as well, and used it to infer specific research directives and define operations appropriate to their test; furthermore, with this much accomplished they were able to demonstrate the importance of what is, in the interactionist conception, the basic phenomenon to be investigated. This work was justly regarded as a major breakthrough. Unfortunately, fruitfulness and precision are not enough. It also matters what happens after the breakthrough. It matters because no single experiment is ever decisive by itself. A single experiment is never in itself decisive because, first, some of its conditions are inevitably unique. It employs particular instances of the general concepts that interest the investigator, it employs particular populations, it is done at a particular time in a particular place. Miyamoto and Dornbusch asked college students in the mid-fifties to evaluate intelligence, confidence, likeableness, and physical attractiveness. In theory, the particulars are inessential aspects of the process and should make no difference. Nevertheless, they may well contribute accidental features to the outcome of the experiment. But to distinguish accidental from essential features of any experiment requires more than one experiment. Second, accepting or rejecting any one hypothesis depends on assuming a rather large number of others; for example, assumptions about the nature of the initial conditions of the experiment, the behavior of the measuring instruments, the importance or unimportance of various conditions under which the hypothesis is tested. Pascal, for example, thought the Puy-de-Dôme experiment was a decisive rejection of the assumption that nature abhors a vacuum.

But to draw that conclusion, one must assume that air pressure is proportional to altitude above sea level, that the height of a column of mercury is proportional to the air pressure, and that it is absurd to reason that the tendency to abhor a vacuum is also proportional to the altitude above sea level. The experiment tests not one but all of these hypotheses. If, therefore, we conclude that the *horror vacui* is rejected by the Puy-de-Dôme experiment, it is because we have independent evidence, provided by other experiments, for the other assumptions we make—provided, for example, by such experiments as Torricelli's investigations of the barometer. Third, every experiment controls some variables for the purpose of investigating the consequences of others. To clarify how some particular aspect of the process works, both the situation in which the process takes place and other aspects of the process itself are held constant. Therefore, important questions always remain when the experiment is completed. In the case of Miyamoto and Dornbusch, for example, what determines which others are significant sources of evaluation? What is the effect of agreement vs. disagreement among multiple sources? How stable are the self-evaluations made by the subjects? What determines how stable they are? What are the consequences of high vs. low self-evaluation? What are the consequences of unstable self-evaluation? Under what conditions would one *not* find that self-evaluation was dependent on evaluations by others? There are, of course, many other questions one might ask, but the point at issue is that no one experiment will answer all of them. Not even a factorial experiment; not even the largest, most efficient factorial experiment even contrived. But if two or more experiments are always necessary, we depend for our understanding of a process on our ability to relate them. If no thought is given to how they are related, the problem of integrating the results into a coherent body of thought becomes serious. Nor is the relation of two experiments a natural outcome of just doing something, anything, that comes to mind. It is difficult to accomplish after the fact; it requires that some direction be given to a program, that the choice of problems, situations, and operations be constrained by what has gone before. A nice sense of novelty in the choice of problem, a nice freedom in the choice of operations and situations, and there is no reason to be surprised that our knowledge of the social self is fragmented, disjointed. It is, of course, possible to integrate such results after the fact, providing one is willing to pay a price. All that is required is a sufficiently judicious abstraction and selection. A rather exquisite example of what can be done in this line is found in Chapter 3 of the present book. But such selection is guided largely by taste. Taste is a considerable scientific virtue, but tastes may differ. What matters is finding a public and impersonal method of resolving such differences. But by this road we return to the fact that some subsequent experiment must be designed in a way constrained by what has gone before. Systematic investigation is as much a necessary condition of profitable scientific inquiry as fruitfulness or precision. There has been relatively little systematic about investigations of the self. (Jones' experiments are an exception, but this work, though in many ways carefully planned, suffers from a starting point so complex that most of it is spent trying to clarify the significance of the first experiment. See Jones, 1966; Jones, 1968; Jones and Pines, 1968; Jones and Ratner, 1967; Jones and Schneider, 1968.) The failure to show much sense of direction is what investigators are really complaining about when they complain of how little has been done and how little is known (cf. Coopersmith, 1967:19). A good deal, as a matter of fact, has been done. The problem is that it does not add up to a unified conception of the process.

The integration of a sequence of experiments is a problem that Webster and Sobieszek solve brilliantly. They begin their work with a study of the simplest possible situation: a single source of known competence to evaluate communicates positive or negative evaluations to two subjects who then work together to make decisions in a manner known to depend on how they have formed expectations for self and other. Two alternative models of this situation are tested, the evidence supporting the simpler of the two. The subjects accept a source if the source is competent to evaluate. They do not accept a source who is incompetent to evaluate, but the incompetent evaluator does not become a negative source—that is, one whose positive evaluations cause negative evaluations of the self or whose negative evaluations cause positive evaluations of the self. This simple starting point is thoughtfully chosen. They could, of course, have started with the intrinsically more interesting case of multiple sources of evaluation. But in that case they would be in some difficulty in trying to interpret the results. The results would depend in part on how a single source affects the formation of expectation-states and in part on the interaction effect of two sources. The interpretation would therefore depend on how much one knew about the effects of a single source, which in this case would be little or nothing. This difficulty is quite general: the interpretation of any complex situation depends on understanding some simpler one. On the other hand, the interpretation of simpler cases does not depend on what one knows about more complex situations. A sequence of experiments therefore has a predetermined starting point. It begins with the simplest case, which, once understood, permits the progressive complication of subsequent experiments. Webster and Sobieszek begin complicating their situation by relaxing the requirement that the source's competence to evaluate be directly known. Instead, competence to evaluate is inferred from status characteristics of the source. The effect is the some; moreover, it is not necessary that the status characteristic be directly relevant to the subject's task for this effect to occur. The way in which Webster and Sobieszek extend their formulation has two notable features. First, the task and interaction conditions of this experiment are identical to the conditions used to test the simpler formulation. This fact is important because it makes a precise comparison of the two experiments possible. Had the task and interaction conditions been different, this comparison would not have been possible. The fact that the experimental setting is standardized makes it possible to compare two quantities from two different experiments with the same confidence that one would feel in comparing two quantities from two conditions of the same experiment.* Second, the only initial condition that Webster and Sobieszek alter is the direct knowledge of the source's competence to evaluate. For example, there is still only one source of evaluations. This is important, again, if one intends to compare experiments. If there is a difference, it can be attributed to differences in knowledge of the source. If there is no difference, one can reasonably argue that the basis of one's knowledge makes no difference, as Webster and Sobiezsek in fact conclude in Chapter 6, because it is unreasonable to suppose that some compensating factor also varied at the same time, which would make the conclusion suspect. The need to compare experiments, then, implies both that one must standardize experimental settings and complicate situations one factor at a time. These two rules determine the next two experiments as well. In these experiments, the theory is extended to multiple sources of a known competence to evaluate. In them, two questions are considered. One has to do with the choice among sources; the other has to do with the effects of disagreement between sources if two are accepted. The experimental setting is in all other respects the same. It is again found that competence to evaluate determines relative acceptance of the two sources; and if two are accepted disagreements between them are resolved by alternating acceptance of their evaluations. That is, the self-evaluation of the subject is an average of the (positive and negative) evaluations made by the two sources. No tendency is found to distort perceptions of these evaluations in favor of positive evaluations.

An exquisite combination of fruitfulness, precision, and systematic investigation will not remove all difficulties in the way of accumulating systematic empirical knowledge of the self. The delicacy of the combination is not the only source of these difficulties, possibly not even the most important source. The subject is in a preparadigm stage of development (in the sense of Kuhn, 1962): there is no accepted definition of its problems, methods, or standards. A preparadigm field is necessarily arrested at a stage in which every new work begins all over again, restating basic foundations because these are in doubt and no work can go on without them. All discourse is forced back to first principles.

---

*Perhaps is should be pointed out that it is sufficient that the conditions be the same theoretically; it is not necessary that they be concretely identical. For example, two concretely different tasks that are both ambiguous binary choice decision-making tasks could be used, providing the scope of the theory is defined in terms only of these abstract properties.

If any research goes on at all, it typically is intended to demonstrate the existence and importance of a phenomenon; one can hardly go forward until this much is accepted. If further progress is made at all, it is questionable to all those who define progress by different standards. The standards themselves are established on nonempirical grounds: Therefore, no appeal to fact will resolve disputes about them and controversy persists; it goes on as if no work had been done at all. One can hardly expect the accumulation of systematic empirical knowledge under these conditions. But what one empirical investigation can accomplish, this one accomplishes. It offers new principles governing the process of self-evaluation; these principles are sufficiently precise to be empirically tested; our understanding of them is extended step by step in a way that, in the end, forms a single, systematic body of empirical knowledge. Not much more could be required of one monograph.

MORRIS ZELDITCH, JR.

Stanford University
Stanford, California

PREFACE

For the last six years our interest has centered around the ways in which individuals come to hold evaluations of self, and how they act on those evaluations. *Sources of Self-Evaluation* is the first major body of work in the area of self to offer an explicit theoretical formulation and to subject the formulation to repeated empirical tests, refining the original theory at each step. The selective summary of literature presented in the first chapters is by no means exhaustive; the self has long been of interest to sociologists, psychologists, and psychiatrists. Our selection was governed by prominent lines of thinking that influenced our own work; completeness was not attempted.

Succeeding chapters set forth the part of the theory to be refined or expanded, together with the experiment used to provide empirical data. In Chapter 9 we examine in the light of our data some of the common-sense literature about the maximization of self. In Chapter 10 the final version of the theory is presented, its relations to the self-concept literature noted, and its limitations explored.

Nobody works in an intellectual vacuum. We are fortunate to have associated with people whose intelligence and interest have been, by turns, inspirational, critical, supportive, helpful, enthusiastic, insightful, and concerned. It is never possible to thank everyone responsible for one's intellectual efforts, but those mentioned below deserve unusually great recognition for their help.

Anyone familiar with the work of Joseph Berger will recognize the importance of his theoretical orientation to our research. Morris Zelditch, Jr., contributed equally to our thinking, and both these men were extremely generous with their time and efforts on behalf of our work.

Bo Anderson read an early version of the manuscript; his suggestions clarified, simplified, and extended our original presentation. Doris Entwisle has worked closely with us on related research, and her suggestion resulted directly in the experiments and theoretical refinement reported in Chapter 8. M. Hamit Fisek gave generously of his advice and consolation at various stages of this work. Our co-experimenters are John Kervin, David Grafstein, Sue Bobrow, and Robert Pollard; their practical and intellectual contributions to the work are significant. Robert Sobieszek provided constant encouragement and support throughout, from the earliest formulation to the completed manuscript.

The research was funded by National Science Foundation grant GS 2169, Office of Education grant OEG-2-7-06160-2, and by funds from Stanford University, Johns Hopkins University, and the University of Rochester.

xvi   PREFACE

Eric Valentine of Wiley-Interscience has our gratitude for his early interest in the work and for his support at various stages of manuscript preparation. Without him, this book would not be a reality.

Sherry Seidel, Janet Terry, Ruth Lewis, and Joanne Yawitz prepared large portions of the manuscript and also kept abreast of numerous details associated with the book. We extend special thanks to them for this work.

Finally, we wish to express our gratitude to the hundreds of young men and women who served as subjects in these experiments. Without their help, the work would have been impossible; without them and people like them, there would be no reason to do the work. We hope they are pleased with the result.

MURRAY WEBSTER, JR.

Johns Hopkins University
Baltimore, Maryland

BARBARA SOBIESZEK

University of Rochester
Rochester, New York

CONTENTS

TABLES

FIGURES

SOURCES OF SELF-EVALUATION

INTRODUCTION

Two very different sets of ideas about the origins and the development of the self and the individual's awareness of himself have influenced most contemporary sociological and psychological thought. One of these, the notion of the *developmental* self, is the orientation adopted today by many psychologists, psychiatrists, and ethologists. According to this orientation, the self—which is roughly equivalent to the set of personal characteristics, or the "personality," of the individual— develops in a way similar to and heavily influenced by the biological growth of the body. From a core set of inherited instincts, psychic energy, a collective conscious (sometimes), and whatever personality predispositions one has at birth, the individual grows with unique traits, habits, attitudes, and values. Freud was a leading exponent of this view, which is illustrated by the following introduction to his system of personality:

> The id is the original system of the personality; it is the matrix within which the ego and the superego become differentiated. The id consists of everything psychological that is inherited and that is present at birth, including the instincts. It is the reservoir of psychic energy and furnishes all of the power for the operation of the other two systems. It is in close touch with the bodily processes from which it derives its energy. Freud called the id the "true psychic reality" because it represents the inner world of subjective experience and has no knowledge of objective reality. (Hall and Lindzey, 1957, pp. 32–33)

Development of the self is viewed as a process of maturation, the growth and channeling of all that the individual was born with. The individual, and the personality traits that he exhibits, are considered to result from an interaction between his innate predispositions and the environmental possibilities and influences afforded by his life circumstances.

> The ego comes into existence because the needs of the organism require appropriate transactions with the objective world of reality. . . . Its principal role is to mediate between the instinctual requirements of the organism and the conditions of the surrounding environment; its superordinate objectives are to maintain the life of the individual

1

and to see that the species is reproduced. (Hall and Lindzey, 1957, pp. 33, 35)

The third and last system of personality to be developed is the super-ego. . . . Its main concern is to decide whether something is right or wrong so that it can act in accordance with the moral standards authorized by the agents of society. (*Ibid.*, p. 35)

For us, the crucial feature of the developmental self orientation is the primacy of inborn needs and traits, the interpretation of maturation and growth as being essentially a modification of what has existed in the individual from birth. According to this orientation, an individual is born with a set of traits or, at the least, with a predisposition to develop certain traits. The end product, the visible personality and the self that is produced, is *at least* as dependent on this biological inheritance as it is on the social influences impinging on the individual and the interactions and experiences that he has.

An entirely different conception of the same processes may be termed the *social* self. Those who adopt this point of view (often called "environmentalists") stress the importance of contact with others for development of the personality. In extreme form, this viewpoint asserts that not only are others essential to the growth and the form of the resulting personality, but they are essential if indeed there is to be any self at all. Adherents to this orientation sometimes argue that there is no meaningful way to speak of the existence of a person or of his personality without reference to the shaping effects of his contacts with others.

At least two forms of environmentalist thought developed in twentieth-century social science. What came to be the earliest dominant form in American psychology, behaviorism, approaches personality development solely in terms of social learning: the individual is no more and no less than what he has been taught by others and what he has learned for himself through social experiences. Apparently in large measure behaviorism represented a reaction against elaborate psychoanalytic formulations, in particular, against the assumption of innate behavior predispositions and "instincts." A behaviorist approach stresses the assumption that human behavior may be studied or analyzed *as if* it were determined only by specifiable external influences: the individual is acted upon more than he acts; and when he does act, the action itself is understandable as a learned *re*action to external stimuli. In answer to the sometimes very emotional objections to this view of people, behaviorists point to the numerous successes of learning theories in accounting for a wide range of complex behaviors (see, e.g., Skinner, 1971).

A somewhat more complicated form of environmentalist thought developed through the writings of William James (1890), through Charles Horton Cooley (1902), George Herbert Mead (1934), and Harry Stack Sullivan (1947), to such contemporary figures as Erving Goffman and Carl Rogers. Like the behaviorists, these investigators reject the necessity for positing innate sources of behavior, primarily stressing the effects of the individual's social interaction in forming his personality. Unlike the behaviorists, however, the idea of a "self-concept" plays a crucial part in the environmentalists' explanations of observable behavior. The individual differs from inanimate objects studied in the natural sciences precisely because he possesses *self*-awareness, a *self*-consciousness that is affected by and in turn affects the social environment. To distinguish this approach from that of behaviorism, and at the same time to emphasize the central importance placed on self-consciousness and the self as mediator of interaction with the external world, it is helpful to give it a name. Writers in this tradition view humans as individuals who interact with one another primarily in terms of symbols— we threaten instead of actually hitting one another; we praise people instead of giving them material goods or love; we identify ourselves to one another in terms of our roles and status positions rather than simply as people. We call this the symbolic interactionist approach, or, simply, the interactionist approach.

As we have noted, ideas similar to those of the interactionist approach appear at least as far back as the writing of William James, but they are most frequently traced to Cooley and Mead. In Cooley's general principle, usually referred to as the idea of the "looking-glass self," a person's self-concept is considered to be dependent on observing the reactions and opinions of others toward the individual. In other words, the personality is formed, not partially, but wholly through the experiences the individual has interacting with others. Whatever traits he has, whatever motivations, drives, attitudes, and characteristic ways of behaving he displays, are taken to be explainable solely as the consequences of his previous interaction experiences with other persons. Significantly, the individual is thought to be *aware* of himself and of his actions, and he is seen as an active agent who exercises a degree of control over the actions he chooses.

Whether there is an original core of traits similar to the id usually remains undetermined; but it is clear that if such a core is believed to exist, it could be composed of nothing more important than a source of energy and a disposition to engage the world in physical activity.

It would be inaccurate to attribute to adherents to the developmental point of view a naive belief that interaction with others has no effect on the personality or the behavior of the individual, and it would be nearly impossible to find a supporter of such an extreme view. By contrast, at least among behaviorists, it is easier to find exponents of the extreme environmental view, which asserts that nothing of what we usually call personality, thought, or the self exists before the organism engages with others in interaction. In distinguishing the environmental from the developmental, the crucial factor seems to be whether the proponent believes that there is any point in investigating whatever inborn or biological differences an individual may possess in trying to understand his personality or to predict his behavior. Someone who does believe that this approach would be useful—for example, a psychologist attempting to determine whether there are innate racial differences in intelligence—is implicitly accepting at least part of what we have termed the developmental system of thought. Someone who would not entertain such a hypothesis as being meaningful, or someone who would not consider investigating the possibility of inborn traits having an important effect on an individual's attitudes or behaviors, is implicitly adopting part of what we call the environmental point of view. Mead made the following distinction between what he called "social" and the "individual" theories of mind:

> The difference between the social and the individual theories of the development of mind, self, and the social process of experience or behavior is analogous to the difference between the evolutionary and the contract theories of the state as held in the past by both rationalists and empiricists. The latter theory takes individuals and their individual experiencing—individual minds and selves—as logically prior to the social process in terms of them; whereas the former takes the social process of experience or behavior as logically prior to the individuals and their individual experiencing which are involved in it, and explains their existence in terms of that social process. (1934, pp. 222–223)

In this sense, it is a question of what is taken as given and what is to be explained in terms of the givens. From the environmental—especially the interactionist—point of view, the social network in which the individual acts is taken as given, and the characteristics of the individual are explained in terms of this network. From the developmental point of view, the individuals and their needs are given, and the social structure is explained as an adaptation of (*a*) the environment to those needs and (*b*) the conflicting needs of various individuals to one another.

Our purpose is not to try to resolve this issue, for it is at least partly metaphysical, thus ultimately not resolvable into a single correct answer. Nor do we wish to enter deeply into the many implications of adopting one of the viewpoints outlined. Rather, our intent is to indicate the intellectual context of the following work and to note that we are explicitly adopting one point of view—not the only possible point of view. We accept, and our work has been guided by, the set of ideas referred to previously as the orientation of the interactionist, or the social self. In what follows, we assume that whatever biological components there may be to the self and to the self-concept, they are not of primary interest here. Taken to be problematic—the matters to be investigated—are questions involving the social nature of the self and the individual's attitudes and behavior in social settings.

One immediate implication of this view is that the processes and the structure of interest are cognitive ones, that is, conscious. We are not concerned with equivalents of the psychoanalytic "unconscious," nor with information of which the individual is unaware, such as uncommunicated opinions of others. More-over, interest is directed toward ideas and behaviors that are centrally involved with the individual's self-conception. Such topics as habitual behaviors, uncon-ditioned reflexes, abilities, and motivations are excluded from study, except in-sofar as they can be directly related to the individual's self-concept.

If we adopt the interactionist point of view, we face three general questions, with many subdivisions, and the answers in large measure define our degree of understanding of the self. The first question is, What are the determinants of the self-concept and of variations in self-concept? The second is, What is the nature of the self-structure, and what determines its stability or changes? The third is, What are the consequences of the various possible "types" of self-concept? Problems involving the first set of questions, determinants of the self-concept, seek to specify the nature of the others with whom the individual interacts and who are important in affecting his self-concept, as well as processes through which their opinions of him become translated into his own thoughts. Problems involving the second set of questions, the nature of the self-structure, ask for a description of what develops through interactions and then influences future interactions. Problems involving the third set of questions, consequences of a given self-concept, are directed toward specifying behavioral effects of this struc-ture for future interaction with others.

We do not claim to have solved all the questions that could be asked of a pro-ponent of the social self point of view, nor do we claim to present a complete theory of the self. We do, however, hope to develop some of the major lines of thought within the interactionist view and to formulate explicitly the questions that others have raised and sought to answer both explicitly and implicitly. Be-yond this, we intend to indicate some significant issues that have not been re-solved satisfactorily and to offer some answers to them. The following work dem-onstrates our conviction that explicit theory is the only possible means to the understanding of phenomena, and we present successive versions of an explicit theory that offers an explanation for some of the substantively interesting and theoretically important problems that have arisen in previous work within the social self tradition.

Chapters 1, 2, and 3 constitute brief, focused summaries of three lines of the-oretical and empirical endeavor that have influenced our own work. Chapter 1 introduces classical theoretical treatments of the self; Chapter 2 summarizes the empirical work in this tradition that is most relevant to our own theoretical re-search program; and Chapter 3 describes the orientation of expectation states theory, from which our theoretical formulation and experimental research pro-gram descends. Readers already familiar with the literature in these fields may wish to go directly to Chapter 4, which is the beginning of our own work.

CHAPTER ONE

THROUGH THE LOOKING GLASS

Self-concept—who an individual thinks he is and the unique traits he believes himself to possess—is at the core of virtually all issues in social psychology. The individual is acted upon by his environment, and specific effects of the environment are mediated by his interpretation of them and how he thinks they are meaningful *to him*. The individual also acts on his environment, and his actions are partially determined by the kind of person he thinks he is, or wants to be.

Similar statements can be made regarding the determinants and the consequences of the self-concept: to a sociologist, the self-concept is determined by environmental influences (mediated by whatever self-concept already exists), and the self-concept in turn is a major determinant of the individual's action within and upon his environment (mediated by whatever possibilities the environment presents). These observations are not novel by this time, and until one begins to describe specifically *how* the self and the environment interact, they are not likely to arouse intellectual dispute, or even much excitement.

But beyond the broad strokes of what we agree "everybody knows" lie considerable areas in which we know surprisingly little. From what precise point in the environment does self-concept come, and just how does it form from external information? Exactly what kinds of consequence for behavior does a particular type of self-concept entail? Although we sometimes have no idea how to answer the more precisely formulated questions about the self, most often we think we know the answer or that the answer has already been provided. But different intelligent and informed investigators offer several intelligent and knowledgeable speculations, and clear-cut empirical (or logical) support is unavailable. With the existing variety of judgments regarding which precise questions ought to be asked and how to go about answering them, have come a corresponding variety of isolated research findings and theoretical assertions. In some cases it is possible to discern common intellectual threads between investigations, in some cases it is possible to formulate the questions that must be asked to fill the gaps between investigations, and in some cases it is impossible to fit knowledge into any comprehensive scheme.

Why should this be true of a subject that has enjoyed the sustained interest of social psychologists for three-fourths of a century? We believe that the vagueness of terminology used by writers in the social self tradition is responsible both for the immediate intuitive appeal of their ideas and for the lack of agreement among writers about "what we know." Paradoxically, if one allows the meanings of terms and assumptions to shift among writers and in various social situations, almost any piece of evidence either confirms the writer or is irrelevant to his argument—depending, of course, on the biases of the reviewer. If one does not define concepts explicitly, anything at all *could* be an instance of them. If assumptions are hinted at, given by analogy, or completely unstated, they appear to contain truth to those already committed; and they are wrong or incomprehensible to critics. Although the early theorists in the social self tradition were brilliant men with profound insights, their work must be regarded as a starting point. Contemporary understanding of the self has been foreshadowed—but *only* foreshadowed—by the ideas reviewed briefly in this chapter. Succeeding chapters consist of increasingly detailed specification of the concepts and the assertions broadly outlined here.

Sociological interest in self-concept is usually traced to the writings of Cooley, especially to what has come to be called the "looking-glass self" idea:

> In a very large and interesting class of cases the social reference takes the form of a somewhat definite imagination of how one's self—that is, any idea he appropriates—appears in a particular mind, and the kind of self-feeling one has is determined by the attitude toward this attributed to that other mind. A social self of this sort might be called the reflected or looking-glass self:
>
> > "Each to each a looking-glass
> > Reflects the other that doth pass."
>
> As we see our face, figure, and dress in the glass, and are interested in them because they are ours, and pleased or otherwise with them according as they do or do not answer to what we should like them to be; so in imagination we perceive in another's mind some thought of our appearance, manners, aims, deeds, character, friends, and so on, and are variously affected by it. (Cooley, 1902, pp. 183–184)

Furthermore, the looking-glass self is tempered by the individual's knowledge of the others and, in some sense, by his assessment of them:

> The thing that moves us to pride or shame is not the mere mechanical reflection of ourselves, but an imputed sentiment, the imagined effect

of this reflection upon another's mind. This is evident from the fact that the character and weight of that other, in whose mind we see ourselves, makes all the difference with our feeling. We are ashamed to seem evasive in the presence of a straightforward man, cowardly in the presence of a brave one, gross in the eyes of a refined one, and so on. We always imagine, and in imagining share, the judgments of the other mind. (*Ibid.*, pp. 184–185)

The significance Cooley assigns to the individual's assessment of the other in this passage seems to come from an implied comparison of the self with the other. Although it is difficult to be certain about the precise *kind* of importance Cooley attaches to the nature of the other, it is clear that he does not intend to suggest that all others with whom the individual interacts are equal in determining his self-concept.

A third major contribution made by Cooley is the notion of what might be called an "internalized other." Through interaction, the individual comes to develop a mental image of others with whom he interacts:

[I] do not see how any one can hold that we know persons directly except as imaginative ideas in the mind. These are perhaps the most vivid things in our experience, and as observable as anything else, though it is a kind of observation in which accuracy has not been systematically cultivated. . . .

I conclude, therefore, that the imaginations which people have of one another are the *solid facts* of society, and that to observe and interpret these must be the chief aim of sociology. I do not mean merely that society must be studied *by* the imagination—that is true of all investigations in their higher reaches—but that the *object* of study is primarily an imaginative idea or group of ideas in the mind, that we have to imagine imaginations. (*Ibid.*, pp. 120–122)

The internal image may be a distortion of reality, and the conceptualization does not specify whether the internal image is stable or changing, nor the determinants of its stability or change. However, the conceptualization is clearly cognitive; the way in which the individual interprets and reacts to the perceptions of others is not solely a behavioristic reflex. Cooley implies that there is a conscious awareness, and that this awareness determines both how the individual reacts to others and the looking-glass self-image he holds.

Mead modified and extended the ideas of Cooley, introducing the concept of the "generalized other," which is prominent in most contemporary discussions of the looking-glass self. Mead was concerned with the processes by which a child learns to see himself as an object; in other words, how he develops a consciousness of self:

> We were speaking of the social conditions under which the self arises as an object. In addition to language we found two illustrations, one in play and the other in game, and I wish to summarize and expand my account on these points. . . .
>
> The fundamental difference between the game and play is that in the latter [actually, both the last phrase of this sentence and later passages make clear that this should read in the *former* . . .—W. & S.] the child must have the attitude of all the others involved in that game. The attitudes of the other players which the participant assumes organize into a sort of unit, and it is that organization which controls the response of the individual. The illustration used was of a person playing baseball. Each one of his own acts is determined by his assumption of the action of the others who are playing the game. What he does is controlled by his being everyone else on that team, at least in so far as those attitudes affect his own particular response. We get then an "other" which is an organization of the attitudes of those involved in the same process. (Mead, 1934, pp. 153–154)

This passage implies that it is impossible to interact with an other unless the individual is able to put himself in the second person's place, to imagine very accurately how the other is about to act. An illustration involving a physical act makes this especially easy to see: a player cannot catch a baseball unless he can anticipate the actions and the intentions of the person throwing it.

Mead's choice of examples and his reference to children's games prompts us to ask whether he considered the self to be an "automatic" and behavioristic set of responses or whether he posited a conscious thought process as governing actions. Elements of both points of view appear in the passage just quoted. Certainly a person could learn to play baseball very well without ever consciously directing his movements; in fact, the player who has to think about every movement before his body makes it will not be able to respond quickly enough to play the game well. Although it is less clear that more symbolic social intercourse could be carried on through a series of conditioned reflexes, at least in principle it seems possible that an individual with a large enough repertoire of behaviors could get by. Much social interaction—especially role-determined behaviors and polite gestures—has become so routine that it requires virtually no thought.

On the other hand, use of the term "attitudes" seems to imply a consciousness on the part of the individual. Since social interaction requires the imagining of future actions of others, it is difficult to see how such interaction could proceed without a consciousness that manipulates images and then decides which of the set of possible future actions to take. Consistent with this is a reference to "internal conversation of the individual with himself in terms of words or significant gestures" (155), which would be impossible from a behavioristic standpoint. Thus, although Mead did not directly address the issue of consciousness versus behaviorism, and although there are some passages consistent with either point of view, on the whole it seems reasonable to conclude that he considered the individual's self to be a cognitive process.

Central to Mead's conception of development of the self is the "generalized other," or the attitudes of the entire set of others with whom the individual interacts: "The organized community or social group which gives to the individual his unity of self may be called "the generalized other." The attitude of the generalized other is the attitude of the whole community. . . ." (1934, p. 154).

From this and later passages it is not possible to be certain exactly how Mead conceptualized the generalized other—whether it is a weighted averaging of the attitudes of all the others with whom the individual interacts, or whether it requires a unanimous community opinion of the specific issue. Apparently this question did not seem particularly important to Mead, for he did not address it directly. We note it because the question of what happens when others disagree in their opinions of an individual is an important theoretical issue that is confronted in later chapters.

However, in at least two important ways the concept of the generalized other extends the idea of the looking-glass self. First, it emphasizes the importance of the social context of self-referent ideas. The individual thinks about himself in categories determined by his social groups, and probably he also applies to himself standards of comparison derived from the range of variation he sees in others.

Second, Mead's discussion of the generalized other and of the importance of the individual's perception of himself in such a context, suggests the idea of social roles, with the individual developing an awareness of the social role he plays within the community. Since the idea of role implies the possibility of various social roles—thus the likelihood that an individual will adopt different roles at different times or within different contexts—the way is opened for one to consider a multiplicity of selves and of self-references.

A final and very important contribution of Mead to the looking-glass self is the idea of a kind of permanence of structure, or a partial resistance to change in the self. The images in Cooley's looking glass could be perfectly malleable, with the individual's self-conception dependent solely on the "reflection" of those with whom he is in immediate contact. Of course such instability is intuitively implausible, and has in fact been empirically disconfirmed, as discussed later. The concept of the self as possessing a semipermanent structure is outlined as follows:

> We want to distinguish the self as a certain sort of structural process
> in the conduct of the form, from what we term consciousness of ob-

jects that are experienced. The two have no necessary relationship. . . .
I do not now want to discuss metaphysical problems, but I do want
to insist that the self has a sort of structure that arises in social conduct
that is entirely distinguishable from this so-called subjective experience of these particular sets of objects to which the organism alone has
access—the common character of privacy of access—does not fuse
them together. (Mead, 1934, pp. 165, 166–167)

That a *semipermanent structure* is built up through the experiences of acting and
being acted upon has two important implications. First, the self is no longer
conceived of as changing with every change in the individual's social environment. Presumably the self is in some measure sensitive to such modifications
(or it would never change as the result of changing experiences); but it does
not change instantly and completely, even if the information coming in from
others changes character radically within a short period of time.

Second, the development of a structure as the result of interaction implies
that the effect of future interaction may not be completely equivalent to the
effect of earlier interaction. Let us consider the illustrative case of an individual
whose work has been praised highly by others and who therefore comes to see
himself as possessing high ability at the task. Once he comes to view himself as
possessing high ability at the task, the effect of further praise (or condemnation)
from others will be different from what it would have been before the individual
came to think he had high ability.

Mead's idea of the self in the social context appears in similar form in the
writing of William James, especially in his discussions of the social self:

A man's Social Self is the recognition which he gets from his mates. . . .
Properly speaking, a man has as many social selves as there are individuals who recognize him and carry an image of him in their mind. . . .
But as the individuals who carry the images fall naturally into two
classes, we may practically say that he has as many different social
selves as there are distinct *groups* of persons about whose opinion he
cares. He generally shows a different side of himself to each of these
different groups. (James, 1890, pp. 294–295)

This passage makes explicit what Mead hinted at—the idea that the individual
may be thought of as having several selves, and that these selves vary with the
particular social context in which the individual finds himself. By extension, it
could be inferred that the individual's self-concept also changes with changes
in the social context; thus not only does he appear as several slightly different
people at different times, but also he conceives of himself as being several different people, or at least he thinks of himself in several distinctly different ways.
This point enables us to speak of situational determinants of various selves. For

example, if we are interested in the individual's level of self-evaluation, it becomes necessary to assert that one individual has several different self-evaluations, dependent on what he is doing and with whom.

A final important concept in the tradition of the looking-glass self is that of a "significant other," a term attributed to Sullivan (1947). Since Sullivan was primarily concerned with socialization of the infant and the child, his application of the term was restricted to parents: significant others are those instrumental in training the child in the attitudes and behaviors necessary for becoming an adult. However, use of the term has gradually been extended to include all those who are instrumental in forming the individual's self-concept. In this sense, a significant other is one whose opinions and actions "matter" to the individual, one whose esteem he values, and whose disapproval he seeks to avoid. Thus it is more self-enhancing for a child to have his work praised by the teacher than by the class dunce, more pleasing to be complimented by a person known to have taste than by an obvious boor, more satisfying to win an award in a national contest than in a local one. This is the central idea that is developed formally in the theory presented and extended in this book.

Our selective review of the writings of various authors reveals the remarkable similarity of most of the central ideas of the social self, and, very often, anticipation by one writer of the developed ideas of another. Indeed, this similarity of thought makes it possible for later researchers, including ourselves, to use the ideas of the social self and to develop a common conceptualization of the processes and the structures involved.

First, we explicitly adopt the interactionist perspective, which asserts that the important influences on the self-concept are social ones and that the important problems are therefore those of learning the social determinants and the social consequences of self-concept. From Cooley comes the central perspective of the looking-glass self—the idea that one's self-concept is directly dependent on the opinions and actions of others. This idea is modified by the consideration that the individual may not correctly perceive the opinions of others and that he will interpret the significance of others' opinions in the light of what he knows of those others.

The second set of ideas, from Mead, involves the concepts of the generalized other and the self-structure. The generalized other places the individual self within a social context, where he plays a role in a community; moreover, it is implied that he may play several different roles within several social contexts. According to the idea of a semipermanent self-structure, the individual does not keep changing his self-image to conform perfectly with the image of him held by whoever he happens to be with at the moment and, implicitly, not only his assessment of the other but his assessment of himself will enter into his interpretation of a given opinion from an other with whom he interacts.

The third set of ideas comes from James and from Mead, and they constitute an attempt to recognize that not all others are equally important in determining the self. Sullivan's "significant other" does not appear to differ in any important way from the other that Mead spoke about, but use of the term draws attention to the possibility of distinguishing significant from nonsignificant others. In terms of specifying the determinants of a self, it becomes crucial to explicate the concept of the significant other and to explain its precise significance in determining the self-image.

Early theorists in the social self tradition were primarily concerned with the first two questions formulated in our introduction: determinants of the self, and the nature of the self-structure. The third set of questions, consequences of particular types of selves, has of necessity been investigated by empirical researchers within this tradition, to whose work we now turn.

CHAPTER TWO

THE SELF–EVALUATION RESEARCH

Within the past twenty years, a substantial number of the empirical studies reported have been based on the theoretical ideas of Cooley, Mead, and others presented in Chapter 1. Some research attempts more or less direct tests of these ideas, and other work focuses on ways of effecting change in self-concept or on selected aspects of self-concept. In this chapter we summarize some representative studies, selecting features of them that form some of the grounds for the theory of sources of self-evaluation outlined in Chapter 4.

Many of those attempting tests of the social self ideas note that the core ideas appear to be relatively straightforward until one tries to make them operational and to conduct empirical research. Then it becomes clear that although the ideas of Cooley and Mead possess considerable intuitive appeal, their generality and broadness of scope do not provide sufficient research directives. Some simplifications and operational assumptions must be added before empirical tests can be undertaken. Beginning with the work of Miyamoto and Dornbusch (1956), attempts to render such ideas operational have become more frequent, more precise in their predictions, and more determinate in their results.

The most interesting features of self-concept, at least to students of social and psychological behavior, are the evaluative aspects. How good the individual thinks he is at given specific tasks, how well he thinks he performs "most things," and even whether he considers himself to have a generally "successful life," receive virtually the total attention of social science. Other self-referent ideas—such as whether the individual regards himself as a child of God or as an advanced animal—are relegated to such primarily nonempirical disciplines as religion or metaphysics. James and Cooley in particular emphasized the evaluative aspects of the self.

If theorists have implicitly focused attention on self-evaluations, this emphasis is quite explicit in most of the empirical research. A major reason for the stress on evaluations appears to be a practical one; namely, to make possible empirical measurement and objective verification. An evaluation may be high or low, good or bad; but these categories are inadequate for describing nonevaluative types of self-referent ideas. Nearly all empirical studies in the looking-glass self tradition focus exclusively on evaluative aspects of the self.

In addition, many empirical studies focus on conceptions of abilities rather than opinions. Again the reason is probably one of measurement: it is certainly easier to measure actual abilities than actual opinions; a person's conception of his abilities is much more readily assessed than his conception of his opinions. There is no reason, however, to suppose that the looking-glass self idea is inapplicable when measurement is difficult; nor must we assume that empirical support is in principle unobtainable.

Research represented here does not exhaust all empirical research concerned with the self—that would be an enormous task, and the result would be of little use to anyone except a beginning student of the field. In particular, we have omitted research from the field of clinical psychology, which often deals with the discrepancy between ideal and actual self, and several types of studies with designs too complicated to permit unambiguous interpretation of results.

In general, two criteria are employed in selecting the studies represented here. First, these are the studies in the literature that are chiefly concerned with evaluative aspects of self-concept and thus present their findings as quantitative data. Second, especially for the more recent research, we have selected studies conducted in highly controlled settings, such as the experimental laboratory. This criterion reflects a desire to avoid possible alternative interpretations of the data, but it also reveals a desire to avoid studies whose results involve factors that are not part of the social self conceptualization. For example, studies of children's self-concept, and especially changes in self-concept through the years in the school system, often report the effects of reference group pressures, distortion of responses on the self-concept measures used, the effects of unknown but presumably influential experiences of success and failure on the global self-concept, and other factors of importance to a particular setting.

Early Research. The first studies in the social self tradition sought to test the basic idea that self-evaluation is dependent on the opinions of others. In terms of the three sets of questions we formulated, these early studies addressed the second: the nature of the self-evaluation structure held by individuals. One of the clearest of the early studies was reported by Miyamoto and Dornbusch (1956). Taking this work as a prototype of research into the self-structure, we discuss the research in some detail, then briefly describe modifications of design and extensions of the findings produced by later, related studies.

Subjects were college students, members of four different living groups or of six different classes ranging in size from 8 to 48 persons. They were asked to rate themselves repeatedly on a set of four characteristics: intelligence, self-confidence, physical attractiveness, and likeableness. The first self-rating was to be the subject's actual perception of himself, the second was to be his perception of the ratings that each other member of the group would give him, and the third was to be his perception of the way "most persons" (an operational measure of the generalized other) would view him. In addition, each subject was asked to rate every other member of his own group, thus yielding a measure of the actual rating of each subject by every other member of his group (comparable to the second self-rating).

Data show strong support for the following predictions. First, the self-rating is quite close to the actual rating of the individual by other members of his group. This finding demonstrates the effects of others' responses on determining the individual's self-perception. Second, the self-rating is close to the *perceived* rating by others, and this association is closer than the association of self-rating and *actual* rating by others. This helps to explicate the relation between perception of others' responses and self-conception. Since self-rating is found to be closer to the perceived rating by others than to actual rating by others, we have data consistent with an interpretation that some distortion and inaccuracies exist in perception and interpretation of others' responses to the individual. The third finding is that individuals' self-ratings are closely related to the perceived rating by "most people" and that this association is even closer than the association between self-rating and perceived rating by other members of the specific membership group. This illustrates the great significance of perceived opinions of the internalized generalized other; the investigators report: "Essentially, the results show that self-conception and generalized other are usually given the identical rating." (256)

Beyond interpretations of data made by the authors, we note two additional points. First, the measures used of the self-concept in this work are of the type referred to earlier as evaluative; they are aspects of the self-concept that can be scaled from high to low. Although it is unlikely that such attributes as physical attractiveness and self-confidence would be termed abilities, they are clearly evaluative—they are present in an individual *to a degree*, and it would probably be possible to elicit some consensus on the amount of each possessed by an individual. Second, these authors, like many later investigators, implicitly focus on the subjects with high self-evaluations. Hypotheses are phrased in terms of individuals with high self-ratings; for example, "The mean of the perceived responses of others will be higher for those persons with a high self-rating than for those with a low self-rating." The same kind of hypothesis presumably would be made for those with low self-ratings, but several factors may operate to complicate and to obscure the picture in such cases. Some later investigators concern themselves with issues involved for low self-ratings, and we return to this problem in summarizing their work and in our own research, reported later.

Moore (1964) conducted a similar study on a different population and using a different set of characteristics. His sample consists of married couples who were asked to use a set of personality trait items to (1) "describe yourself," (2) "describe your spouse," and (3) "describe yourself as you think your spouse would describe you."

Major findings of the study are as follows. First, the self-description is in positive agreement with actual description by the spouse, but *more* in agreement with the individual's *perception* of the description by the spouse. This finding replicates one of the central findings in the Miyamoto-Dornbusch study.

Second, comparison of agreement with perceptions of positive and negative descriptions shows a higher level of agreement between perception of others' opinions and self-description for positive overall descriptions than for negative overall descriptions. No equivalent of this finding is examined by Miyamoto and Dornbusch, and therefore it constitutes an extension of their predictions and findings. (The suggestion that individuals will manipulate their own perceptions of others' evaluations to enhance the self-image is made frequently in the empirical and theoretical literature. We examine this assertion more directly in Chapter 9.)

Third, based on the earlier conjecture that the greater effect of the generalized other (as compared with the effect of a specific group member's opinions) is due to the greater number of members of a generalized other, Moore hypothesizes that the individuals in his sample who have greater extensity of interaction should show a greater discrepancy between perception of spouse's opinions and self-description. When discrepancy scores for females who were employed outside the home were compared with discrepancy scores from unemployed females, the hypothesis was confirmed: discrepancy between spouse's perceived description and self-description was greater for employed than for unemployed females. In terms of increasing determinacy of the social self idea, Moore's third finding is particularly significant, for it helps, in at least a preliminary way, to designate an additional determinant of the effect of others' opinions on the self: the number of others with whom the individual has interaction appears to be inversely related to the degree of influence the opinions any single one of those others will have.

A third study, preceding the Moore study chronologically but logically following it, is reported by Reeder et al. (1960). Subjects were 54 enlisted men at a military base who were members of nine work groups consisting of 5 to 7 members. Each man ranked the members of his group, including himself on two criteria: leadership and "most efficient and useful worker." Next, he estimated the rankings that each of the other men in his group would make. From these questions the investigators obtained information on (1) self-rank, (2) objective group rank, and (3) estimated, or subjective, group rank.

Data support the following hypotheses. First, two of the Miyamoto-Dornbusch findings are replicated: the men with high self-rank actually are ranked higher by others than those with low self-rank; and those with high self-rank perceive that they are ranked higher by others than those with low self-rank.

Second, the authors hypothesize and the data confirm that those with a high subjective group rating receive an objective group rating higher than that given to those with a low subjective group rating. (Although the idea is certainly consistent with ideas in the social self, it is difficult to understand why the authors choose to formulate it in this manner; the support found for it could equally well be interpreted as showing that individuals are fairly accurate in perceiving the objective rating given them by others.)

Other findings in this study reveal an inconsistent pattern of correspondence between the three rankings. In some cases the lack of correspondence could be explained by postulating a tendency to misperceive low ratings from others, as Moore found; in other cases, no satisfactory simple explanation is available.

Following a line of reasoning similar to Moore, Reeder and his colleagues speculate that the inconsistent results might be due to extensity of interaction. To examine this idea, they hypothesized that persons whose self-ratings disagree with the objective group rating of them have recourse to a greater number of reference groups. They constructed an index of the number of significant reference groups, using the following variables to indicate alternatives: education, marital status, urban or rural background, age, and military rank. Those with more education, married, from urban backgrounds, older, and of higher rank are presumed to have access to a greater number of alternative reference groups.

When the sample is divided into those with a large and a small number of alternative reference groups and those showing a large or a small amount of disagreement between the objective group rank and self-ranking, support is found for the hypothesis: persons whose self-ratings disagree with the ratings assigned to them by the group are more likely to have a greater number of alternative reference groups available. Also, this finding is not limited to those whose self-ranking was higher than the objective group rank; it is true of the entire sample. Thus an explanation based simply on a hypothesized desire to maximize the self-evaluation is inadequate.

The analysis by Reeder et al. represents an attempt to make operational the idea of a significant other—an other who is more important than most in determining the individual's self-concept. However, it is not clear from their analysis whether the differential importance of others was a function of the availability of others, as an extensity argument would propose, or whether an other factor could be more important. One factor not explicitly considered by these authors is the evaluative competence that may have been assigned by individuals to members of their work groups and to alternative others. Examination of the categories used to construct the index of extensity for this analysis shows that these categories could plausibly be assumed to classify individuals on whether they were willing to grant members of their work group the right to evaluate them. For example, compare an individual who has a high school education and is from an urban background with a younger individual, possessing less than a high school education, coming from a rural background, and having lower rank. It is plausible that the first individual will be less likely to believe that members of his work group are competent to evaluate his performance. Or, more precisely, he may have thought that by comparison to those in his alternative groups, members of his work group are less competent to evaluate him, thus he will pay less attention to their opinions in his own self-rating. The greater discrepancy shown by the older, higher-ranked man between his self-rank and the objective rank by others, as well as the greater discrepancy between his self-rank and the subjective rank by others, could also be attributed to his unwillingness to grant those work group others the right to evaluate his performance.

If this reasoning is correct, it would not be proper to include marital status in the index, for although it does address an extensity idea, it has no clear relation to perceived competence to evaluate work group performance. Omitting marital status from the index, and observing whether the new index could enable even better predictions of the discrepancy than the old index, could provide useful information for future discrimination between extensity and evaluative competence for these data.

We may also consider the characteristics possessed by alternative others to whom some individuals in this study had access. With the exception of marital status, these alternative others most likely were either higher in demonstrated ability at some kinds of task—for example, college—or were of higher status than the members of the work group—for example, military rank or age. We may conjecture from this study that others of higher perceived ability or of higher status are more likely to become significant others than those of lower perceived ability or low status. The data presented do not allow us to test this conjecture; moreover, there is no satisfactory explanation of why either ability or status should affect likelihood of becoming a significant other. But implicit acceptance of the idea that significant others must have either high status or high ability is reflected in other studies, and later we offer a theoretical explanation for this assumption.

The investigations just cited are representative of many other basic applications of ideas of the social self. These studies generally agree in the results that the self-evaluation is a direct function of (perceived) opinions of others, that such others may not be equally important to the individual, and that individuals may misperceive the others' opinions. Sometimes it appears that the distortion is in the direction of a more favorable self-evaluation, but this is by no means always the case.

Formation and Change of Self-Evaluation.   Preceding studies were concerned primarily with describing the *structure* of the self. Turning now to problems of formation, stability, and change, we find a second set of studies taking as an adequately demonstrated assumption that the self is a function of others' opinions. These investigations into the processes and determinants of change in an existing self-conception are relevant to our first set of questions, *determinants* of the self-evaluation structure.

Our prototype of the formation and change studies is an ingenious experiment by Israel (1956). Subjects were 107 students, members of four different classes at a college for physical education in Sweden. Each class was divided into two experimental groups of approximately 16 to 18 subjects, well acquainted with one another. (Exclusions due to absences diminished some groups by an unreported amount.) Each group member was administered a questionnaire on which the subject was to rank all members including himself on leadership ability and to estimate the level of leadership others thought he possessed, as well as the ranking he *wished* the other members to assign him.

The analyses of interest are those evaluating an attempt to change the individual's self-ranking by reporting to him fictitious rankings from others. Subjects who ranked themselves anywhere except in the last five places in their groups on *wished* ranking were told that the others had ranked them six places below the wished rank chosen; those ranking themselves near the bottom were told others had ranked them five places higher. The effectiveness of this attempted manipulation in changing the individual's self-ranking, according to the data, depends on two factors: first, the manipulation is *more* effective when the individual is strongly attracted to the group; and second, the manipulation is *less* effective when the individual is more accurately able to estimate the others' original ranking of him. Since the self depends on opinions of others, it seems reasonable to suppose that individuals perceiving others' rankings of themselves *in*accurately would be less certain—perhaps also less stable—in their self-ranking.

We can summarize three significant findings from this study. First, there is additional evidence for the basic idea of the looking-glass self and for the idea that the perception of others' opinions is closely related to the self. Second, the effect of others' perceived opinions in changing the self-conception is directly related to the attractiveness of the group. And third, the effect of others in changing the self-concept is inversely related to the accuracy of perception, or to the certainty of the original self-evaluation.

The second finding can be taken as a *scope condition* necessary for the appearance of the phenomena of the first finding. More generally, it can be considered as evidence that the effect of others' opinions in determining the self will be negligible unless the individual feels a high degree of "attraction" to the group.

Another early attempt to study the effect of mitigating factors on the influence of others' opinions was a study by Couch (1958). Subjects were 96 college students who first completed a Twenty Statements Test, in which they wrote 20 responses to the question, Who am I? Then each was paired with another student of the same sex with whom he or she was previously unacquainted, and the two were assigned to write a radio script together. At the conclusion of this task, subjects filled out another questionnaire on which they rated themselves on a 4-point scale for each of 12 items regarding their performance on various aspects of the script-writing task; then they estimated how their partners would rate them at the 12 items.

In terms of our investigation, there are two important findings. First, the data indicate that a relatively short (15-minute) period of interaction does give individuals sufficient time to form an idea of how their partners will rate their performance. Since the interaction period is quite short and is not related to anything important in the subjects' lives outside the study, this fact alone is of significance; it appears that subjects are actively trying to assess how they appear to the other.

Second, Couch notes that the correlation between self-rating and partner's *actual* rating of the individual is much lower than the correlation between self-rating and partner's *perceived* rating of the individual. This finding is directly comparable to and consistent with the Miyamoto-Dornbusch and the Moore study findings.

A study by Backman et al. (1963) manipulated ratings given to subjects, and it suggests one determinant of certainty of self-evaluation, as well as some factors that may be relevant in deciding which individuals become significant others who affect self-evaluation. Subjects were college students who rated themselves on personality items, and told how close friends and relatives would rate them on the same items. Then they filled out personality measurement scales, which they were told would be scored for them by a "professional psychologist" to give them objective information. The "objective information" actually included attempts to alter self-concept on certain personality items. The major results of the study are that subjects do change their self-ranking as a result of the manipulated reports and that they change the low-consensus needs—those which the friends do not agree on—more than they change the high-consensus needs.

Videbeck (1960) reports a study that took more explicit account of the variables associated with effectiveness of an attempted change in the self-evaluation. Subjects were 30 students from introductory speech classes, described by their instructors as superior students. They were asked to rate themselves on a 9-point scale on each of 24 items having to do with adequacy of oral presentation; then they read six poems for a "visiting speech expert."

Some of the major findings of the study are as follows. First, as might be expected, the procedure is effective at changing the individual's self-rating, both positively and negatively. Furthermore, changes are noted both in items directly related to the comments given by the "expert," and, to a lesser extent, in items indirectly related.

A second major set of findings has to do with the positive or negative direction of the changes in self-rating induced by the experiment. Of subjects in the approval condition, 13 of the 15 changed in the predicted direction, whereas 14 of the 15 in the disapproval condition changed in the predicted direction. Thus it can be concluded that these data show no greater tendency to change in a positive direction than in a negative direction. Moreover, the mean amount of change reported on items in the approval condition is $+.49$; the mean amount of change on items in the disapproval condition is -1.30 (Videbeck, 1960: Table 1, p. 355). This comparison suggests that it is easier to *lower* the subjects' self-ratings than to raise them. These data are clearly at odds with one result reported by Moore.

A third set of important facts about this study comes from an examination of the design considerations employed. First, we note that Videbeck was careful to select an "expert" to induce the attempted manipulation; in this, the design is similar to the work of Israel and of Backman et al. Second, he notes that the frequency with which evaluations were received was expected to be a prime determinant of their importance in determining the individual's self-evaluation. In the design, the number of evaluations delivered was constant, guaranteed by having each subject read exactly six poems. The *number* of evaluations from another thus can be distinguished from the variable of *extensity* of interaction, first studied by Moore and later explicated by Backman et al. Third, the distinction of items into those directly related to the evaluations and those less directly related implicitly takes account of a way of conceiving the self-evaluation as being composed of self-evaluations at specific tasks. Videbeck does not mention that the design implicitly made use of a refinement of the idea of multiple selves introduced by James, and the results indicate that some generalization of evaluations does occur from one area to another. Finally, the selection of subjects from speech classes and the chosen task (reading six poems) were two features designed to select only subjects who were quite concerned with their performances. In addition, there was the implicit selection of subjects who probably would want to do *well* at the task. The combination of being interested in one's performance and wanting to perform well may constitute a second scope condition necessary to application of the basic idea of the social self.

Maehr et al. (1962) report a replication of the Videbeck study, using data from 31 boys enrolled in a high school physical education class. All findings of the Videbeck study were replicated except the finding of greater change in the disapproval condition. Thus this study demonstrates the same effects as the Videbeck study, using (1) an entirely different subject pool, (2) a different set of manipulation instructions, and (3) a different attribute for self-evaluation.

Haas and Maehr (1965) describe a series of experiments designed to change aspects of self-evaluation. The subjects were eighth-grade boys enrolled in physical education classes. Results of the first experiment show that the changes

induced because of the treatment were greatest immediately following the evaluations; after that measurement, however, they persisted at the same level for
the duration of the 6-week study.

The second experiment was an extension of the idea in Videbeck's research—
namely, that the number of evaluation treatments is an important variable in
determining the amount of change in the self. This time 30 subjects are told
they performed well on an assigned task. It was administered twice, the second
time two days following the first administration. Comparison of the data from
both experiments indicates the following: for directly related items, change induced by the first treatment of the second experiment was virtually identical to
that induced by the treatment in the first experiment. However after the second
"dosage," subjects in the second experiment showed a greater change in the
predicted direction, and this difference persisted for the duration of the study
(six weeks).

Two findings from the Maehr experiments seem to be especially significant.
First, change in one area of the self-evaluation apparently generalizes into other
areas. This result would be expected from the conception of overall self-evaluation as being composed of specific task evaluations. Second, the effect of frequency of evaluation has been shown to be directly related to the amount of
change induced in the self-evaluation. The third finding—that change induced
by the procedure used in these studies persisted for 6 weeks—seems to have
greater significance for methodology than for theory. In the absence of any
change in evaluations given an individual, one would not expect the effect of
previous evaluations to change with the passage of time unless such evaluations
had been weak to begin with.

Studies summarized in the immediately preceding pages contributed substan-
tially to our ideas for developing a theoretical formulation for the origins of self-
concept. They replicate findings reported from basic research into self-structure
and suggest in particular criteria for determining whose opinions will matter to
the individual: those who are competent to evaluate, who have access to objective evaluative criteria, and who are of high relative status. They point to criteria
we have called scope conditions for inducing change in self-evaluations: attractiveness of the group and desire to perform well at the task. They bring out
and specify the effects of additional factors important in changing self-evaluation: number of evaluations from any one other, nature of evaluations, and effects over time for aspects of self directly evaluated, as well as for those not directly evaluated.

Consequences of Self-Evaluation.   Jones and his associates conducted a set
of experiments using variants of a basic experimental design. In most of these

studies, the individual is made to believe that he is low on one aspect of self relative to other individuals. Manipulation of the low self is performed by an experimenter, who negatively evaluates the individual's performance at the experimental task. Then behavioral effects of the induced self-evaluation are observed. These studies thus are addressed to the third of our questions: *consequences* of a particular type of self-evaluation.

The first study (Jones, 1966) investigated effects of either positive or negative evaluations of performances of individuals whose ability had previously been rated by the experimenter as being either high or low. Thirty-one groups of 4 subjects each (total $n = 124$) were studied in the following laboratory setting. Subjects in each group sat around a table divided to prevent them from seeing one another. Each was provided with switches to send either positive or negative performance evaluations to each other member *and* to indicate his evaluations of his own performance. Each group member also had before him a set of three red and three green lights, to indicate positive or negative performance evaluations received from each of the other members.

The experiment had two phases. In the first phase, subjects took a written test consisting of 20 items. The test was scored by the experimenter, and the score was given privately to each subject. Subjects' scores were either 18 correct out of 20 (High Self) or 8 out of 20 (Low Self). Subjects were informed that one of the others in the group achieved a score of 18, one a score of 13, and one of 8. In the second phase, subjects judged aloud the same type of items used in the first phase, and on the 12 critical trials they evaluated both their own and one anothers' judgments by the switches and lights. Evaluations were controlled by the experimenter, however, such that some subjects were given feedback from other group members consistent with the initial manipulation and some received feedback that was inconsistent. Thus there are two independent variables of interest: the high or low performance evaluation given a subject by the experimenter in the first phase, and the high or low performance evaluations given him by the other group members in the second phase. The two dependent variables of most interest are a subject's evaluations of his own performances and the evaluations he sends to the other group members.

At the end of the second phase of the experiment, subjects were asked to rate their abilities on a 7-point scale, the four conditions of the experiment being ordered as follows: (1) high evaluations by experimenter, high evaluations by others; (2) high evaluations by experimenter, low evaluations by others; (3) low evaluations by experimenter, high evaluations by others; (4) low evaluations by experimenter, low evaluations by others. The difference in mean ratings between any two conditions is significant statistically. In terms of the ideas of the social self, this finding can be interpreted as showing the relative effect of evaluations by others; the observed ordering of conditions is consistent with an assertion that evaluations by both the experimenter and others in the group will affect the self-evaluation and, moreover, evaluations from the experimenter will have a greater effect than those from others.

Evaluations of performances of others reveals an effect of the evaluations of self received from others: subjects receiving a high proportion of positive evaluations from others send a higher proportion of positive evaluations to others than do those receiving a lower proportion of positive evaluations from others. Jones interprets this result in terms of "reciprocation"; that is, subjects are responding to a rewarding experience by giving rewarding responses. To the extent that such an interpretation is correct, of course, subjects are intentionally distorting their evaluations of others' performances to "reward" them with positive evaluations. But any interpretation of this finding, including the interpretation made by Jones, would have been strengthened considerably if a differentiation had been made between the group members who supposedly give the various evaluations to the individual and those to whom the same person gives positive evaluations. Since others in the group were perceived to vary widely in their ability (from the phase I manipulation), and since the "evaluations" sent to others may not have accurately reflected the "true" evaluations the subject made of their actual performance, this finding is not interpreted further here.

In summary, the first experiment by Jones is ingeniously designed to investigate a complex set of phenomena. The controlled interaction using switches and lights and the manipulation of self-evaluation by the experimenter represent significant technical advances for study of the effects of varying patterns of evaluation and interaction. However, the results of the study and the possibility of alternative and sometimes conflicting interpretations of the data, which Jones discusses, all indicate the need for further theoretical development and experimental simplification.

The second experiment (Jones and Ratner, 1967) was intended to investigate other behavioral consequences of a low self-evaluation. Subjects were 40 female college students, formed into groups of three. Each subject was told by a "clinical psychologist" that she was low on "clinical assessment ability." Although results are not always clear-cut, in the simpler "no-commitment condition" they show that subjects with this induced low self-evaluation will give other subjects evaluations that are opposite from the evaluations received from those subjects. That is, if a subject holding an induced low self-evaluation is evaluated positively by another subject, she evaluates that subject negatively; if she is evaluated negatively, she evaluates that subject positively.

A third experiment (Jones and Pines, 1968) showed essentially the same results in a more tightly controlled experimental design.

Still other behavioral consequences of varying types and amounts of positive and negative performance evaluations were presented in a more naturalistic study by Jones (1968). Forty-eight groups composed of four college students were given a clinical case similar to those used in the other studies to be discussed.

The results show a clear effect of the evaluations on quantity of talking in the discussion—the more positive evaluations they received of their comments, the more subjects talked. Moreover, this effect is not correlated with quality of their comments as actually perceived by others; those who talked more as the result of having received (manipulated) positive evaluations from others were given *less* favorable actual evaluations by those others. Beyond these behavioral effects during interaction, the responses of subjects to a postsession questionnaire might have been expected from the ideas of the social self. Those who received high proportions of positive evaluations from others rated themselves higher on "insight into human problems" than those who received mostly negative evaluations. However, this effect is noticeable only in the Complete Feedback conditions; in other conditions (where, presumably, subjects could not compare the proportion of positive evaluations they were getting with the amount others were getting), the evaluations do not result in differences in the self-appraisal items on the questionnaires.

The behavioral effects of the different performance evaluations in this study are particularly interesting, for they begin to suggest one consequence of differing levels of self-evaluation: likelihood of attempting to perform a task. Subjects who were told they were making "good" contributions to the case problem became more likely to offer comments in the future. If this result can be generalized to other interactions, and there is no apparent reason why it cannot, we would expect one observable consequence of having a relatively high self-evaluation to be a high willingness to talk or to offer suggestions when a group task is to be solved.

Second, it is interesting to note that self-appraisal items on the questionnaire show differences between subjects receiving high evaluations and those receiving low evaluations only in the Complete Feedback condition. Since the proportion of positive evaluations received by members was the same in all three conditions, it seems reasonable to attribute this result to a social comparison process that is possible only in the Complete Feedback condition. Subjects in the Self-Feedback condition knew that they were receiving either a high or a low proportion of positive evaluations; but apparently this information was not useful when subjects could not see how the evaluations they received compared with the evaluations others were receiving.

The final study to be reviewed in this section separated the effects of liking from evaluations in a variant of the same basic experiment. Jones and Schneider (1968) induced high school girls to believe they had just performed very poorly at the kind of clinical judgment task on which they were to work. Our discussion refers only to groups in which the manipulation was intended to produce certainty of a low self-evaluation.

In the second phase, subjects were formed into groups of three and took turns giving their oral judgments and evaluating each others' judgments to more of the clinical problems. As in all of Jones's studies except the first one, subjects sent evaluations to each other opposite in nature from the controlled evaluations received from those others. However, in questionnaire responses to a question on liking, subjects reported greater liking for the person who evaluated them positively. This latter result is not particularly surprising, though it points up the importance of distinguishing perceived pleasantness of evaluations from perceived accuracy. We shall have more to say about this distinction in Chapter 3 (task-oriented and process-oriented groups) and in Chapter 9 (believing versus liking a low self-evaluation).

Our review of Jones's experiments has been selective, emphasizing what we believe to be a phenomenon of importance in understanding consequences of the self-evaluation. If we may assume that Jones's subjects described here actually held low self-evaluations, then it is possible to explain their sending "opposite" evaluations in terms of cognitive consistency. If a subject believes the experimental manipulation, then her best guess would be that anyone who agrees with her opinions also has low ability. This line of reasoning is developed more fully and examined in Chapter 5; for the present, we merely note that it is intuitively plausible.

Summary. This completes our selective review of empirical research related to the social self. The findings can be organized in terms of the three sets of issues described in the introduction; namely, *determinants of* self-evaluation, *the nature of the self,* and *observable consequences* of a particular level of self-evaluation.

All studies show evidence that can be interpreted as indicating the critical importance of the opinions of others on the individual's self-evaluation. Furthermore, the importance of others has been shown to be in some sense a direct function of the frequency of interaction with those others and an inverse function of the extensity of interaction with alternative others. There is some evidence that the others with whom the individual interacts are not all equally important in determining self-evaluation, and the term "significant other" has been given to those who are considered to be most influential. However, the characteristics of a significant other have not been spelled out in detail, either conceptually or in terms of empirical evidence. In addition to forming the self, others have been shown to be important both for maintaining a given self-evaluation and for producing change in the level of self-evaluation. Finally, the research by Israel and by Maehr indicates that two of the important scope conditions for demonstrating the effects of others' opinions on the self are a high level of attraction to the others and a high level of motivation, either to learn one's own level of achievement or to attain a high level of achievement.

All studies reviewed have implicitly or explicitly conceptualized the self as a cognitive entity, that is, as a set of self-referent ideas that are held by the individual and of which he can be aware. Second, although the self seems to be sensitive to changes in the evaluations received from others, it is not infinitely flexible, nor is it constantly changing to be in perfect agreement with every modification in evaluations. In other words, a semipermanent *structure* seems to arise as the result of the evaluations received, and the type of structure that arises partly determines the effect of subsequent opinions. Thus it is possible to talk of two individuals—one who possesses a high self-evaluation as the result of having received a large number of positive evaluations and another who possesses a low self-evaluation as the result of having received a large number of negative evaluations—*and* it is possible to assert that the effect of a given subsequent evaluation will not be the same for both these individuals.

Jones's research indicates one major consequence of a given level of self-evaluation: an individual who receives many positive evaluations at a particular task is more likely to attempt future performances than an individual who receives many negative evaluations. This suggests that one consequence of a high self-evaluation may be an increased willingness to perform in the future, and by extension, that a consequence of a low self-evaluation may be a decreased willingness to perform.

A second consequence of a high self-evaluation that appeared in several of the studies is a greater willingness to evaluate one's own future performances positively and a greater willingness to rank oneself highly within the group. If this result suggests a more general tendency for subjects with high self-evaluations to place themselves first in a variety of contexts and to think they are right when there is no objective reason to do so, among other diverse consequences, then it is important to form a precise concept of the tendency. Whether this is the case cannot be determined from the studies so far examined. However, the results of these studies indicate that the possibility merits further examination.

In the next chapter, we introduce a particular view of interaction, translating the information gained from the previous studies into the new conceptualization. This will prepare the way for constructing a theory of some aspects of self-evaluation that is able to explain many of the previous findings summarized and also to predict new empirical consequences.

CHAPTER THREE

SELF–EVALUATION AND PERFORMANCE EXPECTATIONS

Theoretical and empirical work in the social self tradition revolves about two major issues: first, the idea that the individual's conception of his various abilities is built on the perceived opinions of "significant others," and second, the suggestion that the self-evaluation produced in this way has some degree of permanence and directly affects the individual's subsequent behaviors in social situations. Therefore, it is reasonable to begin a theory of the social self by formulating precise concepts both of the characteristics of significant others and of the self-conception that significant others can produce.

The second task has been the object of sustained empirical and theoretical investigation initiated by and focused about Joseph Berger and his associates. These workers have been concerned with developing, testing, and extending a set of propositions to explain certain features of inequality among members of face-to-face problem-solving groups. By adopting this viewpoint for our interests in the social self, we gain a set of concepts and propositions that enable determinate empirical predictions for behavior as a function of ability conceptions. Since, in addition, there is a considerable body of empirical data in support of these propositions, we can focus our efforts on the first task: specifying clearly the characteristics that make an other significant in determining a given individual's ability self-conception. We begin by outlining Berger's way of analyzing interaction and by describing a standardized experimental setting to test the theory; then we indicate parallels between problems of interest in this tradition and problems of interest in the social self tradition. (A more complete summary of this research program than the one given here is Berger et al., 1974.)

Expectation States Theory. Berger's tradition is oriented to explaining the following pervasive fact of social life: among members of a problem-solving group who are previously unacquainted with one another, the interaction process leads to unequal distribution of participation rates and unequal amounts of influence over the group decision and esteem received from other group members. This result is observable in an extremely wide variety of groups, including Bales-type discussion groups of college students, juries, children's play groups, and military teams (see Berger et al., 1972). Essentially, these phenomena are said to occur because during early phases of interaction members form differential ability conceptions, called *performance expectation states*, for one another. Once formed, these expectation states determine distribution of all observable components of power and prestige in the groups. To relate expectation theory to self-evaluation, we must specify precisely how expectation states form through interaction, precisely what an expectation state is, and precisely how expectation states determine future interaction. There are in fact several closely related theories, constructed for a variety of related phenomena. We describe those features most closely related to issues in the social self.

Expectation states theory applies to groups that meet two scope conditions: the members of the group must be *task oriented*, and they must be *collectively oriented*. Task orientation means that the members are engaged in a task that can be completed successfully or unsuccessfully; they are solving a problem or set of problems, and there exists a set of definite and recognizable correct outcomes for their efforts. For example, if members were assigned to solve a set of mathematical problems, the outcome of their work could be evaluated in terms of "correctness" by anyone who knew the standard rules for mathematics. For this reason, the evaluative standards of a task-oriented group can be called "extrasystemic." Members of a group whose purpose in meeting is to have a good time or to get to know one another better are engaged in a task for which success can be assessed only by the group members themselves. Such a task has intrasystemic standards, and groups with only intrasystemic standards usually are not task oriented. Individuals at a social gathering probably would constitute a *process-oriented* group, with intrasystemic standards of success.

The second scope condition, collective orientation, refers to types of interaction that are deemed proper by the group members, or to the manner in which the members try to solve the problems. In a collectively oriented group, it is not only appropriate, it is *required* that members take one anothers' opinions into account in solving the problem. By contrast, it is possible to speak of *individualistic orientation*, in which individuals work by themselves on a problem. A room full of students taking an examination (presumably) would not be collectively oriented.

For informally organized groups meeting these two scope conditions, it is possible to describe the interaction process quite abstractly. At this point we introduce some terminology of expectation states theory.

Imagine a collection of individuals coming together for the first time to meet as a problem-solving group, such as the Bales discussion groups. Their observable interaction will consist of orientation statements that attempt to marshal the group's knowledge and to organize members' efforts, suggestions about how to attack the problem, proposed solutions, criticisms of suggestions offered, laughter, and so on. Some proportion—perhaps 15 to 25%—of the interaction will consist of statements not directly relevant for solving the problem: joking, comments about the weather, concern for the psychological and emotional states of group members. This type of activity, since it is not directly relevant to task problems, constitutes a residual category of interaction for our purposes and is not included in the conceptualization.

Excluding irrelevant types of interaction, we view group interaction as composed of five components:

First, there are *action opportunities*, or socially distributed chances to perform. Asking a member's opinion about how best to solve the group problem constitutes giving an action opportunity to that member. For example, the question "What do you think about this, Bill?" is an action opportunity given to the actor Bill. In a discussion group it is also possible to give an action opportunity nonverbally by looking inquiringly at an actor, or simply by being silent when he looks as though he has something to say. In a more controlled setting, such as the clinical case problems used in some of Jones's research summarized in Chapter 2, action opportunities were distributed by the experimenter when he told each subject to give her best judgment of the probable response of the patient being discussed.

The second component of interaction is *performance outputs*, or problem-solving attempts. If an actor is given an action opportunity, he may accept it and make a performance output. Bill, for example, may say "I think the answer is. . . ." When the task is other than discussion, a performance output would be a different type of problem-solving attempt. For example, in the studies of Videbeck and Maehr, performance outputs were physical: running, jumping, throwing balls, and so on. A performance output is any single unit attempt by an actor to do the activity required by the task; it is an attempt to achieve the group's goal.

A performance output is seldom made without an antecedent action opportunity. It is surprisingly unusual for an actor to try to solve the group problem without first having been "permitted" by other members to do so. In groups that are not strictly task oriented, members seem to make many suggestions without having their opinions solicited. A little consideration suggests a reason for this discrepant behavior. To the extent that members are strictly concerned with solving the group problem and are motivated to do the best possible job, they are not likely to want to hear any but the best suggestions. Not only will they overlook suggestions they feel are not helpful, they will take steps to suppress the individual who makes such suggestions. He will find that his opinions are not asked for, and when he ventures them unrequested he will meet silence, disapproving glances, and quite likely, open hostility. An individual perceived as making good suggestions will receive the opposite treatment: his opinion will be asked frequently, he will be listened to with interest and deference, he will be praised and otherwise encouraged to speak more. In process-oriented groups, irrelevant or low-quality performances are much less likely to be suppressed; they do not detract from any goal attainment.

If an actor accepts an action opportunity and makes a performance output, that performance may be evaluated, either by himself or by another member of the group. This is a *unit evaluation*, since it refers to a single unit act, and it is the third component of the observable interaction process. A unit evaluation may be either positive or negative; it may not be neutral. The actor who has made a suggestion toward solving the group problem may hear another member say, "I think that's right," or "I think he has a good idea." In the tasks used by Videbeck and Maehr, unit evaluations were distributed by the experimenter when he told subjects how well they had performed at each of the tasks. In less controlled situations, each group member is free to evaluate any member's performances, including his own. A unit evaluation is not made without an antecedent performance output, just as performance outputs usually follow action opportunities.

At some point we will want to distinguish public unit evaluations from private unit evaluations. We assume that private unit evaluations invariably are made of every performance output; everybody in the group who knows about the performance output is assumed to evaluate it. Sometimes the private unit evaluation is communicated to the individual making the performance output (e.g., by telling him he did well or poorly), but it need not be. In most cases, it is safe to assume that the private and the public unit evaluations are the same and are coextensive. That is, the individual making the unit evaluation will not disguise his true feelings as, for example, tact might require. This characteristic of public and private unit evaluations may also serve as a distinguishing feature of task-oriented groups. Members of process-oriented groups may seek to avoid offense or embarrassment by keeping certain evaluations private and may even state insincere evaluations publicly. For our purposes, when the term unit evaluation is not specified as either private or public, it is taken to mean that it is both.

The fourth observable component of interaction is *agreement or disagreement* with a given performance output. Many times in discussion groups it is difficult to distinguish positive unit evaluations from agreement, and negative unit evaluations from disagreement. In fact, speech customs frequently dictate that we equate the statements "I disagree with you" and "I think you are wrong." In principle, however, it is possible to distinguish between these two concepts, and in some instances it is useful to do so. In a discussion group, for example, we could be relatively certain that if two people made the same suggestion or guessed the same answer simultaneously, an instance of agreement had occurred.

If the interaction were restricted so that no member could know any other person's performances until after he had made his own performances, it would be still easier to distinguish agreement from positive unit evaluations. And even in the open interaction of a discussion group, an observer frequently feels that he is witnessing an honest expression of agreement between members who have come to the same conclusion, without one of them relying solely on the other for the answer. The observer is likely to have greater confidence in his judgment that he is seeing an honest *dis*agreement when two members offer different and incompatible suggestions for ways to solve the group problem. For difficult tasks, the correct solutions are not at all clear or easy to discover, and it is likely that several members will make performance outputs that are in disagreement.

When disagreement does arise, we may observe *acceptance or rejection of influence*, the fifth component of interaction. If two members make different suggestions, or if two performance outputs imply incompatible courses of action, then one member must back down—that is, make a negative unit evaluation of his own performance output. In a discussion group, disagreement usually means that one of the disagreeing members must say, "I guess I was wrong and you were right." Before the group problem solving can proceed, the member who is to accept influence must accept the course of action proposed by the other. If the disagreement cannot be resolved, the group faces the very difficult problem of choosing between completely disregarding one member or finding a third alternative course of action.

Disagreements can be crucial to a problem-solving group for a reason that lies in the collective orientation condition. Recall that this condition stipulates that it is not only appropriate but *necessary* to take the opinions of every member into account. Thus when a disagreement arises, the group members who are working on a collective task are obliged to take action on it; they must decide which performance output was best. They may decide to ignore one of the suggestions and to follow the other by default, without explicitly announcing that they have thereby chosen to evaluate the first negatively and the second positively; but they may not ignore both suggestions.

All five of these interaction components have the property *scarcity*. If person A is given an action opportunity, person B is at the same time denied an action opportunity. Although there are no strict structural constraints that make agreement or positive unit evaluations scarce, it usually is the case that neither component is in endless supply. Thus such groups exhibit the results of forces producing a differentiation among the members according to the components of interaction. We now describe this differentiating process in more detail.

In the open interaction situation of a problem-solving discussion group, several regular features of the interaction have been reported repeatedly. As the first step toward developing a theory of interaction in problem-solving groups, these regularities are noted and stated in terms of the interaction components introduced previously.

First, after group members have had the opportunity to interact for a short period of time and to become familiar with one another and with the task, the components of interaction tend to be distributed *unequally* among the various group members. Some members come to receive more action opportunities than others, some receive relatively more positive unit evaluations, some make more performance outputs, and so on.

Second, not only is the distribution of the interaction components unequal, it is also *reciprocal*. The members who receive more action opportunities also make more performance outputs, are more likely to receive positive unit evaluations and agreements from others, and are less likely to accept influence in case of disagreement. Simply by counting the number of times a group member talks regardless of what he says, an observer will have a good idea of the ranking of members on likelihood of receiving positive unit evaluations and agreement, and of rejecting influence. Correlations above .80 of the rankings of group members on these components of interaction have been reported

Third, the reciprocal inequality, once it emerges, tends to be *stable*. The members who talk most near the beginning of the group meeting are also very likely to be the ones who talk most at the end of the session; moreover, they are very likely to talk most in subsequent sessions if the group meets more than once. Because of this stability, as well as the reciprocity of the inequality, it is possible to speak of the components of interaction as visible indicators of the *power and prestige structure of the group*.

It is reasonable, therefore, to infer that these inequalities indicate the existence of a hierarchy within the group and that if this hierarchy could be independently determined, it could be used to predict the distribution of the components of interaction. An explanation for these observations will rest on an explanation of the nature and the bases of the hierarchy and how it comes to exist.

At the outset of interaction, the interaction components are probably distributed randomly among the group members. That is, in the first few minutes of interaction, members make suggestions, receive positive and negative evaluations and agreement or disagreement, and accept or reject influence in ways that could not be predicted from any simple theory of group structure or process. We might expect, for example, that some individuals have learned to be more verbal than others, hence will make more performance outputs than others; or that some individuals characteristically are more likely than others to accept influence.

However, the evidence on the relation of action opportunities and performance outputs strongly suggests that individual differences are *not* the most important determinants of distribution of these interaction components after the earliest stages of group interaction. Furthermore, the highly regular relationship of all these components of interaction argues strongly against an interpretation that individual differences are the most important determinant of any single feature of the interaction, such as acceptance or rejection of influence. An explanation of the observed inequalities must reside elsewhere.

A differing type of explanation asserts that the important feature of the early stages of the interaction process is the individuals' formation of an idea of their relative abilities at the group task and of the relative likelihood that any given member will be able to make a useful contribution to the group effort. Once this determination has been made (and of course it can be made incorrectly if a member misperceives the usefulness or the quality of another's contributions), each group member will treat each other member unequally in terms of the components of interaction. He will distribute more action opportunities to those perceived to be likely to make useful suggestions, and he will be more likely to agree with them and to make positive unit evaluations of their performances.

The process may be explained, and also described more precisely, by introducing one final concept—that of a *performance expectation state*. At some point a series of negative or positive unit evaluations of performance outputs is believed to generalize into an overall ability evaluation for the individual making the performance outputs, or into an *expectation state* held for that individual. At some point the individual goes from saying "I think that's correct" to "I think he has high ability"; or he moves from saying "I think that's wrong" to "I think he has low ability at the task." This conception of overall ability *at the specific group task* is what is meant by an expectation state held for the performance of the individual. The statement "I think he has high ability" is significant because it carries with it the implication "I *expect* his future performances to be correct." Thus an expectation state is a cognitive state or belief about ability which is assumed to affect future responses of the individual holding the state.

Expectation states in this conceptualization function as theoretical constructs that are not directly observable but are theoretically linked to other concepts for which empirical indicators can be developed. In expectation states theory, the construct "expectation state" explains the observable features of interaction discussed earlier: once expectations exist and come to be held by the individual group members, all the theoretically important components of interaction will be distributed in accord with the expectations. The higher are the expectations held for the quality of an individual's performance (by both himself and others), the more action opportunities he will be given, the more likely he will be to accept a given action opportunity and to make a performance output, the more likely he will be to receive agreement and a positive unit evaluation for any given performance output, and the less likely he will be to accept influence in case of disagreement.

Expectations are spoken of as having both "self" and "other" components, and they are relative to any pair of individuals. Thus an individual can hold one of four possible combinations of self and other expectations: (1) (relatively) high expectations for his own performance and (relatively) low expectations for the performance of other; (2) low and high expectations for his own performance and that of the other, respectively; (3) high expectations both for himself and for other; or (4) low expectations for both himself and other. The first two types of expectations are called *differentiated* expectations, since they are beliefs that differentiate individuals; the third and fourth types of expectations are *undifferentiated* expectations. For convenience, expectations are written with a plus or a minus sign representing the high and low states, and with expectations held by an individual for his own performance written first. Expectations of the four types thus are written: type 1, $(+ -)$; type 2, $(- +)$; type 3, $(+ +)$; type 4, $(- -)$.

Allowing expectations to take only two states, "relatively high" and "relatively low" means that to fully describe the structure of expectations in a group, it is necessary to follow the (admittedly laborious) procedure of taking all possible pairs of individuals. Even more significant, however, is the theory's emphasis on the *relativity* of expectations; it makes sense to speak of one individual's expectations for himself only *in relation to a specific other individual*. We refer to consequences of this relative conceptualization at several points in this work.

Experimental Tests.   Expectation states theory has been developed in conjunction with a research program involving empirical tests in a social psychological laboratory. A task and an interaction situation are constructed and entered into by volunteer subjects whose behavior is predicted by the theory under consideration. Nearly all research in expectation states theory has employed a variant of one basic experiment and a single dependent variable—rejection of influence in case of disagreement—as the operational measure of expectation states. Using a standard experiment and the same measurement operation often means that the effects of new independent variables can be assessed by making direct comparisons of data across a large number of experiments, thus building cumulative information about the entire theory.

All expectation states theory experiments share the following features. In one or two preliminary phases, the attempt is made to produce a social situation described in the scope conditions of the theory: specifically, a problem-solving group composed of individuals possessing specific information about their task abilities. Either their abilities are unknown (which involves describing their task as requiring an entirely new ability just discovered and unrelated to other skills) or they are given specific expectations by performing the task and receiving public evaluations from the experimenter. The final phase of the experiment measures expectations held by subjects using the proportion of disagreements resolved in favor of self—a standard measure that is predicted to vary directly with the relative expectations held for self and other. For a more complete description of the "basic expectation experiment," see Appendix 1.

The first experiments were conducted to test the "basic expectation assumption": the claim that the pattern of relative expectation states held by subjects would determine important features of their subsequent interaction. (These are reported in Camilleri et al., 1972.) These experiments had two phases. In phase I, pairs of subjects judged a series of slides. After each trial, the experimenter told each subject publicly whether he was "correct." Scores assigned to subjects were either extremely high or extremely low, to produce all four patterns of relative self–other expectations. To produce $(+-)$ expectations, the subject was told that he was correct 17 times out of 20 and the other subject was correct 9 times out of 20. To produce $(++)$ expectations, the subject was told that both he and the other subject were correct 17 times out of 20. For $(--)$ expectations, the subject was told that both he and the other subject got 9 right out of 20. To produce $(-+)$ expectations, the subject was told that he got 9 out of 20 and the other subject got 17 out of 20.

After overall scores had been assigned to subjects and interpreted for them by reference to a table of "national standards," they began phase II, the data collection phase. Subjects were told they were to work together on a second set of slides. They would first make a private initial choice, next they would see their partner's initial choice, and then they would restudy the slide and make a final decision. Because communication was controlled, subjects could be told that their initial choices were in continual disagreement. Thus the experiment consisted of giving each subject an action opportunity, which he had to accept, and of the subject's making a performance output. The feedback of partner's choice constituted a disagreement, and the final choice constituted a disagreement resolution that had to include either acceptance or rejection of influence. Data were collected on the proportion of disagreements resolved in favor of self [called $P(s)$], which is predicted to vary directly with the *relative* self–other expectation states held. Thus the prediction for $P(s)$ from this experiment was: $(+-) > (++) = (--) > (-+)$. Table 3.1 shows that this prediction was confirmed.

TABLE 3.1   REJECTION OF INFLUENCE BY
EXPECTATION STATES

Expectation State	$P(s)$
$(+-)$	.76
$(++)$	.64
$(--)$	.66
$(-+)$	.42

Adapted from Camilleri et al., 1972, p. 34.

Self-Expectation States and Self-Evaluations.   The first crucial process in formation of expectation states is the distribution of unit evaluations for performance outputs. The greater the proportion of positive unit evaluations actor A makes of actor B's performance, *if* B accepts these evaluations, the more likely B is to come to hold high expectations for his own performance. Therefore, the positive or negative unit evaluations that are distributed among members determine expectation states associated with members; hence they determine observable future interaction of the group.

Second, the agreement/disagreement process itself has an important effect on formation of expectation states: as we mentioned, only in cases of disagreement does the necessity arise for making differential evaluations of actors, thus for forming differentiated expectations. If undifferentiated expectations (either high or low) were formed for all actors in the group, there would be no unequal distribution of interaction components. But the unequal distribution does emerge regularly, and there have been both casual and systematic observations of considerable disagreement in problem-solving groups; therefore, it seems reasonable to attribute the differentiated expectations to the necessity for resolving disagreements between actors.

Of central interest here is the way in which individuals form expectations, both for their own performances and for those of others with whom they interact. Formation of performance expectations is in many ways equivalent to the processes referred to in other theoretical and research traditions as forming ability conceptions, the formation of self-expectations being analogous to the formation of a self-evaluation, and the formation of expectations for others being analogous to formation of opinions about others' abilities. In the next chapter, we attempt to reformulate the ideas from the social self tradition into the concepts of expectation states theory, with the goal of extending expectation theory to explain many of the same kinds of situation that have been studied by others in the social self tradition. Using this approach, it should be possible to extend the scope conditions and the determinacy of predictions that are possible from expectation states theory, and at the same time to provide precise answers to some of the major questions that have arisen in work conducted within the social self tradition.

It seems reasonable to suppose that if an actor in a problem-solving group is highly motivated to do the best possible job at the group's task, he will be actively "trying" to form performance expectations for himself and for the other members of the group. That is, if an individual is faced with a task that must be resolved through group effort, he will also decide, perhaps without ever making an explicit statement of the decision, that it is of central importance to determine whose suggestions and opinions are likely to be helpful and whose in all probability will not. In this sense, part of the "subtasks" an actor sets for himself is the deliberate assignment of expectation states to the various group members.

If an actor is concerned with forming useful expectations for himself and the others in the group, he has two basic sources of information available: he can evaluate his own and others' performances himself, or he can rely on the unit evaluations he sees others making. In open interaction in problem-solving groups, there are two types of condition that probably act to increase the reliance on others' unit evaluations. First, it seems reasonable to assume that it is more difficult to make an accurate evaluation of one's own performance outputs than it is of others' performances. Presumably, whenever an actor is willing to accept an action opportunity by making a performance output, he thinks he has a good idea. (Whether the idea sounds good when he says it is a different matter, but in any case, it seems safe to assume that in an open interaction situation, no actor would venture a performance output unless he thought it was a good one at the time.) Second, as the clarity of the evaluative standards diminishes, or as the difficulty of the task increases, it becomes more difficult for an actor to decide whether his own or others' performances are correct. By definition, a difficult task is one for which "right" or "good" performances are not clear, not easily recognizable; and this means that it is more difficult to have confidence either in a given performance output or in the accuracy of one's unit evaluation of a performance output. Also, there are tasks for which correct answers are not at all clear because many steps must be solved satisfactorily to reach the solution to the problem, and the evaluation of the unit steps to a solution is ambiguous. For such tasks, it is also difficult to be certain of one's own unit evaluations of performance outputs. In both these case types, we can suppose that if an actor feels unsure about the unit evaluations he would make of a given performance output, he will be more reliant on the unit evaluations he sees others making. In other words, both for determining an accurate self-expectation and for evaluating performance outputs made either by himself or by others when the task is very difficult or the evaluative standards are unclear, we would expect the opinions of others to become increasingly important determinants of the unit evaluations the actor makes of performances.

The idea of a self-expectation is more limited in several respects than the idea of a self-evaluation spoken of most frequently within the social self tradition. First, expectation states are situation specific: they are always discussed in terms of a single task and a single situation at a given time. By contrast, we sometimes speak of a self-evaluation in a manner suggesting that it is a transsituational phenomenon, possibly even an enduring idea that the individual carries around with him all his life. This difference between self-evaluation and expectation states is due largely to the more precise and explicit scope conditions of expectation theory. Although expectations may sometimes be transferred from one task situation to another, the conditions under which this is possible must be specified before such an assertion can be made.

The relationship between expectations a person holds for his own performance at a specific task and the idea of a self-evaluation may be either close or very distant, depending on the sense in which the latter term is intended. One simple relation may assert that an individual's overall level of self-evaluation is a weighted average of his task-specific performance expectations at various tasks in which he engages. Given such a relation, the relation of a specific task expectation to a self-evaluation would be analogous to the relation suggested earlier between self-evaluation and self-concept; the former is a part of, and consequently a partial determinant of, the latter. In both cases, the latter term is more general, but it usually is used with less precision than the former; people who speak of self-concept differ more widely in what they mean by that term than do people speaking of self-evaluation, and people speaking of self-evaluation have more dissimilar ideas in mind than do people speaking of self-expectations. This narrowing and refining process for terms that originally seemed to have a well-understood, shared meaning has clear precedents in fields characterized by cumulative foci of interest and theoretical development.

A second difference between self-evaluation and expectation states has already been noted: expectation states are relative to pairs of individuals, whereas self-evaluation seldom includes an explicit notion of relativity to a specific other. To specify the complete structure of expectations in a group, we would have to specify the relative expectation states existing for every possible pair of members. This would not be necessary for a nonrelative conception of self-evaluation. On close examination of the idea of a nonrelative self-evaluation, however, it becomes difficult to see how such an idea could have meaning or utility in a given social situation. To say that an individual has a high self-evaluation without specifying that the self-evaluation is high *relative* to the evaluation he holds of some other gives little useful information about his likely interaction patterns with others. Knowing that an individual possesses a high self-evaluation may tell something about his behavior when confronted with an other for whom he has no evaluative information, or about his behavior when confronted with an "average" other, *if* we are willing to make additional assumptions specifying how the individual of a high, medium, or low self-evaluation will treat an "average" other. Even then, however, it would not be possible to make predictions if we take a level of evaluation of the other as a given condition. This relative comparison is information that is used by individuals in governing their approach to others, and we therefore incorporate it in this version of expectation states theory.

We noted earlier that ideas in the social self tradition are not formulated as precisely as those in expectation states theory, nor do they enable such determinate predictions of behavior. On the other hand, questions addressed in the social self tradition have not previously been considered within the expectation theory point of view.* Basically, we need to know whose unit evaluations "matter" when an individual is forming performance expectations and whose evaluations are irrelevant. Put in terms of the social self tradition, this is a question of the characteristics that must be possessed by an effective source of performance expectations. The characteristics of a significant other have not been conceptualized clearly, explicitly, or concisely in the theory and research of the social self tradition; nor have the characteristics of an effective source of expectations been incorporated in expectation theory prior to this.

To specify these characteristics, and to describe precisely the process by which evaluations from an individual possessing the proper characteristics will affect the cognitive structure and future interaction of individuals, are the tasks of the next chapter.

* An unpublished paper, "Status Conditions of Self-Evaluation," developed in the course of expectation states theory work in 1965. Although it was a definite stimulus to our ideas, the paper deals with issues different from those of interest to us here; primarily, it is concerned with social conditions making for a stable self-evaluation. Briefly, the theory presented argues that self-evaluation is produced originally by a *source*, an individual possessing both high status and socially defined right to confer honor or dishonor. However, self-evaluation is stable only if *peers* accept the conferred evaluation of the individual. (See Berger et al., 1970, for the most recent version of this paper.) We present our theory that status is not the major determinant of a potential source's effectiveness (except in the manner described in Chapter 6) and that social rights to evaluate are not crucial. In addition, we assert implicitly that an individual's level of self-evaluation tends to persist unless acted upon and that peer effects are negligible except when peers function as (theoretically defined) sources.

CHAPTER FOUR

SOURCE OF EVALUATIONS AND EXPECTATIONS FOR PERFORMANCE

The first version of the theory, presented in this chapter, explicates the concept of a significant other. It specifies one set of characteristics that an individual must possess if his evaluations are to be accepted by others and used by them to form performance expectations. In addition, it specifies the effects of a significant other on the formation of performance expectations and on observable behavior. The first version deals with the simplest possible situation for which predictions can be made about characteristics of an other who evaluates performance.

Theory and Derivations. Groups to which the theory applies are characterized by four scope conditions. First, the group members are all *task oriented*. We recall from our earlier discussion (Chapter 3) that such group members are performing a valued task for which the possible outcomes are "success" or "failure" *and* that the group members are highly committed to attaining the "success" outcome of the task.

Second, the task is *collective*; it must be solved by group action and consensus. Members of the group see it as legitimate and necessary that every group member consider for use the ideas supplied by every other group member.

Third, since the theory is concerned with formation of beliefs about task ability and not with change in these beliefs, individuals must have *no prior conceptions of their abilities at the given task.* They may hold general ideas about their abilities; but at the outset of the interaction, they must have no information that leads them to believe that they are likely to perform the specific task either well or poorly.

Fourth, since the presence of differentiating status characteristics affects the formation of performance expectations, the scope conditions for the first version of the theory require that the group members be *undifferentiated with respect to observable status characteristics.*

The two contributions of the first source version of expectation theory are the characteristics of the person making unit evaluations of performances, and the differential effects of the unit evaluations from persons with different characteristics. To observe these effects, we must test the theory when several features of the open interaction situation are controlled and when the interaction process is considerably simplified. This does not mean that the theory cannot make predictions for the open interaction of, for example, a discussion group; it should be able to do so. Controlling and simplifying enable us to display more clearly the theoretical processes assumed to be at work. Similarly, simplifying the theory statements allows us to distinguish actors whose roles are more high specialized than would likely be found in an uncontrolled situation. Specifically, the theory speaks of two actors—"person" (p) and "other" (o)—who *perform and interact,* and of a third actor e who *evaluates* their performances. No predictions are to be made for e's behavior, but evaluations that e makes and characteristics that he possesses are predicted to affect all the theoretically important features of future interaction between p and o. As a way of stating the scope conditions concisely, situations meeting those conditions are designated as situations of type S.

DEFINITION 1.   An interaction situation is task situation S if and only if:
   a. There are at least two actors, p and o, performing a task.
   b. There is one actor e evaluating their unit performances.
   c. p and o have no prior expectations for their own or each other's performance at the task.
   d. All actors are task oriented.
   e. All actors are collectively oriented.

Since it is a central contention of the theory that the characteristics of the evaluator are crucial in determining the effect of his evaluations, we designate a special type of evaluator, called a source. The intent here is to distinguish in a formal sense those evaluators (e's) whose evaluations "matter" to p and o from those whose evaluations are irrelevant.

One factor that might be expected to make e a source for p and o might be the latter individuals' knowledge that e possesses access to objective evaluative information they themselves do not possess. In the research by Backman et al., discussed in Chapter 2, subjects took a personality test that was supposedly scored according to an answer key, and in some of Jones's experiments subjects were told that their clinical judgments were compared with standardized answers to the test. For such situations, when subjects believe that an evaluator has access to objective standards for evaluating a performance output, it seems reasonable to believe that they will grant him "sourcehood"; that is, they will almost automatically accept his unit evaluations of performances because they believe that such responses are based on known right answers. This prediction probably would be confirmed by empirical test, but it would constitute a rather stringent limitation on the types of situations to which the theory could make predictions. In most problem-solving groups there is no answer key to which some members can refer in evaluating performance outputs. A more general statement of the important characteristics of a source is necessary.

In the previous examples and in many other empirical studies in the social self tradition, it seems to be crucial for p and o to perceive that the evaluator possesses a high likelihood of being correct when he makes a unit evaluation. This kind of argument is implicitly adopted in all the social self research that attempted to manipulate self-evaluations; for example, Backman et al. used an impressive "clinical psychologist" as their evaluator, Jones used the experimenter, and Israel, Videbeck, and Maehr et al. used experts on physical fitness or public speaking. The investigators have chosen evaluators who were highly competent to evaluate performances because of their special skill or training.

A second possible reason to believe that an evaluator is likely to be correct is the perception that he himself possesses high ability at the task being performed. An individual who is perceived to be very competent may thus seem to be more likely to know whether another individual's performances are good or bad than would an individual who is perceived to have low ability. A definition which encompasses both of these possible bases of source-hood is the following:

DEFINITION 2.   e is a source for p in task situation S if and only if p believes that e is more capable of evaluating performances than p is himself.

The theory asserts that if p does accept e as a source, p will accept his unit evaluations of performances; that is, the unit evaluations of performances made by p will be the same as those made by e. Assumption 1 specifies this effect.

ASSUMPTION 1.   If e is a source for p in task situation S, the unit evaluations of any actor's performances made by p will be the same as those made by e.

To make explicit some of the reasoning behind the assumptions of the theory, as well as to clarify exposition of the ideas, we represent them in the form of balance diagrams, following conventions developed by Cartwright and Harary (1956).

In Figure 4.1 and succeeding balance diagrams, unit evaluations of performance outputs are represented by directed lines, and unit relations by brackets.

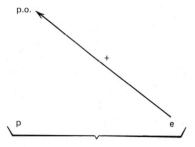

Figure 4.1   Evaluation of a performance output by an evaluator whom p has accepted as a source.

Since p has accepted e as a source, there is a unit relation "acceptance" between p and e, represented by the bracket connecting these two points. In this diagram, e has positively evaluated a performance output, as represented by the + sign on the line connecting e and p.o. Since all unit relations that form are positive by definition, there is no need for a sign on the p-e bond.

Assumption 1 states that if p has accepted e as a source, the unit relation between p and e exists; and when e evaluates a performance output, the p–p.o. bond will also form *and* will take the same sign as the e–p.o. bond. This is represented in Figure 4.2 by the addition of the p–p.o. bond, which has the same sign as the e–p.o. bond. Note that by Assumption 1 if p has *not* accepted e as a source, the p–e unit relation will not have formed, and the theory does not predict how p will evaluate the performance output. This case is considered further in later chapters.

The effect of unit evaluations of performance is specified in Assumption 2: when p evaluates the performance outputs of any actor, he will eventually come to hold a similar expectation state for that actor. In this situation, of course, that actor could be either p himself or o. If p does form expectations for the actor, Assumption 2 says that they must be in accord with the unit evaluations of the performances. Less formally, Assumption 2 says that p will eventually move from saying "I think he's right" to "I think he has high ability" and "I expect him to be right in the future." Assumption 2 specifically rules out going from a series

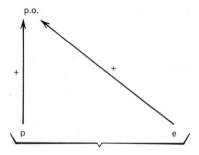

Figure 4.2   p's evaluation of the performance output.

of either positive or negative unit evaluations to a contradictory expectation state—for example, from "I think he's right" to "I think he has low ability."

ASSUMPTION 2.   In task situation S, if p makes unit evaluations of the performance outputs of any actor, p will come to assign to that actor an expectation state that is consistent with those evaluations.

Assumption 2 does not assert that p will form expectations on the basis of a single unit evaluation. The meaning intended is that formation of an expectation state requires a series of consistent unit evaluations. In this sense, formation of performance expectations is a function of the number of unit evaluations and of such other factors as the consistency of evaluations and the time interval between evaluations. However, we are not centrally concerned with all these factors, nor with a more precise specification of the numerical properties of the process of formation.

Figure 4.3 is a diagrammatic representation of Assumption 2. The actor o has been added to the diagram of Figure 4.2, and a unit relation between him and the performance output indicates that the performance output is associated in p's mind with o. The performance output could equally well have been made by p, in which case the other actor in the diagram would be designated by p' (p as an object of orientation to himself). In that case, p would be concerned with evaluating his own performance and with forming expectations for himself.

Assumption 2 says that in the course of interaction a generalized evaluational bond will form between p and o, and this bond will be formed in a balanced fashion. In other words, if p is evaluating a series of performance outputs of o, he will develop a generalized evaluation of o or will form an expectation state for the actor o. Moreover, this generalized evaluation or expectation state will be consistent with p's evaluation of o's performance outputs. This is shown in Figure 4.4, with the expectation state represented by a double line to distinguish it from a unit evaluation (single line).

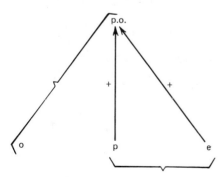

Figure 4.3   p's perception of a unit relation between an actor and an evaluated performance output.

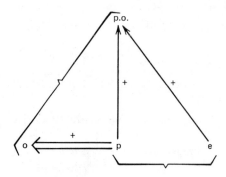

Figure 4.4 Formation of an expectation state for the actor o.

Next we specify formally the circumstances under which p will accept the actor e as a source, and the consequences of p's forming expectations for himself and the actor o. This is the task of Assumptions 3 and 4. Once p has assigned expectation states, these two assumptions assert that the states will determine probabilistically all important features of the observable future interaction. The states tend to be self-maintaining—once they exist, they affect the very conditions that led to their formation.

Assumption 3 specifies the effect of p's expectations for other actors on his observable interaction with them, and Assumption 4 specifies the effect of expectations p holds for himself and others on his observable interaction with those others.

ASSUMPTION 3: In task situation S, if p holds higher expectations for an actor o_1, than for an other actor o_2, then:
  a. p will be more likely to give o_1 an action opportunity than o_2.
  b. p will be more likely to evaluate positively o_1's future performance outputs than o_2's.
  c. p will be more likely to agree with o_1's performance outputs than with o_2's.
  d. p will be more likely to accept o_1 than o_2 as a source.

ASSUMPTION 4. In task situation S, the higher the expectations an actor p holds for himself relative to the expectations he holds for an other:
  a. The more likely p is to accept a given action opportunity and make a performance output.
  b. In case of disagreement with o, the more likely is p to reject influence.

This completes the theory. It differs from previous versions of expectation theory in two ways, both of them derived from ideas in the social self tradition. First, this version adds and defines the concept of a source—an actor whose evaluations of performance will be accepted by others in the system. Second, it makes acceptance of an actor as a source probabilistically dependent on expectations held for him. The higher the expectations held for any actor in the system, the more likely is he to become a source, that is, to have his unit evaluations of performances used by others to form conceptions of ability for the actors in the system.

According to Assumption 3d, the higher the expectations held by p for an evaluator, the more likely is the evaluator to become a source for p. Then the definition of a source (Definition 2) and the other parts of Assumptions 3 and 4 specify the consequences of e's becoming a source: he is predicted to be able to determine the expectations held by p for himself and o, and these expectations are predicted to affect future interaction between p and o.

Note that Assumption 3d does not preclude the possibility that an evaluator for whom p holds low expectations will become a source for p. There are at least two ways this could occur. First, if that actor has access to evaluative information, such as an answer key, his ability level at the task is irrelevant; the theory is intended to predict that any evaluator possessing such information is very likely to be accepted as a source, regardless of p's perception of his task ability. Second, and more interesting, is the possibility that p will think that even an evaluator for whom he holds low expectations has more ability than he himself does. Recall that it is one of the boundary conditions of task situation S that p has *no idea* of his own ability. Therefore, it is still possible that an individual could decide, on learning the group task, that even an evaluator of low ability (i.e., one for whom he holds low performance expectations) has more ability than p himself does. This occurrence would be especially likely, for instance, when p perceives the task to be very difficult.

Derivations from the basic source theory were chosen for test to yield maximum information about the two most important and most problematic features of the theory. First, we say that whether an evaluator's opinions will "matter" is dependent on the expectations held for the quality of p's own performance; this assertion is central to the theory and represents an important idea for test. The second significant assertion is that expectations held by individuals in interaction will determine features of the observable interaction between them. Since behavioral effects of known expectation states have been recorded in other expectation theory studies, data collected from our experiment can be compared with previous data to assess the relative strength of expectations produced by an evaluator.

Let us now introduce some abbreviated notation. An evaluator for whom p holds high expectations will be referred to as a High Evaluator (HE); an evaluator for whom p holds low expectations will be referred to as a Low Evaluator (LE). If p's performances have been evaluated positively and o's have been evaluated negatively by e, then *relative to o*, p will be said to be in a $(+-)$ condition. Note that we do not say that p holds a $(+-)$ *expectation state*, for this may or may not be true. According to the theory, whether p does hold the expectation state depends on whether he has accepted the evaluator as a source; the *consequences* of his acceptance or nonacceptance constitute part of the empirical tests. Notice further that we are concerned with *differential* relative expectation states. The $(++)$ and $(--)$ conditions would be expected to produce identical effects on behavior, and for our version of expectation theory they are not of further interest.

Combining notation for evaluators with that for the evaluations made of p's and of o's performances yields the following four experimental conditions: (1) if p has received positive evaluations and o has received negative evaluations from an evaluator for whom p holds high expectations, from p's point of view, we have the HE $(+-)$ condition; (2) if p and o have received negative and positive evaluations, respectively, p is in the HE $(-+)$ condition; (3) if the evaluations are the same as in condition 1 but p holds low expectations for the evaluator, p is in the LE $(+-)$ condition; (4) if the evaluations are the same as in condition 2, but p holds low expectations for the evaluator, p is in the LE $(-+)$ condition.

We now proceed to the derivations from the theory that are subjected to test in the first source experiment. Combining Assumptions 1, 2, and 3d of the theory yields a prediction that when p holds high expectations for e, performance evaluations by e are quite likely to affect p's expectation state. If the expectations held by p for e were "infinitely high," and if the number of performance evaluations made by e were also infinite, p's expectation state would be completely determined according to these assumptions. Since these conditions would not possibly obtain in any empirical situation meeting the conditions of S, we use the less certain term "quite likely." Addition of Assumption 4b, relating acceptance of influence to conditions of disagreement, enables derivation of the following empirical consequence:

DERIVATION 1.   In case of disagreement with o, the probability of p's rejecting influence is greater in the HE $(+-)$ condition than in the HE $(-+)$ condition.

Also, since even an evaluator for whom p holds low expectations is assumed to have some probability of becoming a source, the same set of assumptions also yields:

DERIVATION 2.   In case of disagreement with o, the probability of p's rejecting influence is greater in the LE $(+-)$ condition than in the LE $(-+)$ condition.

However, the theory also predicts that an e for whom p holds low expectations is less likely to become a source, hence less likely to be able to produce these expectation states and consequent behaviors, than is an e for whom p holds high expectations. Holding constant the nature of the performance evaluations and varying the expectations p holds for the evaluator, we expect the HE to be more effective than the LE:

DERIVATION 3.   In case of disagreement with o, the probability of p's rejecting influence is greater in the HE $(+-)$ condition than in the LE $(+-)$ condition.

DERIVATION 4.   In case of disagreement with o, the probability of p's rejecting influence is greater in the LE $(-+)$ condition than in the HE $(-+)$ condition.

Combining these four derivations yields:

DERIVATION 5.   In case of disagreement with p and o, the probabilities of p's rejecting influence will be in the following order: HE $(-+)$ < LE $(-+)$ < LE $(+-)$ < HE $(+-)$.

Experimental Procedures.   In the first source experiment, 20 subjects were assigned randomly to each of the four conditions. All 80 subjects, who were males between ages 18 and 24, were students recruited from a junior college in California for a "study in group interaction." Subjects were contacted and scheduled by telephone for the study, and the groups were conducted at the Stanford Laboratory, several miles from their home college.

The "basic source experiment," which is modified for all subsequent experiments reported here, consists of two phases. In phase I, both members of a pair of subjects judge a set of 20 slides, and these performances are evaluated by "person #3," a fictitious third subject. Person #3 is described as being either highly competent to evaluate performance (the HE conditions), or as possessing low competence (the LE conditions). To one subject in each group, #3 gives mostly positive evaluations [the $(+-)$ condition]; to the other, mostly negative evaluations [the $(-+)$ condition]. In phase II, the expectations held by each member of the pair of subjects is measured, using the $P(s)$ measure. These expectation states are predicted to vary directly with two factors; first, whether person #3's evaluations are accepted (which depends on the HE–LE manipulation), and second, whether those evaluations of the subject are mostly positive or mostly negative. Details of the basic source experiment are given in Appendix 2.

Results reported here and in later chapters reflect exclusion of data from subjects who do not meet one or more scope conditions of the theory. For this first source experiment, data from 4 subjects (5% of the sample) were excluded. Criteria for exclusion are described in detail in Appendix 3.

By the design of the study, the experimenter has granted the fictitious person #3 the right to evaluate performances of both subjects in every group. The experimenter thus has granted person #3 a special social position that has been denied to both real subjects, for they are not permitted to evaluate any unit performances in the first phase. Moreover, the evaluator's opinions are the only possible information available to subjects in the first phase of the study. If a subject is interested in evaluating his own unit performances in the first series of slides, the only usable information he has (other than his own judgment of the slide) is the evaluation from person #3. However, we have predicted that this design feature alone, is not sufficient to guarantee that person #3 will be listened to. The theory predicts that his unit evaluations will be accepted by subjects and used to form expectation states or ability conceptions only when the evaluator is described as being of high ability.

Results.   For each source experiment, we present two types of data analysis. Major tests of the theory are conducted from predictions that the $P(s)$ figures for conditions of the experiment will vary in the ways predicted by the theory. Other sources of information—relevant both to testing the theory and to specific experimental conditions—can be obtained from experimental data. Such statistics as variance about the mean likelihood of accepting influence, likelihood of alternating responses in the situation, and shape of the distribution of subjects with various response patterns can be examined for added information. However, the theory does not enable derivation of predictions concerning the variance across subjects in various conditions without several additional, nontheoretical assumptions. Since these assumptions are often of the type that does not permit a high degree of confidence, it would not be appropriate to consider such statistics to be strictly relevant to the confirmation status of the theory. Therefore, when data other than those on rejection of influence are presented, the necessary additional assumptions are noted, and these data should be interpreted more cautiously than data on rejection of influence.

Rejection of Influence.   The five derivations from the theory can be tested by using the overall mean $P(s)$ data by condition (Table 4.1), which are in accord with all five derivations. Table 4.2 presents the results of two nonparametric tests of the various predicted comparisons. The first four comparisons between pairs of conditions are tested using the Mann-Whitney U statistic, and the fifth derivation is tested using the Jonckheere test, which tests the differences between all con-

TABLE 4.1   OVERALL $P(s)$ FOR SUBJECTS
BY CONDITION

Condition	$P(s)$	n
HE $(+-)$	.80	19
HE $(-+)$	.46	18
LE $(+-)$	.65	19
LE $(-+)$	.58	20

ditions and also the predicted ordering of conditions. Rows 1, 3, and 5 show that the confidence level of the difference of the first, third, and fifth predictions is beyond .05; row 2 indicates that the confidence level of difference of the second prediction is .062; and in row 4 the confidence level of the fourth prediction is .085.

Besides these overall mean figures, the $P(s)$ data can be examined for trends in time for rejection of influence. According to the theory, expectation states should be formed before the beginning of the interaction between p and o, for all evaluations of their performances should have taken place by that time. Therefore, differences in $P(s)$ should be apparent at the beginning of the series of disagreement trials, and the theory gives no reason to expect that the lines will show changes through time. Figure 4.5 plots $P(s)$ lines for the four conditions, by blocks of five trials.

For all conditions, $P(s)$ drops slightly from first to second quarters. After that, with the exception of the LE $(-+)$ condition, there is little evidence of change in slope through time. The most persuasive evidence for predictions is the consistent lack of overlap of any lines of the different conditions. Possible reasons for the drop between the first and the second quarters are discussed below.

Comparisons also can be drawn between data from this experiment and

TABLE 4.2   CONFIDENCE LEVELS OF PREDICTED DIFFERENCES

Predicted Comparison	n's	U	P
HE $(+-)$ > HE $(-+)$	19, 18	38.0	$p < .05$
LE $(+-)$ > LE $(-+)$	19, 20	135.5	$p = .062$
HE $(+-)$ > LE $(+-)$	19, 19	61.0	$p < .05$
LE $(-+)$ > HE $(-+)$	20, 18	141.5	$p = .085$
HE $(+-)$ > LE $(+-)$ >	19, 19,		$p < .05$
LE $(-+)$ > HE $(-+)$	20, 18		

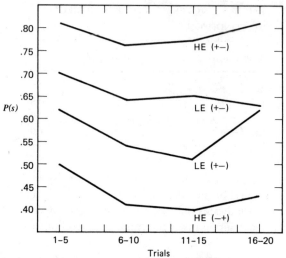

Figure 4.5 $P(s)$ curves by blocks of five trials.

those from previous work. An experiment differing from this one in that the experimenter evaluated subjects' performances in phase I was reported by Camilleri et al. (1972). Table 4.3 compares overall mean $P(s)$ data from HE conditions of our experiment with data from comparable conditions of the previous experiment. For both the $(+-)$ and the $(-+)$ expectation conditions, $P(s)$ data do not vary appreciably whether the evaluator is the experimenter, as in the previous study, or the HE, as in the present study.

Comparisons with the previous experiment must be drawn cautiously, since there were differences in subject population and experimenters, as well as detail differences in the instructions and the number of trials in each phase of the experiment, but the similarity of data is striking. For the HE $(+-)$ condition, the figure is .80; for the Exp $(+-)$, .76. For the HE $(-+)$ condition, the

TABLE 4.3 $P(s)$ OF SUBJECTS ACCORDING TO
EVALUATOR OF PERFORMANCES

	Evaluator	
Expectation Condition	HE (present)	Exp. (previous)
$(+-)$	.80	.76
$(-+)$	.46	.42

figure is .46; for the Exp $(-+)$, .42. Presumably the most important character-istic of the experimenter is not his own level of ability. Rather, his performance evaluations were accepted because subjects believed he had access to an answer key (i.e., to objective evaluative information). The similarity of results, therefore, may suggest that for this experimental situation at least, the effects of evaluations from an evaluator are very nearly identical, whether the evaluator's basis for being perceived as "competent to evaluate" is access to objective evaluative information, as the experimenter had, or possession of high task ability.

Variance Across Subjects. Another method of determining differences between the four conditions of the experiment is to compare the amount of variance in the data from each condition. Table 4.4 presents the variance about the mean *number* of self resolutions per subject [not $P(s)$].

There is considerably greater variance in each $(-+)$ condition than in the corresponding $(+-)$ condition. Comparison of rows 1 and 2 shows greater variance in the HE $(-+)$ condition than in the HE $(+-)$ condition and com-parison of rows 3 and 4 shows greater variance in the LE $(-+)$ condition than in the LE $(+-)$ condition. Also, comparisons of row 1 with row 3, and of row 2 with row 4, permits the following more general comparisons of variances: (1) for the $(+-)$ state, there is *less* variance in the HE condition than in the LE condition; (2) for the $(-+)$ state, there is *greater* variance in the HE condition than in the LE condition. Comparison of all rows of Table 4.4 reveals the fol-lowing ordering of conditions by amount of variance: HE $(-+)$ > LE $(-+)$ > LE $(+-)$ > HE $(+-)$.

TABLE 4.4   VARIANCES OF THE MEAN NUMBER
OF SELF RESOLUTIONS PER SUBJECT

Condition	Variance	n
HE $(+-)$	3.50	19
HE $(-+)$	20.48	18
LE $(+-)$	6.89	19
LE $(-+)$	12.36	20

In Table 4.5 we use Snedecor's *variance ratio* between possible pairs of condi-tions to assess the magnitude of differences of the variances. At the .05 level of confidence, variances are different in the HE $(+-)$ and the HE $(-+)$ condi-tions (row 2), and the HE $(+-)$ and LE $(-+)$ conditions (row 3). With the possible exception of the HE $(-+)$ and the LE $(+-)$ pair in row 4, confidence in other variance differences does not reach the .05 level.

TABLE 4.5   VARIANCE RATIO BETWEEN PAIRS OF CONDITIONS

Conditions	F	df	Confidence Interval (two-tailed)
HE $(+-)$, LE $(+-)$	1.97	18, 18	$.10 < p < .20$
HE $(+-)$, HE $(-+)$	5.86	18, 17	$.002 < p < .02$
HE $(+-)$, LE $(-+)$	3.53	18, 19	$.002 < p < .02$
HE $(-+)$, LE $(+-)$	2.97	17, 18	$.02 < p < .10$
HE $(-+)$, LE $(-+)$	1.66	17, 19	$.10 < p < .20$
LE $(+-)$, LE $(-+)$	1.79	18, 19	$.10 < p < .20$

Since the theory predicts that populations of the $(+-)$ and the $(-+)$ conditions will be different, perhaps in this sense the results of rows 2, 3, and (possibly) 4 are in accord with expectations. However, although assumptions of the theory do predict that the $(+-)$ and $(-+)$ populations will differ, they do not predict that this difference necessarily will be reflected in the amounts of variance. Therefore, it does not seem wise to attach great importance either to the comparisons that do exceed the .05 level or to those that do not.

Within any condition, change over time in amount of variance across subjects can be discussed in many ways. We present here one simple interpretation. If variance within any or all conditions either increases or decreases steadily through time, it can be taken as an indication that some consistent effects are being produced by the interaction process itself, as contrasted with effects produced by the principal experimental manipulations. For example, if variance was increasing linearly within all conditions, it would be reasonable to suppose that the process of resolving the series of disagreements was affecting the expectation states held by subjects at the beginning of the series of trials. Or, if the overall amount of variance within any condition is the result principally of a particular time period, such as the first or the last quarter of trials, we would have to consider this finding in evaluating the overall variance differences between conditions. Table 4.6

TABLE 4.6   VARIANCES ABOUT THE BLOCK MEAN NUMBER
OF SELF RESOLUTIONS PER SUBJECT

Condition	1st Quarter	2nd Quarter	3rd Quarter	4th Quarter
HE $(+-)$	.55	.70	.54	.66
HE $(-+)$	1.90	1.32	1.76	2.69
LE $(+-)$	.60	1.18	1.18	.77
LE $(-+)$	1.19	1.78	.99	1.78

presents the variances about the mean number of self resolutions, by blocks of five trials.

First, we note in Table 4.6 that the relative overall variances of Table 4.4 are generally preserved when the series of trials is broken into blocks of five. Within every block, the HE $(-+)$ condition shows greater variance than the HE $(+-)$ condition; and in every quarter except the third, the LE $(-+)$ condition shows greater variance than the LE $(+-)$ condition. Thus the overall variance *ordering* in Table 4.4 also appears within almost every block of trials.

Second, since the ordering is generally preserved within the blocks, it can be concluded that the relative overall variances of Table 4.4 were *not* produced by any single quarter but accurately reflect the amounts of variance in the data for each condition.

Finally, examination of the quarters shows no clear-cut evidence of systematic increase or decrease in variance through time. Therefore, Table 4.6 gives little support to the thesis that the disagreement interaction process itself is producing simple changes in expectation states held by the subjects.

Another partial explanation for the observed ordering of conditions by amount of variance depends more closely on the formulation of the theory, especially with respect to acceptance of the evaluator as a source, and the effects of the expectations that are held for potential sources. Assumption 3d states that the higher the expectations held for an evaluator, the more likely is he to become a source. By assumption 1, we suppose that the unit evaluations of performances made by p will be the same as those made by the source. Then by the addition of Assumption 2, the theory as presently formulated predicts that the evaluations made by a source will be very likely to affect the expectations p holds for himself and for o. Of course p may not accept the evaluator as a source—this depends on the expectations p holds for e—but *if he does* accept e as a source, e's evaluations will be very likely to affect p's expectation state.

Alternatively, we might argue that any evaluator is likely to have some effect on p's expectations, but the degree of that effect will be determined by the expectations p holds for the evaluator. In other words, the difference between these two formulations is in the conceptualization of a "significant other": whether, according to the present theory, only certain individuals can be significant others and all significant others will have a considerable effect on the individual's expectations, or, as the alternative might assert, being a significant other is a matter of degrees and all others are to some degree significant in determining an individual's self-expectation. That is, we want to know whether everybody's evaluations matter somewhat, or whether only some people's evaluations matter—and these matter a great deal.

It would be difficult to discriminate between the two formulations by using data from the HE conditions of this experiment: both predict that the HE will be very likely to induce expectations as the result of his evaluations. Predictions would be quite different for the LE conditions, however. The present theory predicts that both LE conditions will contain some subjects who hold expectations based on evaluations from e and some who hold either undifferentiated expectations or expectations formed on the basis of spurious, theoretically irrelevant factors. The alternative, on the other hand, would predict that the LE will produce "weak" expectations for all or for nearly all subjects in each condition.

Other expectation theory research has found that the disagreement interaction situation used for this experiment will produce differentiated expectations in subjects who are initially undifferentiated. Thus for one test of the original formulation we could examine the variance by blocks, to detect an increase through time in the two LE conditions; such an increase might be produced when the subjects who originally did not form expectations based on the evaluator's opinions formed $(+-)$ or $(-+)$ expectations as the result of resolving the series of disagreements. The block variances of the LE conditions shown in Table 4.6 reveal no simple increase in variance; the amount of variance through time is essentially constant in these two conditions, as would be predicted from the alternative formulation.

On the other hand, the two formulations also make different predictions for the rejection of influence data, especially for the first few trials, before interaction effects of the disagreement resolution have a chance to emerge. Using the $P(s)$ criterion, the ideal time to test the two formulations would be immediately following the manipulation phase of the experiment, before there has been any interaction between subjects. If the present formulation is correct, there should be two populations visible at this point. Such analysis assumes that each of the two populations will contain individuals who display $P(s)$ figures with only a small range about their respective mean values.

Since it is impossible to examine data before any interaction has had a chance to occur, we select instead, data from the first quarter of the critical trials as the best available approximation. Because the test conditions are not ideal, and because numbers of subjects and of trials to be used are quite small for the type of analysis performed, results of the analysis cannot be interpreted with the confidence allowable for those from previous analyses.

In using variance data, we must also assume that there will be less variance across subjects who have formed differentiated expectations than across those who have not. If this assumption is made, the present theoretical formulation predicts that each of the two LE conditions will show two populations at the outset: those who have formed expectations based on e's evaluations and those who have not. The alternative view might predict that each condition will contain a single population of subjects who have formed a "weak" expectation state. More precisely, the present theory predicts a bimodal distribution of subjects according to the number of trials on which they accept influence; the alternative predicts a unimodal distribution.

Figure 4.6 is a bar graph of subjects in each of the two LE conditions, arranged according to their total numbers of stay responses for the first five trials (i.e., according to how often during the first five trials they rejected influence). For the LE $(-+)$ condition there is some evidence for the predictions of a bimodal distribution. However for the LE $(+-)$ condition, Figure 4.6 shows no such evidence.

Psychological Tension in the Interaction Situation. A possible explanation for the greater variance in both $(-+)$ conditions is the conjecture that this state involves more psychological tension than the $(+-)$ state. In this section we consider two possible pieces of evidence for such tension.

First, on a relatively intuitive level, we might examine the likelihood of alternations for various conditions. An alternation is defined as resolving the disagreement on any trial n in a way differing from the resolution on trial $n - 1$; for example, resolving trial $n - 1$ in favor of self and trial n in favor of the other. The proportions of alternations in various conditions cannot be directly compared, however, for they are related to the likelihood of accepting influence in the following way: the closer the $P(s)$ figure to .50, the greater the probability of an alternation, assuming an independent trials process. Since data from expectation theory experiments in general, and from this experiment in particular, do meet the independent trials assumption, the expected and observed proportions of alternations can be compared, with the expected figure adjusted to take into account overall mean $P(s)$ figures for each condition.

The formula for expected proportion of alternations, assuming an independent trials process, is: expected $P(\text{alt}) = 2P_i (1 - P_i)$, where $P_i = P(s)$ for condition i. Table 4.7 presents expected and observed frequencies of alternations for the conditions of the experiment.

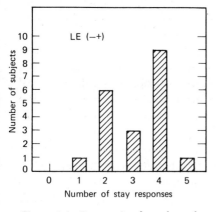
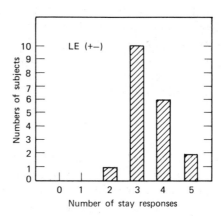

Figure 4.6   Bar graph of number of stay responses per subject in the LE conditions for trials 1 to 5.

TABLE 4.7   EXPECTED AND OBSERVED PROPORTIONS
OF ALTERNATIONS

Condition	Expected P (alt)	Observed P (alt)
HE $(+-)$	.32	.34
HE $(-+)$	.50	.48
LE $(+-)$	.46	.48
LE $(-+)$	.49	.46

Table 4.7 shows no tendency for greater alternating behavior in the $(-+)$ conditions than in the $(+-)$ conditions; all values appear to be within the range that might occur by chance. Therefore, if $(-+)$ states do involve more tension than $(+-)$ states, there is little evidence that this difference is expressed in high rates of alternating behavior.

We can also examine data for evidence of psychological tension by studying variances within conditions. In Table 4.4 variance in each of the two $(-+)$ conditions is greater than that in the corresponding $(+-)$ condition; that is, variance is greater in the HE $(-+)$ condition than in the HE $(+-)$ condition, and also greater in the LE $(-+)$ condition than in the LE $(+-)$ condition. With the evaluator (HE or LE) held constant, the $(-+)$ condition shows greater variance than the $(+-)$ condition. We may therefore inquire whether the $(-+)$ expectation state itself is producing the higher variances observed for both evaluators.

One interpretation of variance within a condition argues that there is an inherent imbalance in the $(-+)$ expectation state. To illustrate this idea, consider Figure 4.7a, a balance diagram schematizing the relations between p and himself, with p' representing an actor as he views himself, when p holds low expectations for himself. In this figure, the sign on the evaluation bond represents the low self-expectation. Let us assume that any individual has some kind of unit relationship with himself (e.g., possession or similarity), indicating this relation with a bracket, as in Figure 4.7b. Since unit relations are positive, the relational unit involving p and p' has both a positive and a negative component, thus is imbalanced. As a consequence, tension is generated within this single cycle.

Since the unit relation cannot be dissolved, the only two possible ways p has of resolving the imbalance and achieving balance are to change the sign of the expectation bond to positive or to dissolve it by putting performance expectations out of his mind. The former course would mean that in the experimental situation he would become $(+-)$ instead of $(-+)$. The latter course would mean becoming individually oriented instead of collectively oriented, for expec-

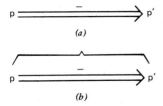

Figure 4.7   (a) Balance diagram of an individual with low self-expectation. (b) Addition of a unit relation.

tations become nonrelevant to final choices when the subject is individually oriented.

In terms of data from this experiment, either undetected individual orientation or "escaping" from the (−+) condition would contain at least two sets of subjects: those with the (−+) expectations and those with some other pattern of expectations. It seems reasonable to assume that for subjects who are individually oriented or who hold (+−) expectations, $P(s)$ would be higher than for those who hold (−+) expectations. Strictly speaking, of course, an increase in variance would require only that the $P(s)$ figures *differ* for any of these possibilities and for the (−+) condition, and that assumption would certainly be likely to be supported.

We believe that there is reason to expect higher variances within the (−+) conditions than within the (+−) conditions. However, this analysis alone cannot account for the finding that variance was greater in the HE (−+) condition than in the LE (−+) condition, nor for the finding that variance was greater in the LE (+−) condition than in the HE (+−) condition. In other words, an explanation has been constructed for only part of the observed ordering.

Adding further assumptions permits a more complete accounting for the observed ordering of conditions by variance, though still not for the complete ordering. The observed ordering was

$$\text{HE } (-+) > \text{LE } (-+) > \text{LE } (+-) > \text{HE } (+-);$$

the "imbalance" assumption accounts only for the greater variance shown by the (−+) conditions than by the (+−) conditions, or:

$$\text{HE } (-+), \text{LE } (-+) > \text{LE } (+-), \text{HE } (+-).$$

The original assumptions of the theory predict that the high evaluator will be more likely to induce subjects to form expectations that are consistent with this evaluation than will the low evaluator. If fewer subjects in the LE conditions form the expectations than in the HE conditions, this would produce greater variance in the LE conditions. Therefore, by adding the assumptions of the theory to the "imbalance" assumption, the right side of the observed ordering may also be explained:

$$\text{HE } (-+), \text{LE } (-+) > \text{LE } (+-) > \text{HE } (+-).$$

However we cannot account for the entire observed ordering without the additional assumption that variance produced by subjects with $(-+)$ expectations in the HE $(-+)$ condition is greater than the variance produced when subjects do not form expectations in the LE $(-+)$ condition. We are not prepared to espouse this interesting conjecture at this point, since it involves acceptance of too many untestable assumptions, as well as the question of a negative source, an important theoretical issue discussed in Chapter 5.

This exercise of explaining the variance orderings is completely *ad hoc* and has no direct relation to the theory. It does provide a partial accounting for the data, suggesting that in this empirical setting, there is reason to believe that the $(-+)$ condition produces psychological tension for the individual.

Summary and Conclusions.   Data from the first source experiment indicate a high degree of support for the derived predictions of the theory. Subjects in the $(-+)$ conditions were more likely to accept influence than were those in the $(+-)$ conditions, and this difference was more pronounced for those in the HE conditions than for those in the LE conditions. Those in the HE $(-+)$ were about 2.7 times as likely to accept influence as those in the HE $(+-)$ condition; for the LE $(-+)$ and the LE $(+-)$ conditions, the difference was much less. The observed ordering of conditions by rejection of influence was also as predicted.

Overall results of empirical tests are supportive of the theory as presented; the major predictions on rejection of influence are confirmed in terms of the $P(s)$ differences between conditions. Analysis of $P(s)$ data in terms of time trends indicate the same type of support, especially because the mean $P(s)$ curves never overlap for any of the conditions. These results can be summarized as follows:

1. The expectations held for the evaluator and for p and o produce a difference in observable behavior.

2. The differences between conditions in acceptance of influence are substantial, are in the predicted direction, and are maintained through the series of trials.

We interpret the results of the first experiment slightly differently in terms of the social self and in terms of expectation theory. First, of course, we note that terms of the two approaches differ in some minor ways, and translation is necessary before application of the results is possible. Second, in drawing conclusions for the social self, we must relax, cautiously, some of the rigorous scope conditions necessary for application of formal expectation theory. Strictly speaking, for example, we can apply this theory, and the findings of experimental tests, only to task-oriented situations (i.e., the individual is a member of a group and is highly motivated toward achieving the group goal). The social self tradition is also interested in situations marked by difficulty in ascertaining that the task-orientation condition is met (i.e., in a variety of evaluative situations it is impossible to know for sure that an individual is task oriented). Keeping this caution in mind, we examine some implications of this work which seem *likely* to be true.

The major significance of this work is to demonstrate that not everyone's opinions matter to the individual who is concerned with evaluating performances. The differences between the two LE and the two HE experimental conditions show quite clearly that unit evaluations from an individual perceived to have high ability at the task are much more likely to produce observable effects in future interaction, and presumably to have produced unobservable effects in actors' cognitive conceptions of ability. This result also provides a partial answer to the question of what people, or *kinds* of people, constitute significant others: at least one requisite characteristic of a significant other in this situation is the belief by others that he is competent at the task. When his perceived competence is low, the evidence of this study indicates that his evaluations will most probably be ignored by others.

Second, variance differences between conditions, and the balance diagrams we have presented, raise an interesting issue. In simplest statement, this issue arises from the intuitively appealing idea that it is somehow less pleasant to have a low opinion of one's own ability than to hold a high opinion. The balance diagrams offer to explain this situation by suggesting that simultaneous awareness that one is related to onself and does not evaluate one's self highly produces an imbalanced cycle in the p–p' relation. Such imbalance is then posited to produce tension and an attempt to resolve the tension by making a change. This interpretation is partially congruent with the observed ordering of conditions from this experiment on amount of variance. But there is no evidence for the idea in the alternations, which also would be expected to reflect the tension.

Finally, the empirical consequences of a given self-evaluation have been somewhat clarified by this research. The social self tradition has already been described as generally lacking consistent or determinate predictions for precise behavioral consequences of the individual's conceptions of his own ability. The perspective of expectation theory, especially Assumptions 3 and 4 of the version offered here, does yield the possibility of deriving such predictions. Rejection of influence—the measure used in this study of expectation states—is one such consequence. The set of assumptions used here could also have derived predictions for amounts of interaction, likelihood of receiving action opportunities or agreements, or several other observable consequences. Whether these parallel predictions from expectation theory have been tested is not important, and this research did not test them. Much more significantly, the theory enables determinate predictions to be made dealing with features of future interaction *as the direct result* of previous evaluations and of the individual's performance expectations.

In the next chapter we consider an interesting theoretical issue that emerged from some of the interviews conducted with subjects following this experiment, involving their interpretation of evaluations from the LE.

CHAPTER FIVE

THE NEGATIVE SOURCE EXPERIMENT

The Problem. Unexpectedly, some subjects of the first source experiment seemed to regard the low ability evaluator as a "negative source." That is, they seemed to form expectations *opposite* to his unit evaluations: if he gave them a large proportion of positive evaluations, they formed low expectations for their own performance, and if he gave them a high proportion of negative evaluations, they formed high expectations for their own performance. These subjects often reported in the postexperimental interviews that they felt the evaluator was more likely to be wrong than right, thus his evaluations should be interpreted to mean the reverse of what he said.

This information suggests that the LE conditions may have produced at least three types of expectations for subjects: some did form expectations consistent with the LE's evaluations, some seemed to ignore him, and a third set seemed to form expectations that were *inconsistent* with the evaluations received. The first two types of expectation patterns were predicted from the theory; the third "opposite" type was not.

The following interview excerpt illustrates what we have termed the "negative source phenomenon." The subject had had 17 out of 20 of his unit performance outputs in phase I positively evaluated by the LE.

Group no.: X40   Condition: LE $(+-)$ Interviewer: Webster

I: Did you find that it was helpful to you in phase I to know how #3 evaluated your choices?

S: Well, I don't know. (laughs)

I: Well, did you find that it hindered you?

S: No, but, uh, being that he, in this case, got a low score and, uh, we were only 3 off, uh, it would appear that I got a fairly low score.

This subject's overall $P(s)$ was .50; the average $P(s)$ for subjects in the LE $(+-)$ condition shown in Table 4.1 is .65.

For a subject in the LE $(-+)$ condition (i.e., for one whose performances were negatively evaluated), this "opposite" interpretation seemed to cause the formation of high expectations for his own performance. On the questionnaire he filled out immediately after the evaluations in phase I, this subject indicated that he felt he had *greater* ability than his partner.

Group no.: X40   Condition: LE $(-+)$ Interviewer: Sobieszek

I: Did it help you . . . to know #3's evaluations of your answers?

S: You mean for the second part? When I took it again?

I: Throughout the study.

S: Well it just—I didn't take what he said very seriously.

I: Why not?

S: 'Cause he got an 8—and an 8 was very rare and low—at least that's what it said.

I: So did you have any idea of how good you were at it? . . . From what he said?

S: I thought maybe I'd be a little better than what he said.

I: Did you think it was helpful to you in phase II to know what the other person's initial choice was before you made your final decision?

S: No, not really.

I: Why not?

S: Mainly because the other—party, the third party—gave him a high score.

I: Uh-huh (affirmative).

S: And he got a low score himself, so I didn't think much of him.

This subject's overall $P(s)$ was .75; the average $P(s)$ for subjects in the LE $(-+)$ condition was .58 (see Table 4.1).

The plausibility of these feelings is apparent. The LE manipulation consisted of telling subjects that the evaluator had achieved a score of 8 correct out of 20 on the first set of slides. The score was interpreted for them as being "a rare score, which would fall into the *lower* category for an individual performance." The "lower" category also appeared on a chart that described a score of 0 to 10 as RARE, POOR.

Since it is a central tenet of the social self orientation that the *interpretation* of opinions of the significant other determines the self, an issue such as the negative source is intriguing, implying as it does that some individuals, when they give an opinion, are more likely to influence people in a negative way than in a positive way. Intuitively, this idea has been expressed many times: "If that stupid person thinks my opinion is right, then I'm worried," or "I'm especially proud of the fact that my opponent has disagreed with every idea I've put forth." The belief that certain people possess such poor powers of discrimination or are so likely to be wrong that they are reliable indicators of a right answer (because they always fail to choose it), is certainly an established one in folklore.

It is possible to construct a fairly rigorous theoretical explanation of the phenomenon of the negative source. To do this, we use the same kind of balance diagrams we used to explicate the process of forming ability conceptions from the opinions of others. In the process, we confront an issue deliberately overlooked the first time through: the issue of making predictions regarding an individual who is receiving evaluations from someone for whom he has a low opinion.

In the original theoretical formulation, we considered only the case of the individual who holds a high opinion of the evaluator. In such a case, the high expectations held for the evaluator make the unit relation "acceptance as a source" very likely to form, by Assumption 3d.

When p holds low expectations for e, two predictions are possible. The original theory predicts that existence of low expectation relations between p and e will prevent formation of the "acceptance as a source" unit relation. A negative source formulation, on the other hand, would predict that existence of a low expectation for e would produce a tendency for a unit relation "acceptance as a negative source" to form. If we permit this unit relation to have a negative sign, at least for discussion purposes, we can construct a balance diagram in which p believes the opposite of whatever e says about performance outputs and will come to assign performance expectations to the actor associated with the p.o.'s that are inconsistent with the positive or negative nature of e's evaluations.

If o (of Figure 5.1) were p', then the figure would illustrate the subject's report in the first interview segment quoted—the subject has received positive evaluations from e of the unit performances made by himself (p') and, as a consequence, says he has formed *low* expectations for his own performance. As is, the figure illustrates the case in the second interview segment quoted: p sees the performances by o positively evaluated by the LE, and consequently forms *low* expectations for o.

The first formulation of the source theory makes no provision for a negative source. Assumption 3d says that the higher the expectations held for an actor, the more likely he is to be accepted as a source; no prediction is made for the actor who is not accepted as a source. Neither does the present theory provide

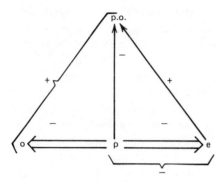

Figure 5.1 Effects of a negative source low evaluator.

for acceptance of a low evaluator as a negative source. Unless expectations held for an evaluator are high enough to foster his acceptance as a source, the present theory predicts that his unit evaluations will be ignored by actors when they form performance expectations for themselves and for one another.

A theoretical reformulation designed to take into account negative sources would have to resolve several issues that can be conveniently ignored in the more simple approach of the first theory. The largest problem is determining when the possibility of becoming a source ceases and when the possibility begins to exist for the evaluator to become a negative source. Clearly in the first experiment the evaluator was described as possessing a negative ability; he had received a score of 8 correct out of 20 on a set of binary problems. Even by pure guessing, he should have had a score of 10 out of 20 in this situation. But what of the individual who did receive a score of 10 out of 20? Would his evaluations be considered irrelevant in forming expectations, since he was correct exactly half the time? Or, since it is plausible to define a score of 10/20 on a test as being RARE and POOR, would this also be sufficient for him to become classified as a negative source? Is there a middle ground where we can be certain that an evaluator will be ignored and that above and below this area the possibility exists for him to become either a source or a negative source? If so, how wide is the middle ground, and does it extend equally far above and below the exact "chance likelihood" score of 10? All these questions, and others like them, make reformulation to account for the negative source a difficult task.

Before undertaking such a reformulation, we should note that the evidence for existence of a negative source is anecdotal. Interviews of this study were designed primarily to determine whether the scope conditions of the theory had been met. Although interviews can suggest ideas for future theoretical work and more rigorous empirical testing, and have frequently done so, such information must be interpreted with extreme caution. There are simply too many factors that can affect a subject's answers to questions in the postexperimental interviews used for this work. From data of the first source experiment alone, it was impossible to determine (1) whether the negative source actually existed in this experiment, or whether he was simply a rationalization offered by some subjects to explain their behavior in the situation; (2) if the phenomenon did exist, under what conditions, and for what proportion of the subjects in the LE conditions the evaluator was perceived this way; (3) what precise effect evaluations from a negative source would have on the expectations and the behavior of an individual in this experimental situation. The broad outlines of a reformulation incorporating the negative source are clear, but the prior question whether reformulation should be undertaken at all could not be answered from available data.

Thus we must ask, What kind of information will help to clarify the issue of the negative source? and What kind of experiment will provide such information in an unambiguous way? We have noted difficulties in relying on the interview in this experiment, and there did not seem to be any simple way of improving the quality of this information from subjects. Furthermore, in designing the situation for this research, a strategy decision was made to depend as little as possible on subjects' reports of their interpretation of the situation, seeking behavioral data, instead.

If we consider the hypothetical effect of a negative source on the $P(s)$ data from this experiment, we can design an experiment to establish whether the negative source must be conceptualized as part of the theory. By contrast with the two HE conditions of the first experiment, the LE conditions were expected to show the same types of $P(s)$ differences, but to a smaller extent. In the original theory, this happens when some subjects in the LE conditions ignore the evaluator.

However, if some subjects were forming expectations opposite to those which the LE's evaluations would produce, this would also lead to the observed decrease in difference between the $(+-)$ and the $(-+)$ conditions. If we extend the situation, we ask what the effect would be of an evaluator with even less ability than the LE in our first experiment, an individual whose lack of ability at the task is truly amazing. From the original formulation, we would expect that as the ability of the evaluator decreased, the proportion of subjects in each condition who ignore him would increase, thus that the $P(s)$ difference between the $(+-)$ and the $(-+)$ conditions would *decrease*. A greater proportion of subjects should hold undifferentiated expectations. On the other hand, from a negative source theory, we would expect that as the ability of the evaluator decreased, the proportion of subjects in each condition who form expectations opposite to his evaluations would increase, and the $P(s)$ difference between the $(+-)$ and the $(-+)$ conditions would *increase in an opposite fashion*.

This was the design of the negative source (NS) experiment. All details were the same as those of the first source experiment, except that the ability score of the NS evaluator was announced to subjects as 4 out of 20. This manipulation, which gave him an ability far less than chance would have given, was designed to emphasize that if there was to be such a thing as a negative ability, this person certainly possessed it.

Fifty subjects were run in the negative source experiment, 25 assigned randomly to each of the NS $(-+)$ and the NS $(+-)$ conditions. The subject pool was the same as that of the first source experiment. Since the manipulation involved giving the evaluator a less plausible score than that for the first experiment, greater losses for suspicion were anticipated, and in fact were found. In addition, some subjects had trouble understanding the experimental instructions, did not believe the evaluations came from person #3, or did not believe the phase II disagreements were real. Data from seven subjects who clearly did not meet conditions of the theory were excluded from analyses, bringing the number in the NS $(+-)$ condition to 20, and the number in the NS $(-+)$ condition to 23.

Results.   Data from the negative source experiment were compared with those from the first source experiment, and comparisons were drawn between the two conditions of the negative source experiment. Table 5.1 shows the mean $P(s)$ values for subjects in the two previous LE conditions and for subjects in the two conditions of the negative source experiment.

TABLE 5.1 $P(s)$ FOR SUBJECTS IN LE CONDITIONS
OF THE TWO EXPERIMENTS

Unit Evaluations	Evaluator's Score	
	8	4
$(+-)$	.65	.69
$(-+)$	.58	.63
Difference	.07	.06

First, the difference between the $(+-)$ and the $(-+)$ conditions is only slightly smaller for the negative source experiment than it was for the first source experiment. The differences in the first and the second experiments are .07 and .06, respectively. This finding can be interpreted in two ways, which are relevant to the question of whether theoretical reformulation is desirable. The first question is whether the $P(s)$ figures are closer together in the negative source experiment than they were in the first experiment; this result would be predicted by the original formulation. The figures are closer, but the difference is so slight as to be meaningless (.01). The second question is whether the $P(s)$ figures are "reversed," as would be predicted only by the negative source formulation; that is, whether the $P(s)$ of the $(+-)$ condition is *less* than the $P(s)$ of the $(-+)$ condition. They are not; and this is the single most important factor in deciding whether reformulation is necessary. Since such a reversal would clearly be necessary for support of the negative source idea, we conclude that the results of test of the major differences in the two predictions do *not* provide justification for the reformulation.

Statistical tests of differences between the $(+-)$ and the $(-+)$ conditions can also be used to assess the magnitude of differences. Table 5.2 shows the results of the Mann-Whitney U test on both conditions of each experiment (rows 1 and 2), and of the test applied to the two comparable conditions of both experiments (rows 3 and 4).

Before offering interpretations of Table 5.2, two cautions should be noted. First, both conditions of the negative source experiment show slightly higher $P(s)$ values than comparable conditions of the previous study, which will produce differences between comparable conditions in rows 3 and 4. Attaching great significance to small differences in these two rows should be avoided. Second, for row 2, and possibly for rows 3 and 4, the two formulations of the theory would predict no differences between the populations. It is not permissible to interpret failure to achieve a usual level for rejection of the null hypothesis as evidence for the hypothesis that there is no difference between the conditions. At the same time, we are going to be interested in establishing a lack of difference between conditions; we simply must guard against interpreting the results of the statistical test as "proving" a lack of such difference. With these two cautions in mind, we examine the following comparisons.

TABLE 5.2   MANN–WHITNEY U TESTS OF DIFFERENCES OF CONDITIONS
OF THE FOUR LE CONDITIONS

Predicted Comparison	n's	U	Z	p (one-tailed)
LE $(+-)$ LE $(-+)$	19, 20	135.5	—	.06
NS $(+-)$ NS $(-+)$	20, 23	191.5	.95	.17
LE $(+-)$ NS $(+-)$	19, 23	216.5	.05	.31
NS $(-+)$ LE $(-+)$	23, 20	174.0	1.47	.09

First, we note that neither the difference between the two LE conditions of the first experiment nor the difference between the two NS conditions of the present experiment attains the usually accepted .05 level for confidence that a difference *does* exist. In other words, using only this statistic, we could not conclude that either the LE or the NS had the effect of producing differentiated expectations for subjects in this experiment. This result is consistent with the original formulation of the theory; it would be inconsistent with a negative source formulation.

Second, using this statistic we cannot conclude that the effect of the LE was significantly different from the effect of the NS. The p values in rows 3 and 4 do not attain the customary .05 level for rejection of the null hypothesis. We might interpret this result simply by saying that the change from assigning e a score of 8 to assigning him a score of 4 was not large enough to produce a significant change in $P(s)$ data with the samples of the two experiments. However, since the $P(s)$ values did change from the first experiment to the second, we have to temper the interpretation of the statistic with this information.

Overall, from the results of the statistical tests performed on data from the two conditions of each experiment, there seems to be no justification for making the negative source reformulation. Neither the difference between the two NS conditions nor the difference between comparable expectation conditions of the two experiments produced the kind of changes that would be predicted by a negative source formulation.

Comparisons can also be drawn between the process data from the negative source experiment and the first source experiment. Figure 5.2 shows curves for the four conditions, by blocks of five trials. The most important attribute of these curves has already been discussed for the first source experiment—namely, at no time do the curves from the two LE conditions of that experiment overlap. For the negative source experiment, however, the curves do overlap and cross in the third quarter of trials. This result is consistent with the original formulation; it would be inconsistent with a negative source formulation, since this would predict a consistent and enduring (though reversed) difference in $P(s)$ between the two NS conditions.

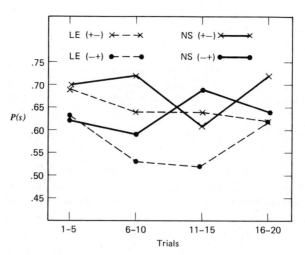

Figure 5.2 $P(s)$ curves for four LE conditions, by blocks of five trials.

Second, we note that the $P(s)$ figures for both the negative source conditions increase over time, from .70 to .72 for the NS $(+-)$, and from .62 to .64 for the NS $(-+)$ condition. The increase is not large and is not regular in either condition; thus it probably would not be wise to attach a great amount of importance to the change. From the original formulation of the theory, however, we might expect that subjects in the NS experiment would pay little attention to the evaluator and that any *effect* of his evaluations would decrease through time. Perhaps such "drifting" is reflected in the changes in the $P(s)$ figures of the negative source experiment. In general, results of the process analysis of data on rejection of influence are more consistent with what would be expected from the original formulation than from a negative source formulation.

Although we have less confidence in self-report information in these experiments, because the negative source question arose in this area (interviews), we also can examine overall mean $P(s)$ data from subjects in the two experiments as a function of subjects' reports of their interpretation of the evaluations. At the end of each phase of the experiment, a questionnaire is distributed, and subjects are asked questions designed to elicit information on the success of the manipulations, among other things. Two of these questions are particularly relevant to the issue of the negative source: (1) "How would you estimate your ability to do this sort of task compared to that of your partner?" and (2) "Suppose you were to work on a second series of Contrast Sensitivity slides similar to those you have just completed. How well would you expect each of [you] to do at the second series?" The first question measures the overall evaluation of performance held by the subject after the evaluations from person #3 have been delivered. The second question measures his expectations for future performance at the same task.

Subjects in the two experiments can be classified for each question according to whether they answered "in line" with evaluations given them by person #3, "opposite" from his evaluations, or whether they indicated "no difference" between themselves and their partners after hearing the evaluations. Table 5.3 shows the mean $P(s)$ for subjects in each of the four conditions, by their responses to the two questionnaire questions.

Data in Table 5.3 point to several interesting results. In both sections, $P(s)$ data correspond roughly to the questionnaire response. That is, subjects who responded "in line" with the evaluations also show the kind of $P(s)$ differences that would be predicted from the original theory formulation, whereas those who responded "opposite" to the evaluations show $P(s)$ differences that would be expected from a negative source formulation. Data in row 1 of both sections show the $P(s)$ for the $(+-)$ condition to be greater than the $P(s)$ for the $(-+)$ condition, and in the second row of each section we see the opposite result. This finding might lead to the interpretation that both experiments produced a negative source effect for some subjects.

TABLE 5.3   MEAN $P(s)$ FOR QUESTIONNAIRE RESPONSES[a]

	(a) Estimated Ability			
Response	LE (+ −)	LE (− +)	NS (+ −)	NS (− +)
In line	.68 (11)	.53 (14)	.71 (10)	.58 (9)
Opposite	.57 (5)	.74 (4)	.45 (2)	.73 (5)
No difference	.68 (3)	.60 (2)	.72 (8)	.64 (9)
	(b) Estimated future Performance			
Response	LE (+ −)	LE (− +)	NS (+ −)	NS (− +)
In line	.67 (14)	.56 (11)	.66 (15)	.55 (11)
Opposite	.55 (3)	.70 (5)	.52 (3)	.65 (8)
No difference	.68 (2)	.52 (4)	.65 (2)	.64 (4)

[a] The n's are in parentheses.

Before accepting this interpretation, we should examine the results in row 3 of sections (a) and (b)—the data from subjects who indicated on the questionnaire that there was no difference between themselves and their partners. The response of "no difference" could come from at least three sources. First, the respondent may be reflecting his true feelings and giving information that could be used to predict his probable future behavior. Second, he could be obeying a normative injunction against making differential evaluations or invidious comparisons, especially the kind requiring one to distinguish himself from another person with whom he is in interaction. Third, he could be refusing to give the experimenters information on his feelings through a desire to maintain privacy or to avoid giving the appearance of having been influenced by the experiment—a rather common desire among subjects, in our experience. If the "no difference" response on the questionnaire were produced by any reason other than the first one here, it would not be wise to consider it a reliable indicator of expectations produced in this situation.

Examination of $P(s)$ data in row 3 of both sections indicates that for all four possible comparisons of (+ −) and (− +) conditions (two experiments, two questions), the $P(s)$ is higher for the (+ −) condition than for the (− +) condition *among the subjects who indicated that they did not hold differential ability conceptions*. For the comparison between conditions of the negative source experiment on the question of estimated future performance, the difference is negligible (.65 vs. .64); but for the other three comparisons it is substantial. It seems reasonable to interpret the results appearing in row 3 of both parts as indicating that the questionnaire is a less reliable measure of expectations than behavioral data on acceptance of influence, at least for subjects who deny any differences between themselves and others. For others, those in rows 1 and 2, it might be that responses on the questionnaires truly reflect their assessments of the situation; we do not want to generalize too readily the interpretation from those who refused to make a differential evaluation. However, results of this interpretation of row 3 should make one wary of too hastily accepting the interpretation that rows 1 and 2 support the negative source formulation. Most conservatively, we conclude that we cannot decide the question of reformulation based only on the results of this analysis by questionnaire response. Thus results of the questionnaire analysis can be called entirely indeterminate. Less conservatively, they can be considered to be slightly in favor of the interpretation that for 8 of the possible 12 comparisons—that is, for the comparisons possible in rows 1 and 3, but not those possible in row 2—the results are consistent with the original formulation.

Variance Across Subjects. Next we examine the first block of trials of both conditions of the negative source experiment for the shape of their distributions of subjects according to number of self resolutions. These are shown in Figure 5.3.

The original formulation predicts a unimodal distribution, composed entirely of subjects who ignored the evaluator. The predictions from a negative source formulation are not completely clear. If the experimental manipulation of a score of 4 correct out of 20 can be considered to have produced a negative source phenomenon in all subjects, a unimodal distribution would be expected. On the other hand, if some subjects did accept the NS as a negative source and others accepted him as a source, a bimodal distribution would be expected. Neither distribution in Figure 5.3 appears to be bimodal. Thus we conclude that this analysis is consistent with the original formulation and possibly is inconsistent with a negative source formulation.

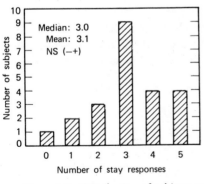 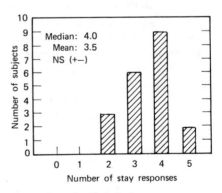

Figure 5.3 Distribution of subjects according to number of self resolutions.

Data on variance across subjects in the two experiments can be examined for some effects that are not directly derivable from the theory, yet still might be expected from the two possible formulations. We take first the total amount of variance across subjects in the two experiments. The original formulation might lead us to anticipate that more subjects in the LE conditions than in the NS conditions would form expectation states corresponding to the evaluations; hence LE conditions would show greater variance than corresponding NS conditions, for they would contain two populations. NS conditions would contain a single population—those holding undifferentiated expectations—and would have the smaller variance. These predictions involve at least two assumptions. First, it must be supposed that variance shown by subjects who have formed the expectation states will be lower than or equal to that for subjects who hold undifferentiated expectations or expectations unrelated to the experimental manipulations. As suggested in analysis of data from the first source experiment, this assumption may not be justified; there is some reason to believe that the $(-+)$ expectation state, especially, will exhibit large amounts of variance. The second assumption that must be made before deriving the prediction that variance will be greater for the NS than for the LE conditions is that variance due to imperfect experimental techniques—undetected person orientation, slight deviations in procedure—is equally likely to occur in both experiments and with both sets of subjects. This assumption seems plausible. Neither assumption is testable from our data; hence interpretations of the data on variance must be made cautiously. A negative source formulation would probably also predict less variance in the NS conditions than in the LE conditions, since subjects would be expected to form the "opposite" expectation states.

Table 5.4 presents overall variance about the mean number of stay responses per subject from the two experiments. Comparison of rows 1 and 2 indicates that variance is *smaller* within the corresponding conditions of the negative source experiment. This result is consistent either with a negative source formulation or with the original formulation, if the other necessary assumptions stated previously are accepted.

Next we examine changes in variance through time for the negative source experiment. The original formulation suggests the likelihood of an increase in variance through time in both conditions of the negative source experiment, as

TABLE 5.4   VARIANCE ABOUT THE MEAN
NUMBER OF STAY RESPONSES

	$(+-)$	$(-+)$
LE	6.89	12.36
NS	5.99	9.32

some of the subjects who originally held undifferentiated expectations came to form differentiated expectations because of the disagreement interaction. Presumably some would form $(+ -)$ and some $(- +)$ expectations within each condition, thus leading to the differentiation of two populations, and consequently, to an increase in variance. A negative source formulation would predict that the populations within each condition would be fixed by the original evaluations, hence that variance within each condition should be relatively constant. Table 5.5 shows the variance by blocks of five trials for the two conditions of the negative source experiment. The $(- +)$ condition appears to offer some reason to believe that variance is *decreasing* as a function of time in this experiment. However, the figures for the $(+ -)$ condition do not reveal any simple decrease as a function of time, for the figure for the third quarter is highest for this condition. Thus variance data through time appear to be inconsistent with the original formulation for the $(- +)$ condition, and either indeterminate or consistent with a negative source formulation for the $(+ -)$ condition, depending on whether we interpret row 1 of Table 5.5 as showing a constant value through time or as showing no interpretable trend.

TABLE 5.5   VARIANCE ACROSS SUBJECTS BY BLOCKS
OF FIVE TRIALS

	Trials			
	1–5	6–10	11–15	16–20
NS $(+ -)$	.79	.78	1.21	.67
NS $(- +)$	1.81	1.50	.89	.72

Overall, results of examination of the variances yield no clear pattern for the original formulation or for the reformulation. We therefore retain the original, less complicated formulation.

Summary and Discussion.   To summarize results of our analyses of the negative source experiment, we find no clear reason from a comparison of experiments to conclude that theoretical reformulation to take account of the negative source is either necessary or desirable. The most important tests of whether reformulation is necessary come from the $P(s)$ data, since these are predicted from the theory, and from the reversal that would be expected from a negative source formulation. The data show no tendency toward such a reversal, either in the overall $P(s)$ figures or in the process data through time. These data clearly support the original formulation. Examining the $P(s)$ data according to questionnaire response brings out some results that would be predicted by a negative source formulation and some that are predicted by the original formulation. However, we must conclude that any classification of subjects according to questionnaire response in this experimental situation is a procedure with inherent risks of unreliability or inaccuracy. Therefore, neither the questionnaire analyses supporting the original formulation nor those supporting reformulation, merit the confidence we place in mean $P(s)$ figures.

Less direct evidence comes from examining variance in both experiments. The overall variance was slightly lower in the negative source experiment—a result that would be in accord either with a negative source reformulation or with the original formulation. The time changes in variance from the negative source experiment, and also the time changes from the LE conditions of the original experiment (Table 4.6), are generally consistent with what we would expect from a reformulation. Any interpretation of variance figures requires making assumptions about the subject populations, about the experimental situation, and about the nature and effects of expectation states. Since we cannot test these assumptions, and since there are intuitive reasons to believe that some of them are false, it seems wise not to rely heavily on variances in deciding whether to reformulate the theory.

Finally, there are considerations of simplicity and of parsimony. If all other considerations were met, one should prefer the simplest theory, and the one with the smallest number of assumptions. For this case, since no clear need has been demonstrated to undertake the difficult and complex task of theory reformulation, we have grounds for retaining the original formulation.

Thus we conclude that the theory does not need to take account of a negative source phenomenon and that reformulation need not be undertaken. We also conclude that the intuitively appealing idea of the negative source does not seem to appear in these experiments. Though there are many reasons to believe that a negative source is plausible, we find no evidence that it actually produces the effects that would most reasonably be expected.

The decision not to reformulate the theory does not imply that there is no negative source. It simply indicates that the set of situations for which the theory makes predictions does not activate such a phenomenon in a consistent manner. A full investigation of the idea on its own merits could begin with an assessment, for example, of the kinds of situations in which a negative source does operate. For our purposes, the original theory may stand, and in the next chapter we begin extending the theory, with the aim of increasing the scope of situations for which it can make predictions.

CHAPTER SIX

STATUS CHARACTERISTICS OF EVALUATORS

Theory and Derivations. In this chapter we consider an extension of the propositions of the original theory designed to increase the variety of situations for which predictions can be derived. We take as reasonably well confirmed the first source theory.

We still may ask how an actor decides whose evaluations to use in the absence of any information about the evaluator's ability. Frequently an actor does not know the ability of those who are evaluating his own and others' performances, and a confirmed answer to this question would considerably broaden the scope of the theory. The following set of propositions serve to extend the first source theory, both increasing the scope and retaining the formal structure, which has received empirical confirmation in the first two source experiments.

As in the first source theory, we want to explain the *formation* of expectations, not change in existing expectations. Thus we deal with situations in which the actors initially have no conceptions of their own or of one anothers' abilities. Furthermore, the theory is limited to groups whose members are task oriented and collectively oriented. These scope conditions and antecedent conditions are contained formally in the definition of situations to which the theory is intended to apply. We modify part c of Definition 1 as presented in Chapter 4.

DEFINITION 1.   c.   No previous expectations are held by p and o for their own or any other actor's ability at the task.

Definition 2 and Assumptions 1 to 4 are unchanged from those in Chapter 4 for this extension of the theory. According to the theoretical structure, if p could make a decision about the ability of e, then by Assumption 3d he would be able to decide whether to accept e as a source. However, since we have specified that p not be given this information, an inferential process must occur if p is to reach any conclusion about e's ability. Then we must determine what kind of information p might consider useful in making the inference.

A version of expectation theory dealing with situations of initially undifferentiated expectations has been constructed (Berger et al., 1972), and for extension of the source theory it is useful to adopt a modification of ideas in that theory. This version asserts that under certain conditions, in the absence of direct information about the task ability needed to solve the problem, actors will form expectations based on the state of a single status characteristic possessed by the individual. That is, when an actor needs to determine the ability level of another in the absence of direct evaluative information, the actor will come to hold a high or low expectation that is consistent with the high or low overall status of that other. In the case of a status characteristic that is directly and clearly relevant to the task, this assertion seems plausible. However, the theory asserts further that it is not necessary for the status characteristic to be seen as directly relevant to the task ability required if it is *not known* to be *nonrelevant*. This rather counterintuitive assertion states that p will place the burden of proof in an unfamiliar situation on a demonstration that the status characteristic is *not* relevant to task ability, and in the absence of such a demonstration, p will conclude that it *is* relevant.

In terms of accepting an evaluator as a source, a similar assertion would be as follows: if p does not know the ability of the evaluator, but does know that he possesses the high state of a status characteristic, then p will infer that the evaluator has high ability; and on the basis of this inference, p will form high expectations for e, thus will be likely to accept him as a source. As in other theoretical and empirical work, this assertion is assumed to be true regardless of the task, and in the absence of information about the relevance of the status characteristic to the task. Cases of the status characteristic being known to be directly relevant to task ability also fall within the scope of the theory. However, this knowledge is *not* required for use of the theory in making predictions.

The first step is to arrive at a precise definition of the term "status characteristic." We simply require that it be a property of an individual which may be used to describe him and that the property possess different states which are evaluated. For simplicity, status characteristics are treated as if they had only two states—positively evaluated and negatively evaluated. However, this simplification need not restrict the generality of the theory, for it will always be possible to substitute the words "preferred" and "nonpreferred" for the high and low states, respectively.

DEFINITION 3.   A characteristic D is a *diffuse status characteristic* if and only if the states of D are differentially evaluated by all the actors in S.

We need to know the circumstances under which p will think that knowledge of states of D is helpful in assigning performance expectations to himself and to any other actor. It seems reasonable to assume that information of states of

D is not particularly helpful if p knows that he and o (or, he and e) possess the *same state*, but only when they possess different states. That is, knowing that one's partner in an interaction situation possesses a status equal to one's own on some diffuse status characteristic (such as race or sex) does not seem to be sufficient "reason" to conclude that he possesses *equal ability* at a task that is not specifically related to D. By contrast, there is both theoretical and empirical reason to believe that knowledge that the other actor possesses a *different* state of D *will* lead to a differential performance expectation. In other words, we are making an assumption about a psychological process similar to what is sometimes called the "halo effect"—the nonlogical "generalization" of evaluations from one characteristic to another. We assert that this process does not operate in the case of status equals; such people do not use this knowledge to infer that their task abilities are equal. Freese and Cohen (1973) implicitly made use of this idea in a recent experiment. However, we do not know of any relevant, direct test of such an assertion.

Assumption 5 asserts that only when the evaluator has a state of D different from that which p possesses will p try to reason from the status characteristic to an expectation state for him; this is the meaning of the term "salient." A salient characteristic is one that p "notices" and tries to use to form an ability conception. Assumption 6 then proposes the link between D and an expectation state.

ASSUMPTION 5.   In S, D will become a *salient* factor to p for assigning performance expectations to himself and o if and only if he and o possess different states of D.

ASSUMPTION 6.   In S, p will assign expectation states to any actor on the basis of a salient D if and only if p does not believe that D is nonrelevant to the task.

In Assumption 5, the actor designated as o could as well have been designated by any other letter, including e. The thrust of Assumption 5 is that p will *not* try to reason from a status characteristic to a performance expectation for any actor who possesses the same state as p himself does, but he *will* try to reason from a status characteristic to a performance expectation for any actor who possesses a different state from that which p possesses.

The negative formulation of Assumption 6 reflects its reliance on the "burden of proof" concept: as long as p does not know that the states of D are not relevant to the task, he is said to assume that they are relevant, and it is posited that he will assign high or low expectations, respectively, to actors who possess the high or low states of the characteristic.

This completes the task of extending the theory to cases in which performances are evaluated by an actor whose specific task ability is unknown. If p is aware that he and the evaluator possess different states of some single characteristic D, the theory predicts that he will infer from this to an ability level, hence to an expectation state, for the evaluator. Once he has done this, p will either accept or reject e's evaluations in a manner equivalent to that which he would use if he possessed information about e's ability.

Two special cases are still outside the scope of the theory. First, this extension cannot be used to derive predictions when p has no information about either the ability or the status of an evaluator or when p and e possess the same state of D. The former case is relatively unlikely to occur in most natural situations, hence is probably not a major limitation on usefulness of the theory. The latter case is probably more likely to occur, and some extension of the theory beyond that which we are prepared to offer in this work would be a useful contribution. Second, this theory extension does not give information that could be used to derive determinate predictions when p and e differ on more than one diffuse status characteristic. Such situations do occur with considerable frequency in natural situations, and a theory capable of predicting for them would also be very valuable. However, the problem is difficult theoretically, for interaction between individuals who differ on several salient status characteristics at once is very complex. Berger and Fisek (1970) and Webster, Roberts, and Sobieszek (1972) report early attempts to specify the form of a combining process for cases of two or more characteristics.

From the theory extension, it is possible to derive the prediction that actors will respond to evaluators of unknown ability but high status just as they respond to evaluators of known high ability. Similarly, they should respond to evaluators of low status much as they respond to evaluators of known low ability.

For derivations, we use the following notation: an evaluator of known high status but unknown ability is referred to as a high status evaluator (HSE); similarly, an evaluator of unknown ability but known low status is LSE. The two actors p and o have their performances evaluated either by the HSE or by the LSE, in the same patterns as in the first source experiment; that is, with a high proportion of positive evaluations to one of them [the (+ −) condition] and a corresponding high proportion of negative evaluations to the other [the (− +) condition]. Thus the four conditions of the study are similar to those for the first source experiment: HSE (+ −), HSE (− +), LSE (+ −), LSE (− +).

Combining Assumptions 1, 2, and 3d yields the prediction that when p holds high expectations for the evaluator, he will be quite likely to accept those evaluations and to base on such evaluations the expectations he forms for his own and for o's performances. Adding Assumptions 5 and 6 allows us to predict that p will form high expectations for an evaluator who possesses the high state of the characteristic and that evaluations from such an e will be quite likely to affect p's expectation state. Then Assumption 4b, relating acceptance of influence to expectation states, enables derivation of the following empirical consequence:

DERIVATION 1.   In case of disagreement with o, the probability of p's rejecting influence is greater in the HSE $(+-)$ condition than in the HSE $(-+)$ condition.

The case of the LSE is somewhat more complex, but still manageable. Assumptions 5 and 6 predict that p will form low expectations for e's performance, but this does not preclude acceptance of e as a source. The reason for this is the same as that stated in the first source version of the theory—namely, by definition of situation S, p has no idea of his own ability; thus it is possible that an actor in this condition will decide that the LSE has more ability than he himself possesses, and this fulfills Definition 7. Then by Assumption 3d, p will accept the LSE as a source. Thus we have

DERIVATION 2   In case of disagreement with o, the probability of p's rejecting influence is greater in the LSE $(+-)$ condition than in the LSE $(-+)$ condition.

Since similar unit evaluations are predicted to be more likely to be "effective" coming from the HSE than from the LSE, we can also say

DERIVATION 3.   In case of disagreement with o, the probability of p's rejecting influence is greater in the HSE $(+-)$ condition than in the LSE $(+-)$ condition.

DERIVATION 4.   In case of disagreement with o, the probability of p's rejecting influence is greater in the LSE $(-+)$ condition than in the HSE $(-+)$ condition.

Combining these four derivations yields

DERIVATION 5.   In case of disagreement between p and o, the probabilities of p's rejecting influence will be in the following order:

$$\text{HSE } (+-) > \text{LSE } (+-) > \text{LSE } (-+) > \text{HSE } (-+).$$

Experimental Procedures.   Test of these derivations was conducted in an experiment in which 100 subjects participated, 25 assigned randomly to each of the four conditions. All subjects were males between the ages of 16 and 18, recruited from several private high schools in Baltimore, Maryland. They were contacted by telephone and scheduled for groups, all conducted at the Social Relations Laboratory, The Johns Hopkins University.

Each group consisted of two subjects from the same high school. To minimize the effect of any previous general expectations individuals might have for each other, group members were prevented from seeing each other before the experiment.

After the standard introduction to the experiment had been read by the first experimenter, the second experimenter interrupted over the intercom as follows:

SECOND EXPERIMENTER: Pardon me, Dr. Gordon. We're ready in here.

FIRST EXPERIMENTER: Who is the person who is acting as the evaluator for this group?

SECOND EXPERIMENTER: Person #3's name is William Mason. [He's a junior at Johns Hopkins. *Or*, He's in the 8th grade at _____ Junior High School.]

The first experimenter wrote the name of the college or junior high school on the board in the space labeled "Person #3 _____." This constituted the HSE–LSE manipulation—using a status characteristic that might be termed "level of academic attainment." The rest of the experiment duplicated the first source experiment.

Based on the interview criteria, data from three subjects were excluded from analysis. One subject expressed a definite belief that the disagreements were not real and thus did not try to resolve them; one expressed a definite belief that the evaluator did not possess the status characteristic attributed to him; and one apparently seriously misunderstood the instructions (he said he thought that person #3 did have an answer key to the slides). Analyses from the other 97 subjects are given below.

Results

Rejection of Influence.   Table 6.1 presents the statistic employed for major test of the derivations from the extended theory, the mean $P(s)$ for each condition. Data are in accord with predictions of Derivations 1, 2, and 3 but not with D4. The overall mean $P(s)$ for the LSE $(-+)$ and the HSE $(-+)$ conditions do not differ as predicted.

Table 6.2 lists the results of nonparametric statistical test of the five derivations. Rows 1 through 4 report the one-tailed probability results of the Mann-Whitney U test, and row 5 reports the results of the Jonckheere test for differ-

TABLE 6.1   OVERALL $P(s)$ BY CONDITION

Condition	n	$P(s)$
HSE $(+-)$	24	.78
HSE $(-+)$	25	.50
LSE $(+-)$	25	.70
LSE $(-+)$	23	.50

ences between all conditions and the predicted ordering of conditions. By these tests, the differences between conditions support Derivations 1, 2, 3, and 5, but not D4, using the conventional .05 level for rejection of the null hypothesis.

To assess the effects of the status-based source, we next compare data from this experiment with data from previous experiments. Table 6.3 presents the overall mean $P(s)$ for the comparable conditions of the first source experiment and also of the experiment reported by Camilleri et al. (1972), which differed from the source experiments in that the *experimenter* evaluated performances in phase I, not the evaluator, as in the source studies. (Data in columns 2 and 3 have already been presented in Table 4.3.) We note again that conclusions from comparisons with Table 6.3 must be drawn cautiously because of subject population differences and other historical factors. Table 6.3 reveals that there is little difference in mean $P(s)$ between comparable HE and HSE conditions of the two source experiments and between comparable conditions with the experimenter evaluating performances. For the high ability evaluator, the relevant figures are .80 and .46; for the high status evaluator, .78 and .50; and for the study in which the experimenter acted as evaluator, .76 and .42. Differences between comparable LE and LSE conditions are greater, with the low status evaluator showing greater effectiveness, as measured by the difference between the $(+-)$ and the $(-+)$ conditions, than the low ability evaluator. For the low ability evaluator, the figures are .65 and .58; for the low status evaluator, .70 and .50.

TABLE 6.2   STATISTICAL TESTS OF DERIVATIONS

Derivation	Prediction	n's	Z-Transformation	p
1	HSE $(+-)$ > HSE $(-+)$	24, 24	5.27	< .05
2	LSE $(+-)$ > LSE $(-+)$	25, 23	2.55	< .05
3	HSE $(+-)$ > LSE $(+-)$	24, 25	2.77	< .05
4	LSE $(-+)$ > HSE $(-+)$	23, 25	0.21	.42
5	HSE $(+-)$ > LSE $(+-)$ >	24, 25,	5.32	< .05
	LSE $(-+)$ > HSE $(-+)$	23, 25		

TABLE 6.3   COMPARISON OF STATUS, ABILITY, AND EXPERIMENTER EVALUATORS

		$P(s)$ by Evaluator			
Status	$P(s)$	Ability	$P(s)$	Experimenter	$P(s)$
HSE (+ −)	.78	HE (+ −)	.80	(+ −)	.76
HSE (− +)	.50	HE (− +)	.46	(− +)	.42
LSE (+ −)	.70	LE (+ −)	.65		
LSE (− +)	.50	LE (− +)	.58		

Considering first the comparisons having to do with the theory extension goals of this research, the relation of the two HSE conditions supports the first derivation of the extended theory; the $P(s)$ difference between the HSE (+ −) and the HSE (− +) conditions appearing in Table 6.1 is large and is in the direction predicted. In addition, comparison of results from the HSE conditions of this study with results from the two previous studies shows very small differences between comparable conditions. In Table 6.3, the value of $P(s)$ for the (+ −) condition is within .02 of the observed .78 of this study in both previous cases, and the value for the (− +) condition is within .08 of the present .50 in both previous cases.

In view of the considerable differences in theoretically irrelevant features of the situation—including subject population characteristics, the slide task, and the pattern of agreements and disagreements in the second phase of the experiment—the similarity of $P(s)$ data is especially striking. This similarity of results, by the influence measure used in all studies, can be given the following very important interpretation: in this controlled interaction situation, the effect of evaluations from an evaluator appears to be virtually the same whether the evaluator's basis for an accurate evaluation is (1) possession of access to objective information regarding correct answers (like the experimenter of the Camilleri et al. study); (2) high task ability (like the evaluator of the first source study); or (3) possession of the high state of a diffuse status characteristic (like the evaluator of this study). We return to consideration of some implications of this finding later.

The LSE conditions, considered by themselves, show the differences predicted by Derivation 2 of the theory: the $P(s)$ difference between the LSE (+ −) and the LSE (− +) conditions is substantial and is in the direction predicted. Comparison of data from the comparable conditions of the previous source study in Table 4.3 indicates that the effect of the low status evaluator is greater than the effect of the low ability evaluator in this situation. However, since the theory gives no way to derive a determinate prediction for such a comparison—it does not tell whether the present manipulation of "eighth grader" should be more or less effective than the previous manipulation of "a score of 8 out of 20" in producing low expectations for the evaluator—any interpretation of this comparison would have greater significance for measuring characteristics of the methodology of this experiment and of the subject population than for testing the theory.

A finding *not* in accord with one derivation is the lack of a difference between the HSE $(-+)$ and the LSE $(-+)$ conditions. The mean $P(s)$ figure for both these conditions is .50, and from row 4 of Table 6.2 we see that the data distributions fell considerably short of the difference required to attain the conventional .05 level for rejection of the null hypothesis. This result shows that the LSE was more effective in inducing expectation states than was anticipated; this greater effectiveness, moreover, was especially noticeable in the LSE $(-+)$ condition.

Of several interpretations of this finding, one that seems to be especially worthy of further consideration is the possibility that some subjects in the LSE conditions made another characteristic of the evaluator salient in assigning expectations to him. That is, some subjects in the LSE conditions may have activated a characteristic that caused them to assign *high* expectations to the LSE, thus to be very likely to accept him as a source.

Recent theoretical work on expectations at Stanford, especially that of Freese (1969) and of Berger and Fisek (1974), provides a clue. According to these investigators, there is some theoretical and empirical reason to believe that there are at least two possible causes of formation of a particular pattern of expectations: in the absence of direct information about a given individual's ability, others may form expectations for his performance based *either* on a diffuse status characteristic, as in our theory, *or* on a specific social characteristic, such as ability at a nonrelated task. For this experiment, the latter possibility means that some of the subjects in the LSE conditions may have used some characteristic other than academic status to form their expectations for the evaluator, the characteristic they did choose causing them to form high expectations for the evaluator.

Since special care was taken in the design of our study to avoid giving any status information on the evaluator but the single characteristic manipulated, it seems unlikely that another diffuse status characteristic became salient. The two schools used in describing person #3 in the HSE and the LSE conditions were chosen to be close to those attended by the subjects on such other status characteristics as socioeconomic status, quality of teaching and of students, and race and sex of students. Therefore, it seems unlikely that subjects would have inferred any ability information about the evaluator on the basis of what they were *told* about him, unless they chose to use the one diffuse status characteristic intentionally manipulated. However, it is possible that subjects could have used a specific social characteristic to assign expectations, and could have used this in a way neither anticipated when the experiment was designed nor specifically noticed when it was being conducted.

Once data are collected and the interviews completed, it is impossible to determine precisely what proportion of subjects in the LSE conditions did use a specific social characteristic to assign expectations to the evaluator, but at least it is clear that the possibility existed for them to make salient other cues besides the evaluator's academic status. One such set of cues is contained in speech patterns, and in fact some subjects spontaneously mentioned that they had used the voice to infer other characteristics of the evaluator.

To provide some information that could be used for a more systematic assessment of this possibility, the transcribed interviews from both LSE conditions were analyzed for mention of the high state of any specific social characteristic. [Our reason for looking for mention of the *high* state of a characteristic should be clear from the kind of result for which we were seeking an explanation: the unexpected finding was that the LSE was more effective than the theory led us to expect, especially in the LSE $(-+)$ condition, in producing the expectation states consistent with his evaluations.]

Interviews included the question, "Can you tell me anything you remember about person #3?" and answers of some subjects contained references to the high state of a social characteristic that they inferred on the basis of his voice. Remarks such as the following were classified as indicating activation of the high state of a specific social characteristic:

> Didn't sound nervous—that was one thing that would convince me that he had a good evaluation. . . . Definite. He was more, like, he made up his mind. . . . When he spoke over the intercom he sounded very sure of himself, so I figured he'd do a good job. . . . Quite good. . . . Efficient. . . . Sounded mature for his age. . . . He's uh, he sounded, sounded, very intelligent for an eighth grader. Like he had a lot on the ball.

Such remarks could have been prompted by either of two factors: a rather precise diction and absence of the prevailing Baltimore accent, and the assumption of the role of person #3 by an individual considerably older than an average eighth-grade student.

Five subjects in each of the LSE conditions made remarks that were classified as indicating activation of the high state of a specific social characteristic. Table 6.4 shows that the effect of evaluations for these subsamples, especially that from the LSE $(-+)$ condition, was greater than the effect for all subjects in the LSE conditions.

In interpreting data in Table 6.4, three cautions should be kept in mind. First, the size of the cells is much too small for drawing definitive conclusions about the process of activation of a specific social characteristic. Second, it must be remembered that the interview was not designed to elicit information on specific social characteristics. Spontaneous mention of such a characteristic appears to be a reasonable way of getting information on activation where it is salient; it tells nothing in cases of subjects less willing to offer information, however, and the interview was not designed to follow up such mentions systematically. As we have seen in two previous source experiments, subjects' interpretations of their reasoning and their behavior in these experiments are often not reliable enough to base theory tests on; subjects can construct a reasonable explanation of their behavior if asked to do so, but this explanation is not a sufficient basis for predicting the behavior of others. Third, and most important, the secondary analysis of data in Table 6.4 was undertaken only as a way of acquiring information for a preliminary check of an unanticipated finding. These results should be considered suggestive rather than conclusive. It may well be necessary to control the perception of specific social characteristics as well as of diffuse status characteristics in designing these studies in the future

TABLE 6.4 SUBJECTS MENTIONING HIGH STATE OF A SPECIFIC SOCIAL CHARACTERISTIC

| Condition | P(s) | |
	Mentioning	Not Mentioning
LSE (+ −)	.72 ($n=5$)	.70 ($n=20$)
LSE (− +)	.32 ($n=5$)	.55 ($n=18$)

Data on rejection of influence can also be examined for trends in time. According to the theory, expectation states should be formed before the beginning of interaction between p and o, just as in the first source experiment. Therefore, the $P(s)$ curves should look very much like the curves for the first source experiment: they should show the differences between conditions at the outset of interaction, and throughout the series of trials. Figure 6.1 plots $P(s)$ curves for the four conditions, by blocks of five trials.

Separation of conditions for this study is not as clear-cut as it was for the first source study, although the three conditions HSE (+−), HSE (−+), and LSE (+−) are all in the relative positions expected from the derivations. The LSE (−+) condition shows the same relations to the other conditions through time exhibited in the overall mean $P(s)$ figure in Tables 6.1 and 6.2; that is, the figure for this condition, except for the second quarter, is lower than might be expected. The second quarter of trials for this condition was surprisingly high by comparison with the mean for this condition: it reached about .61, the value

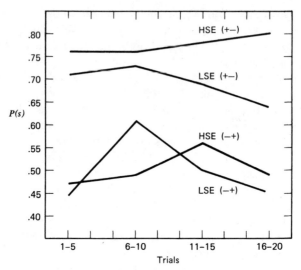

Figure 6.1 $P(s)$ curves by blocks of five trials.

expected for the overall mean. Other analyses, including variances given later, do not indicate anything else unusual either about the second quarter or about the entire series of trials for this condition. Thus no additional interpretations of process data for this experiment are offered.

Variance.   Examination of data on variance about the mean number of self resolutions for this experiment reveals some differences for these data from the first source study. The overall variances for the four conditions of the two studies and the variance data from this experiment alone, by blocks of five trials, appear in Tables 6.5 and 6.6, respectively. We see that the ordering of conditions by overall variance is generally preserved through time. Exceptions are the first

TABLE 6.5   VARIANCES ABOUT MEAN NUMBER OF
STAY RESPONSES

Ability Experiment		Status Experiment	
Condition	Variance	Condition	Variance
HE $(+-)$	3.50	HSE $(+-)$	4.43
•HE $(-+)$	20.48	HSE $(-+)$	10.75
LE $(+-)$	6.89	LSE $(+-)$	11.41
LE $(-+)$	12.36	LSE $(-+)$	14.73

TABLE 6.6   VARIANCE BY BLOCKS OF FIVE TRIALS

Condition	Block			
	1	2	3	4
HSE (+ −)	.78	.69	.95	.87
HSE (− +)	1.23	.84	1.50	1.17
LSE (+ −)	.84	.91	1.59	1.36
LSE (− +)	1.18	1.50	1.72	1.75

block for the LSE (+ −) condition, where the variance is a bit lower than expected from the overall ordering, and the first block for the HSE (− +) condition, where the variance is a bit higher.

In terms of changes through time, only one condition, the LSE (− +), shows variance data increasing consistently. The two HSE conditions display no evidence either of simple increase or of decrease, and the LSE (+ −) condition shows an increase for the first three quarters only. A simple interpretation of the difference between the HSE conditions and the LSE conditions in terms of variance changes through time might assert that the manipulation "effects" of the LSE are less lasting than the effects of the HSE. This is not the kind of differential effectiveness predicted by the theory; the assumptions lead to the prediction that fewer subjects will pay attention to the LSE than to the HSE, but they are indeterminate with respect to how long evaluations will continue to produce changes in behavior during the experiment. A simpler interpretation would assert that the increase in variance evident in the LSE (− +) condition and possibly also in the LSE (+ −) condition could indicate that subjects in both conditions who had ignored the evaluations were beginning to form either (+ −) or (− +) expectations as the result of having to resolve disagreements.

We have two comments on the variances in Table 6.5 and 6.6. First, for every condition except the HSE (− +), the status experiment produced somewhat higher variances than the ability experiment. Since there is no theoretical reason to expect this difference, we conjecture that it reflects a difference in subject population. Recall that subjects for the first source experiment were junior college students, whereas those for the present experiment were high school students. Most simply, data in Table 6.5 seem to suggest that in this experimental situation, high school students exhibit more variability of response than do college students. The deviant cell, HSE (− +), may have been lower than the HE (− +) cell merely because the latter was abnormally high. Second, variances of conditions shown for this experiment are ordered in a way more simply interpretable from the theory, along with a small number of additional assumptions, than are those from the first source experiment. The observed ordering for this experiment is: HSE $(+-)$ < HSE $(-+)$ < LSE $(+-)$ < LSE $(-+)$. If we repeat the assertion that the HSE conditions will contain a greater proportion of subjects who hold differentiated expectations than the LSE conditions, the central inequality is to be expected; that is, HSE $(+-)$, HSE $(-+)$ < LSE $(+-)$, LSE $(-+)$. Then, from the considerations advanced in Chapter 4 that the $(-+)$ condition is more "stressful" to the subject, we can explain the other two inequalities and the overall ordering. Since predictions regarding variance are not strictly derivable from the theory, we present the results of these analyses only to help to explicate relations between the first source experiment and the present one testing the theory extension.

Finally, data from the first block of trials can be inspected for evidence of two populations within each of the LSE conditions. It will be recalled from the discussion in Chapter 4 that according to the theoretical formulation, each condition should produce two sets of subjects: those who have formed expectations based on the evaluations in the first phase, and those who have not. We might expect to see this differentiation of effect in the first block of five trials, before those subjects holding undifferentiated expectations form expectations as the result of the disagreement resolution interaction.

Figure 6.2 shows the distribution of subjects by number of resolutions in favor of self for the two LSE conditions of this experiment.

Neither condition of the experiment shows a distribution indicating the presence of two populations. Since this is the third experiment in which no such evidence appears, this result is not surprising. At this point we can conclude either: (1) the theory formulation is somewhat inaccurate for leading us to expect two populations when the evaluator is not very credible, or (2) this inspection for bimodality somehow masks the existence of the two populations that actually are being produced in the experiment. From the data, it is impossible to decide between these alternatives.

However, we can suggest some reasons for the indicator's undersensitivity

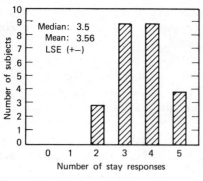 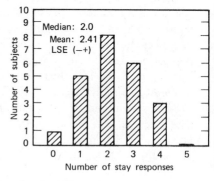

Figure 6.2   Number of self resolutions per subject for the LSE conditions, trials 1 to 5.

and also some possible ways of reformulating the theory to prevent the expectation of two populations. First, the ideal time to examine the data for bimodality would be on the first two or three trials, and with a very large sample of subjects. In these studies, because of the relatively small sample sizes, we may have had to wait for too much interaction, and perhaps there were too few subjects, to indicate the bimodality. Second, we do not know what $P(s)$ figure to expect from subjects who have not formed the expectation states consistent with the evaluator's evaluations. Subjects who ignore the LSE may hold expectations that produce a wide range of $P(s)$ figures, and this would give us data with a mode different from data of those who accept the evaluator as a source, as well as considerable variance on either side of the mode. Of course there is no way of knowing how much variance about the mode in these conditions is "natural" for subjects who accept the evaluator, and how much might be produced by existence of a set of subjects with a wide range of undifferentiated expectations in the experiment.

On the other hand, our simple and concise formulation of the theory may not be the best possible way to conceptualize the phenomenon of acceptance of an individual as a source. The process of acceptance is envisioned in the present formulation as once-and-for-all: an individual perceived to possess higher ability than p is accepted, and once accepted, every unit evaluation he makes will influence p's evaluations. One possible alternative means of acceptance of a source is what might be called an "independent probabilities model." According to this conception, *any* unit evaluation has a chance of being accepted by p, and the exact probability of acceptance is determined by the expectations held for the individual making the unit evaluation. Thus instead of accepting a source and thereafter believing everything he says, p may decide anew, every time he has to evaluate a unit performance, whether to accept the evaluator's opinion. Such a process is more difficult to conceptualize theoretically, but it possesses considerable intuitive appeal. Moreover, it leads to a prediction of only one mode in the distribution of subjects for each condition, because the condition would contain responses independent of the individual subject. A second possibility is that the LSE and the LE do in fact produce certain expectations in all subjects, but the expectations are "weaker" either in terms of their effects on $P(s)$ data *or* in terms of longevity of effect on $P(s)$ data than are expectations produced by the HE or the HSE. This kind of formulation also leads to prediction of one mode within these conditions of the experiments. However such reformulation would entail major changes in the construct "expectation state"—changes that do not seem to offer any other advantages in the current conceptualization.

Discussion.   In terms of the theory extension goals of this research, it seems fair to conclude that the work was reasonably successful. The addition of a small number of propositions enabled removal of one rather strict limitation on the original theory; namely, that individuals know the ability of an individual evaluating them before deciding whether to accept him as a source. Predictions for conditions of the experiment were generally confirmed, with the exception of the LSE $(-+)$ condition, where values of $P(s)$ were lower than expected. It was possible to show for this condition that there was some theoretical and empirical reason to expect the manipulation procedure used to produce the type of deviation observed from the predictions of the theory.

Owing to the structure of the extended theory, it is predicted that the effect of the HSE occurs *because* individuals have formed high expectations for him, and the lesser effect of the LSE occurs *because* individuals have formed lower expectations for him. Therefore, we may argue that the process of going from conceptions of ability of the evaluator to the observable behavior in the $P(s)$ data is the same in both experiments. Following this line of reasoning, we can feasibly consider the empirical tests of this source experiment to be, in some ways, a replication of the tests of the first source experiment, and the confirmed predictions of this status version of the theory can be taken to increase the confidence in the predictions from the first version of the theory as well.

In terms of extending expectation theory, the results of this study appear to confirm the prediction that a "burden of proof process" operates in determining acceptance of the evaluator. Previous research by Berger and Fisek (1970), Berger et al. (1972), and Moore (1968) has indicated that this process operated in the way predicted for individuals in direct disagreement interaction with each other. This study shows that the burden of proof process also operates in an equivalent way in determining acceptance of a potential source. More generally, the results of this study suggest not only that the status characteristic affects observable interaction but that it affects the cognitions of the individuals whose performances were evaluated in this experiment.

In terms of the social self, the extended theory enables us to predict whether an individual will be a significant other when we know either his task ability *or* the state of a diffuse status characteristic that he possesses. An extension of this version of the theory, which is not undertaken in this work, would include the concept of a specific social characteristic and would enable predictions for the case of an evaluator when we know: (1) his perceived ability, (2) his perceived diffuse status, (3) whether he has access to objective evaluative information, (4) his perceived state of a specific social characteristic. From such a theory, it would very likely be possible to make predictions for most naturally occurring, simple social situations of a single evaluator. In the next chapter, we extend the theory to enable predictions for more complex situations, in which the individual faces evaluations from more than one potential source.

CHAPTER SEVEN

MULTIPLE SOURCES AND THE FORMATION OF PERFORMANCE EXPECTATIONS

Theory and Derivations. To this point, we have been concerned in the theory and research with the simplest possible situation for which conceptions of ability are formed, that of one evaluator and two individuals in interaction. We now undertake expansion of the theory to include cases of multiple evaluators, each of whom gives individuals unit evaluations of performance. In an interaction situation of the type that fits the scope conditions of expectation theory, multiple sources of evaluations are probably the rule rather than the exception; every actor in a group probably feels that he possesses the right (if not the obligation) to tell others what he thinks of their performances. An extension of the theory that enables predictions in the case of more than one evaluator therefore increases the formal scope of the theory and its practical utility, as well.

As in the case of the status characteristics extension of the theory, we seek in this chapter to broaden the theory by adding as little as possible to assumptions of the previous versions. This strategy enables us to retain the earlier confirmation and to make direct comparisons of data from subsequent tests to earlier versions of the theory.

The kind of group to which this version of the theory applies is composed of at least four members. Two of the members, p and o, interact with each other; and their expectations and observable behavior form the subject of the theory. The other members of the group are evaluators, potential sources for p and o. The theory addresses situations in which there are at least two such e's, e_1 and e_2. The theory is not concerned with their performance expectations, and the e's only function is to make performance evaluations of p and o. The situation has two kinds of actors: those who have the right to evaluate (e_1 and e_2) and those who both evaluate and perform the task (p and o).

In the first version of the source theory, we used a single evaluator, for whom

95

expectations were either high or low. The contribution of the present extension of the theory is to generalize to situations involving *two* evaluators for whom either *similar* or *dissimilar* expectations are held. We change part b of Definition 1 to incorporate this extension; part c is the same as that given in Chapter 4.

DEFINITION 1.   b.   There are at least two actors e_1 and e_2, who have the right to evaluate task performances of p and o.

c.   p and o have no prior expectations for their own or each other's performances at the task.

Definition 2 is the same as in previous versions. The first assumption specifies the process by which evaluations from an evaluator can affect the expectations held by an actor in the situation. Assumption 1 of the first version of the theory can be adopted directly for the first part of Assumption 1 of this version:

ASSUMPTION 1a.   In S, if *only one* actor e is a source for p, then the unit evaluations made by p of any actor's performances will be the same as those made by e.

But in situation S as defined for this extension of the theory, there is more than one e, therefore more than one potential source for p. This assumption from the previous version of the theory does not tell what happens if both evaluators become sources for p; therefore, extension of the theory requires that Assumption 1 have separate assertions to deal with other possible cases. Two cases are logically possible if all evaluators become sources: either they agree on their unit evaluations of a given performance output, or they disagree. Part b of Assumption 1 specifies the effects of all sources' agreeing on a unit evaluation.

ASSUMPTION 1b.   In S, if both e_1 and e_2 are sources for p, and both e_1 and e_2 make the *same* unit evaluations of any actor's performance, p will make the same unit evaluations of that performance as e_1 and e_2.

Assumption 1b is a fairly simple extension of the idea in the first (one-source) version of the theory. When at least two sources make different unit evaluations of a performance, the case is more complex and could be formulated in a number of ways. As a first statement, we choose the simplest possible assertion for such a case. In Chapter 8 we attempt to refine this statement further.

ASSUMPTION 1c.   In S, if e_1 and e_2 are sources for p and e_1 and e_2 make *different* unit evaluations of any actor's performance, p will not make a unit evaluation of that performance output.

Balance diagrams can be constructed to illustrate the reasoning behind Assumptions 1a, 1b, and 1c. As in other balance diagrams in this book, directed lines represent unit evaluations of performance, and braces indicate acceptance of an evaluator as a source; unit relations (braces) are all positive, and evaluations (lines) may be either positive or negative.

In Figure 7.1a, p has accepted one of the evaluators as a source, and that evaluator (e_1) has made a positive evaluation of a performance output. By Assumption 1a, p should positively evaluate that performance output, as illustrated in Figure 7.1b. Notice that the left cycle of the diagram is then balanced, hence stable, regardless of the evaluation made by e_2. Since the unit relation has not formed between p and e_2, the right cycle is vacuously balanced, and also stable.

Figure 7.2a represents the case of both evaluators having become sources and both agreeing in their unit evaluations of a performance output. Assumption 1b then says that p will evaluate the performance output in the same way as the evaluators. This is illustrated in Figure 7.2b, where two cycles have been formed and both are balanced and stable.

The case of p having accepted as sources two evaluators who make different performance evaluations is illustrated in Figure 7.3a. Assumption 1c says that under these conditions p will not assign a unit evaluation to the performance output. Notice in Figure 7.3b that no matter how p evaluates the performance output, one cycle of the diagram would be imbalanced and tension producing. As the first statement of the assumption to cover the situation of disageeing sources, therefore, we have chosen a formulation in which p will not make any evaluation that would cause his cognitive structure to become imbalanced.

Assumptions 2, 3 and 4 are also the same as those assumptions in the earlier versions of the theory. The wording of Assumption 3d will be changed slightly (see Chapter 10) to emphasize that accepting or rejecting one evaluator as a source does not affect the probability of accepting or rejecting the second evalu-

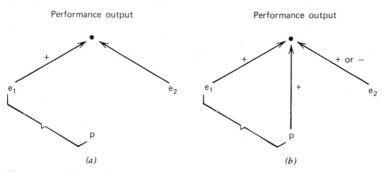

Figure 7.1   Balance diagram—one source.

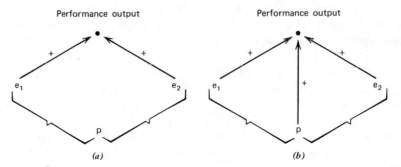

Figure 7.2   Balance diagram—two sources agreeing.

ator as a source. Again, we note the *possibility* that the probabilities are contingent. The simplest alternative assumes that they are not. Our "next step" (Chapter 8) sheds further light on this problem.

This completes the theory revision. It is more general than the first statement in that it enables prediction to all cases within the scope of the first statement, as well as to situations more complex than those for which the first statement could be used. This formulation allows prediction to situations featuring *either* one or (at least) two evaluators. If there are two or more evaluators, we can make predictions when the e's are of the same or of different competence and when the evaluators agree or disagree in their unit evaluations.

The simple extension of the interaction situation made by changing Definition 1 and examining cases of exactly two evaluators yields ten possible cases, in addition to the four cases tested in the experiment reported in Chapter 4. The research designed for the first test of this theory extension selected four cases that would yield maximum information on the predictive power of the theory

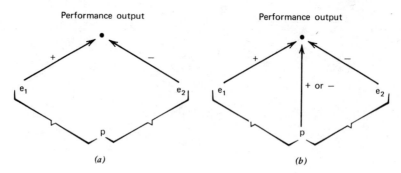

Figure 7.3   Balance diagram—two sources disagreeing.

and would be of greatest substantive interest. In these four cases, e_1 has high ability and e_2 has low ability. In two cases, e_1 and e_2 agree in their unit evaluations, and in two cases e_1 and e_2 disagree. In all four cases, e_1 and e_2 give differential evaluations to p and o, as they did in the three earlier experiments.

Before drawing the derivations for tests, let us clarify the notation used for conditions. For this experiment, an evaluator described as having high ability is designated simply by H, and one described as having low ability, with L. The pattern of evaluations given to p and o is the same as in previous experiments, with p first and o second. For example, H $(-+)$ L $(+-)$ indicates that the high ability evaluator gives p low evaluations and o high evaluations, and the low ability evaluator gives p high evaluations and o low evaluations. Thus the $+$ or $-$ signs in parentheses designate the expectation states which each evaluator is attempting to produce. Using this notation, the four cases selected for testing are H $(+-)$ L $(+-)$, H $(+-)$ L $(-+)$, H $(-+)$ L $(+-)$, and H $(-+)$ L $(-+)$.

Two sets of derivations can be made from this version of the theory: those referring to conditions in which there are two evaluators, and those referring to conditions in which there is only one evaluator. The first set of conditions, created in the experiment designed specifically for test of the extended version of the theory, is referred to as primary derivations. The second set of conditions, created for the test of the first statement of the theory in Chapter 4, is referred to in this chapter as secondary derivations, for these predictions are also possible from the extended version of the theory. We consider the set of primary derivations first.

From Assumption 3, combined with Assumptions 1 and 2, subjects in the H $(+-)$ L $(+-)$ condition are very likely to form $(+-)$ expectation states, and subjects in the H $(-+)$ L $(-+)$ condition are very likely to form $(-+)$ expectation states. In these conditions, p is presented with two evaluators. He is quite likely to accept the high ability evaluator as a source and less likely to accept the low ability evaluator. Whether he has accepted one or both of the evaluators, by Assumption 1a or 1b, p is quite likely to make unit evaluations that agree with those of both evaluators. These unit evaluations become generalized to expectation states (Assumption 2); and with Assumption 4, the theory makes the following prediction:

DERIVATION 1.   Subjects in the H $(+-)$ L $(+-)$ condition are more likely to reject influence than subjects in the H $(-+)$ L $(-+)$ condition.

In both the H $(+-)$ L $(-+)$ condition and the H $(-+)$ L $(+-)$ condition, the high ability evaluator has the greater probability of becoming a source, and subjects in those conditions are more likely to form expectation states consistent with the high ability evaluator than with the low ability evaluator. Therefore, subjects in the H $(+-)$ L $(-+)$ condition are quite likely to form $(+-)$ expectation states, and those in the H $(-+)$ L $(+-)$ condition, to form $(-+)$ states. Again adding Assumption 4:

DERIVATION 2.   Subjects in condition H $(+-)$ L $(-+)$ are more likely to reject influence than subjects in condition H $(-+)$ L $(+-)$.

Next, in condition H $(+-)$ L $(+-)$ most subjects are expected to form $(+-)$ expectation states, none to form $(-+)$ expectation states— this is precluded by Assumption 2—and a few to retain their undifferentiated expectation states by ignoring both evaluators. By comparison, condition H $(+-)$ L $(-+)$ contains a somewhat different distribution of subjects. Most subjects will accept the high ability evaluator as a source and will form $(+-)$ expectations, a smaller number will accept only the low ability evaluator as a source and will form $(-+)$ expectations, and some will accept neither, hence remaining in the undifferentiated state, designated (0 0). Finally, an additional number will accept both evaluators, and by Assumption 1c will also retain undifferentiated expectations because their sources have disagreed.

Thus in the H $(+-)$ L $(+-)$ condition, more subjects will hold defined $(+-)$ expectations than in the H $(+-)$ L $(-+)$ condition. By a similar line, we expect that more subjects in the H $(-+)$ L $(-+)$ condition will hold defined $(-+)$ expectations than in the H $(-+)$ L $(+-)$ condition. The theory therefore yields the following two derivations:

DERIVATION 3.   Subjects in condition H $(+-)$ L $(+-)$ are more likely to reject influence than subjects in condition H $(+-)$ L $(-+)$.

DERIVATION 4.   Subjects in condition H $(-+)$ L $(+-)$ are more likely to reject influence than subjects in condition H $(-+)$ L $(-+)$.

The complete ordering of these four conditions can be stated by combining Derivations 1 to 4:

DERIVATION 5.   H $(+-)$ L $(+-)$ > H $(+-)$ L $(-+)$ > H $(-+)$ L $(+-)$ > H $(-+)$ L $(-+)$.

For secondary derivations, we could present the four derivations selected for test of the first source theory. However a more interesting comparison is between the two-evaluator conditions and the earlier single-evaluator conditions. For a complete comparison of conditions from the two experiments, we would have to know empirical values for the probabilities of accepting the high and the low ability evaluators as sources. However, we are not in a position at this time to determine empirical values of the acceptance probabilities.

Even without knowing these values, it is possible to construct partial orderings of conditions from the assumptions of this theory, if we further assume that probabilities of accepting as sources the high and the low ability evaluators, respectively, are fixed across each condition of the two studies. That is, if we can make the intuitively plausible assumption that whatever the probability of accepting the high ability evaluator as a source may be, it has the same value in both experiments, we can still construct a partial ordering of the conditions from the two experiments.

In general terms, the present formulation implies, other things being equal, that: (1) two agreeing evaluators will have a greater effect on the population in an experimental condition than will a single evaluator; (2) evaluations from an evaluator described as having high ability will have a greater effect on the population in an experimental condition than the same evaluations from an evaluator described as having low ability. These ideas are presented more precisely as:

Given situation S,

1. Adding an agreeing evaluator increases the probability of forming expectations consistent with the evaluations;

2. Adding a disagreeing evaluator decreases the probability of forming expectations consistent with the first evaluator;

3. Adding an agreeing high ability evaluator increases the original probabilities more than adding an agreeing low ability evaluator;

4. Adding a disagreeing high ability evaluator decreases the original probabilities more than adding a disagreeing low ability evaluator.

From this line of reasoning, and using the assumptions of the present version of the theory, we should observe that the H $(+-)$ L $(+-)$ condition is more effective in producing the $(+-)$ expectation state than was the earlier HE $(+-)$ condition. Furthermore, the HE $(+-)$ condition should be more effective than the H $(+-)$ L $(-+)$ condition. Similarly, H $(+-)$ L $(+-)$ should be more effective in producing $(+-)$ expectations than was LE $(+-)$. In producing $(-+)$ expectations, H $(-+)$ L $(-+)$ should be more effective than HE $(-+)$, which should be more effective than H $(-+)$ L $(+-)$. And, to complete the partial ordering that can be made from these assumptions, H $(-+)$ L $(-+)$ should be more effective than LE $(-+)$, and LE $(-+)$ should be more effective than H $(+-)$ L $(-+)$. Thus we have the following secondary derivations, ordered in terms of rejecting influence:

$$H\ (+-)\ L\ (+-) > HE\ (+-) > H\ (+-)\ L\ (-+);$$
$$H\ (-+)\ L\ (+-) > HE\ (-+) > H\ (-+)\ L\ (-+);$$
$$H\ (+-)\ L\ (+-) > LE\ (+-) > H\ (-+)\ L\ (+-);$$
$$H\ (+-)\ L\ (-+) > LE\ (-+) > H\ (-+)\ L\ (-+).$$

Two observations concerning these secondary derivations are in order. First, we noted at the beginning of this section that a complete ordering of all eight conditions is not possible from assumptions we now are willing to make. Second, the theory predicts the ordering of the four cases selected in the primary derivations. As a generalization of the first version of the theory, it would also predict the four single-evaluator cases; the ability to predict the four previous cases is a necessary condition for this theory to be a generalization of the earlier version, and the theory does meet that condition. We have chosen not to regard the ordering found in the earlier research as independent evidence in support of this formulation, since these results were known to us when the extension was formulated. However, we do claim that the secondary derivations presented here, predicting comparisons between sets of cases, constitute independent tests of the extended version of the theory.

The secondary derivations predict four partial orderings, each of which contains two pair-wise inequalities. Given the predictions of the theory, the eight inequalities are not independent. Suppose, for example, that H $(+-)$ L $(+-) >$ HE $(+-)$. Since the earlier theory stated that HE $(+-) >$ LE $(+-)$, it follows that H $(+-)$ L $(+-) >$ LE $(+-)$. We therefore select a subset of six independent pair-wise comparisons from the total, to involve comparisons between the closest pairs. This subset offers a more stringent test of the theory, for errors of prediction or variance in the data will be more likely to disconfirm predictions between close pairs of conditions. The subset, ordering in terms of probability of rejecting influence, is:

$$H \ (+-) \ L \ (+-) > HE \ (+-);$$
$$HE \ (+-) > H \ (+-) \ L \ (-+);$$
$$H \ (-+) \ L \ (+-) > HE \ (-+);$$
$$HE \ (-+) > H \ (-+) \ L \ (-+);$$
$$LE \ (+-) > H \ (-+) \ L \ (+-);$$
$$H \ (+-) \ L \ (-+) > LE \ (-+).$$

Experimental Procedures. Both the primary and secondary derivations of the theory were tested in an experiment with 84 subjects, 21 assigned randomly to each of the four conditions selected. All subjects were female junior college students between the ages of 18 and 21, recruited from large lecture classes and scheduled by telephone.

The experimental design was maintained as closely as possible to that of the basic source experiment. Availability of subject pools dictated the use of female subjects for this experiment, whereas previous source experiments used male subjects. It was not anticipated that using female subjects would introduce un-foreseen effects, because data from earlier expectation theory experiments using female and male subjects showed no striking differences in behavior in the experimental situation. Such effects may nevertheless exist, however; thus caution should be observed in interpretation of data.

As in the basic source experiment, each group consisted of two subjects who were seated such that they could not observe each other. In the first phase of the experiment, the two experimenters explained to subjects that they were to participate in a two-part study. In the first part, they would receive evaluations of their answers to a task problem from two evaluators, persons #3 and #4. The evaluators were described as "two other junior college girls, like yourselves." The evaluators were described as having taken a special test to determine their ability at the task, as in the basic source experiment. At the appropriate point, the second experimenter left the room to learn the evaluators' performance scores, soon afterward interrupting as follows:

EXPERIMENTER: Pardon me, Dr. Gordon. Persons #3 and #4 have finished the first set of slides. Out of 20 slides, *person #3* got a total of 17 correct and 3 incorrect. This is a very unusual score and would fall into the *upper* category for an individual performance. *Person #4*, out of the 20 slides, got a total of 9 correct and 11 incorrect. This is also an unusual score and would fall into the *bottom* category for an individual performance.

Since it was unreasonable to expect subjects to remember both evaluators' scores and the scores both subjects received from each of the evaluators, an additional change from the basic source experiment was incorporated. The scores received by the evaluators were posted on a chalkboard with the headings: "#3's score" and "#4's score."

The remainder of phase I duplicated the basic source experiment, save that subjects received feedback from *both* evaluators simultaneously, according to a prearranged and fixed feedback schedule. Person #3 always gave subject #1 a score of 17 out of 20 positive evaluations and #2, 9 out of 20 positive evaluations. Person #4 gave one subject 16 out of 20 positive evaluations and the other subject 8 out of 20, and these evaluations either agreed with #3's evaluations or disagreed, thereby placing subjects into each of the four conditions noted previously. The evaluation totals for each subject from each evaluator were then posted on the chalkboard, labeled "#3's (or 4's) evaluations." Phase II of the experiment was exactly the same as in the basic source experiment.

Three subjects were excluded from analysis for failing to meet scope conditions of the theory. One of these, in condition H (+−) L (−+), was suspicious of the experimental situation. She did not believe the evaluations were real, nor that the evaluators existed. Another, in condition H (−+) (+−), was excluded for the same reason. The third, in condition H (−+) L (−+), did not understand the instructions of the experiment and was not task oriented. Analyses were performed on a total of 81 subjects.

Of the remaining 81 subjects, three were classified as "person-oriented," or failing to show collective orientation toward solution of the task. In these cases, a definite classification was not possible as a result of contradictory and inconsistent questionnaire and interview responses. Following the general inclusion principle described in Appendix 3, data from these subjects were retained for primary analyses. We present one table with them excluded, for a comparison with data from the first source experiment.

Results

Rejection of Influence. Comparison of $P(s)$ figures for each of the four conditions of the experiment (Table 7.1) tests the five primary derivations of the theory. As the figures show, each of the first four derivations is supported by data, and the overall ordering of conditions is also supported. Table 7.2 presents the results of a Mann-Whitney U test performed on the pairs of conditions as a way of assessing reliability of differences between conditions.

TABLE 7.1   OVERALL $P(s)$ FOR SUBJECTS BY CONDITIONS

Condition	$P(s)$	n
H (+−) L (+−)	.80	21
H (+−) L (−+)	.76	20
H (−+) L (+−)	.58	20
H (−+) L (−+)	.42	20

TABLE 7.2   MANN-WHITNEY U-TEST ON MAGNITUDE OF DIFFERENCES, MULTIPLE-SOURCE EXPERIMENT

Predicted Comparison	n's	U	Z-Value	p
H (+−) L (+−) > H (−+) L (−+)	21, 20	25.00	−4.838	$p < .001$
H (+−) L (−+) > H (−+) L (+−)	20, 20	87.00	−3.069	$p = .001$
H (+−) L (+−) > H (+−) L (−+)	21, 20	188.50	−0.564	$p = .288$
H (−+) L (+−) > H (−+) L (−+)	20, 20	125.00	−2.042	$p = .02$
H (+−) L (+−) > H (+−) L (−+)>			5.37	$p < .001$
H (−+) L (+−) > H (−+) L (−+)				

Three of the four predicted comparisons achieve significance at or beyond the customary .05 level (one tailed). The fourth, although not significant at the .05 level, was in the predicted direction. The overall ordering (row 5) is significant beyond the .001 level. The data therefore furnish substantial support for the primary ordering derivations of the theory.

Secondary derivations of the theory involve comparison between data from this experiment and the basic source experiment. These data are presented in Table 7.3a and 7.3b. The first predicted inequality, H (+−) L (+−) > H (+−), is not supported by the data in Table 7.3a. The $P(s)$ figures for both these conditions are .80, and all remaining inequalities are as predicted.

TABLE 7.3a $P(s)$ BY CONDITIONS OF MULTIPLE-SOURCE EXPERIMENT, PERSON-ORIENTED SUBJECTS INCLUDED

Condition	$P(s)$	$P(s)$	Condition
H (+−) L (+−)	.80	.80	HE (+−)
H (+) L (−+)	.76	.65	LE (+−)
H (−+) L (+−)	.58	.58	LE (−+)
H (−+) L (−+)	.42	.46	HE (−+)

TABLE 7.3b $P(s)$ BY CONDITIONS OF MULTIPLE-SOURCE EXPERIMENT, PERSON-ORIENTED SUBJECTS EXCLUDED

Condition	n	$P(s)$	$P(s)$	n	Condition
H (+−) L (+−)	20	.80	.79	18	HE (+−)
H (+−) L (−+)	19	.75	.66	18	LE (+−)
H (−+) L (+−)	18	.54	.58	20	LE (−+)
H (−+) L (−+)	20	.43	.44	17	HE (−+)

The same kinds of comparison can be made using data from these experiments but excluding subjects tentatively classified as "person oriented." To the extent that the person orientation classification is accurate, exclusion of these subjects will permit finer comparisons of data between the conditions. Table 7.3b contains the same data as Table 7.3a, minus those from the person-oriented subjects. As can be seen, the data in Table 7.3b support all derivations of differences between conditions of the one-source and the two-source experiments.

Variances.   Table 7.4 presents variances about the mean number of self responses for subjects in each condition. The lowest variance of all four conditions occurs when both evaluators are attempting to produce (+−) expectation states; the greatest variance, when both are attempting to produce $(-+)$ states (rows 1 and 4). When the evaluators disagree in their evaluations (rows 2 and 3), there is more variance in the H $(+-)$ L $(-+)$ condition than in the H $(-+)$ L $(+-)$ condition. The theory predicts that in the first two conditions [H $(+-)$ L $(+-)$ and H $(+-)$ L $(-+)$] most subjects will form $(+-)$ expectation states, and in the last two, $(-+)$ expectation states. We can summarize the variances by noting that there is more variance in the $(+-)$ conditions when the evaluators disagree, and more variance in the $(-+)$ condition when they agree.

TABLE 7.4   VARIANCES ABOUT THE MEAN NUMBER
OF STAY RESPONSES

Condition	Variance	n
H $(+-)$ L $(+-)$	7.39	21
H $(+-)$ L $(-+)$	13.88	20
H $(-+)$ L $(+-)$	9.10	20
H $(-+)$ L $(-+)$	19.53	20

Combining all rows of Table 7.4, we obtain the following ordering of variances:

$$H (-+) L (-+) > H (+-) L (-+) >$$
$$H (-+) L (+-) > H (+-) L (+-).$$

Without specific knowledge of the probabilities of accepting each evaluator, precise predictions concerning ordering of variances are not possible. We would expect, however, that conditions in which evaluators disagree would have higher variances than conditions in which they agree, or, H $(+-)$ L $(-+)$ > H $(+-)$ L $(+-)$, and H $(-+)$ L $(+-)$ > H $(-+)$ L $(-+)$. The first ordering holds, but the second does not. The magnitude of variance in the H $(-+)$ L $(-+)$ condition is not predicted; it is consistent, however, with results of the basic source experiment, in which the highest observed variance was in the H $(-+)$ condition, where most subjects are assumed to form $(-+)$ expectation states.

In summary, variances show no consistent or significant differences, save the high variance in the H $(-+)$ L $(-+)$ condition. In the discussion of the results, we consider a possible explanation for this finding.

Trends Through Time.   The theory as formulated makes no predictions of systematic changes in behavior through time. It does not, however, preclude the possibility of such changes, and information concerning them would be useful in refining the theory. We interject the note of caution that the experiment used

20 critical trials, and this number may not have been sufficient to allow development of consistent time trends. Therefore, any conclusions drawn are tempered by this observation.

In examining time trend data, we inspect means, variances, and alternations for each condition by blocks of five trials. Three properties of the behavior of subjects are considered: changes in rates of accepting influence through time, reflected in the mean $P(s)$ per quarter; the possible emergence of subpopulations in the conditions through time, reflected in changes in variances per quarter and in overall distributions of responses per condition; and changes in stability of response patterns through time, reflected by the rate of alternation responses per subject per condition.

Figure 7.4 presents the $P(s)$ curves for each condition through time. Since the theory predicts no systematic changes in rate of accepting influence through time, the $P(s)$ orderings predicted should be apparent from the first block of five trials and maintained for each block of trials. Inspection of $P(s)$ by quarters indicates that the predicted ordering obtains in the first block of trials and persists without exception through each quarter. At no point do the lines representing $P(s)$ cross. There is a slight decline in $P(s)$ from the first quarter to the last quarter in all four conditions. This decline, ranging from a low of .02 to a high of .04, in no way changes the ordering of conditions and has no apparent theoretical basis. In view of the magnitude of the changes, we are inclined to attribute it to random response variation.

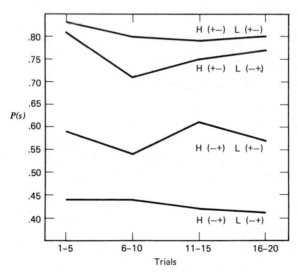

Figure 7.4 $P(s)$ by quarters.

Examining variances through time yields information on effects of the inter-action process on formation of expectation states. The theory predicts that the expectation states formed will be maintained throughout the critical trials. Some subjects, however, faced with nearly constant disagreement from an other, may change expectation states already formed. Variances about the block mean num-bers of self responses are one way to ascertain whether there are a significant number of such subjects. If so, we should observe sharp and consistent changes in variances through time. The complexity of the situation for this experiment makes it necessary to obtain as much information as possible from the data, so Table 7.5 presents both observed *and expected* variances for each quarter. The expected variance assumes an independent trials process and is calculated by $NP (1 - P)$, where N is the number of trials in the block and P is the proportion of self responses in the block.

TABLE 7.5   OBSERVED AND EXPECTED VARIANCES BY QUARTERS[a]

Condition	Block			
	1	2	3	4
H (+−) L (+−)	.63	.80	1.25	1.30
	(.70)	(.80)	(.83)	(.80)
H (+−) L (−+)	.89	1.30	1.56	1.19
	(.77)	(1.01)	(.94)	(.89)
H (−+) L (+−)	.47	.96	1.31	1.08
	(1.21)	(1.24)	(1.19)	(1.22)
H (−+) L (−+)	1.64	1.54	1.88	1.58
	(1.23)	(1.23)	(1.22)	(1.20)

[a] Expected variances are in parentheses.

We must be cautious in comparing observed and expected variances in the H (−+) L (+−) condition (row 3 of the table), since the assumption of inde-pendent trials does not hold for this condition.* There is no obvious explanation of why this condition alone violates the assumption.

* Chi-square values associated with the one-step transition matrices for each condition (df = 1) and their significance levels are:

H (+−) L (+−) =   1.5, $p < .20$;
H (+−) L (−+) =   0.5, $p < .30$;
H (−+) L (+−) = 13.3, $p < .01$;
H (−+) L (−+) =   0.0, $p < .90$.

There is an increase in observed variance in three of the four conditions from the first to the last quarter, but an *F*-ratio comparison of variances between the first and last quarters shows no significant differences at the .05 level, two tailed between quarters.

Comparison of the observed and expected values for the first two conditions, H (+−) L (+−) and H (+−) L (−+), shows that although the observed values generally exceed the expected values, the differences, using the *F*-ratio, are not significant. The highest observed variance is in the H (−+) L (−+) condition. This variance is highest throughout each quarter, with no persistent increase or decrease through time.

There is some indication, then, of consistent increase in variances through time in three of the four conditions. This information alone does not provide definitive evidence for emergence of subpopulations. We turn next to other features of data to shed light on this issue.

The distribution of responses for each condition may provide substantiation for the evidences of potential bimodality indicated in the variances through time. We do not acquire information for the emergence of subgroups, but for their existence at the end of the interaction process. Figure 7.5 presents the overall distributions of self responses for each condition.

The distributions of responses provide some indication of the existence of subgroups in the H (+−) L (−+) condition and in the H (−+) L (−+) condition. In the former, the distribution clusters around 17–20 stay responses and around 11–15 stay responses. In the latter, there is a cluster of responses around 13, and another at 7. These two conditions, referring to Table 7.4, had the highest observed variances. The evidence in the H (+−) L (−+) condition is not clear. A shift of one subject could sharply change the shape of the distribution, and we conclude that there is no clear-cut evidence of existence of subgroups in this condition.

Another way to account for the increase in variance in conditions is to reason that the experimental manipulations into the conditions involve a certain amount of psychological tension for subjects, and the interaction process itself increases that tension. Subjects ought then to manifest increases in response instability. The proportion of alternation responses, discussed in Chapter 4, provides some measure of such tension or instability. Using the formula for calculating expected alternations presented earlier, we compare observed and expected alternations for each condition. Table 7.6 presents the relevant data.

Inspection of the table fails to indicate a consistent trend in the stability of responses for the H (+−) L (+−) condition through time. The observed alternations are very close to expected alternations, with a slight drop in the last quarter. Neither is there a consistent trend in the H (+−) L (−+) or H

Number of Self Responses	Conditions			
	H (+−) L (+−)	H (+−) L (−+)	H (−+) L (+−)	H (−+) L (−+)
20	XX	XXXX		
19	XXX	X		
18	XXX		X	
17	XX	XXX	X	
16	XX	XX		
15	XX	XXX		X
14	XXXX	X	XX	X
13		X	XXXX	XXX
12	XX	X	XX	X
11	X	XX	XX	XX
10		X	XXXX	XX
9			X	
8			X	
7		X	X	XXXX
6			X	XX
5				X
4				
3				X
2				
1				
0				XX
	($n = 21$)	($n = 20$)	($n = 20$)	($n = 20$)
Mean	16.01	15.25	11.55	8.50
$P(s)$	(.80)	(.76)	(.58)	(.42)

Figure 7.5 Overall distributions of self responses.

$(-+)$ L $(-+)$ conditions through time, although in both conditions the observed alternations are higher than expected in the first two quarters. Considerable differences between the observed and expected alternations exist in the H $(-+)$ L $(+-)$ condition; but evaluation of these differences is difficult, considering the failure of the independent trials assumption on which the statistic is based.

To summarize, the data on alternation responses show no consistent changes over time, indicating that no systematic changes in response stability occur as a result of the interaction process.

TABLE 7.6 OBSERVED AND EXPECTED PROPORTIONS OF ALTERNATIONS BY QUARTERS AND OVERALL[a]

	Block				
Condition	1	2	3	4	Overall
H (+ −) L (+ −)	.30	.31	.31	.26	.30
	(.28)	(.32)	(.33)	(.32)	(.32)
H (+ −) L (− +)	.38	.44	.38	.34	.38
	(.30)	(.40)	(.38)	(.35)	(.36)
H (− +) L (+ −)[b]	.66	.57	.50	.61	.58
	(.48)	(.50)	(.48)	(.49)	(.49)
H (− +) L (− +)	.51	.52	.43	.50	.49
	(.49)	(.49)	(.49)	(.48)	(.49)

[a] Expected proportions are in parentheses.
[b] Independent trials assumption does not hold.

Alternative Formulations for Accepting an Evaluator as a Source.   The theory asserts that the probability that any evaluator will become a source, thereby influencing the formation of performance expectations, is a direct function of the relative expectations held for the evaluator. Incorporating the effects of multiple sources, the theory allows for the possibility that more than one source will be activated in a given situation. Assumption 3d states that the probabilities of evaluators becoming sources are functions of the expectations held for them, and the probabilities are both nonzero and independent.

When situation S features multiple evaluators for whom p holds differential expectations, there are at least two reasonable *alternative* formulations to account for their effects on p's expectations. One formulation might maintain that only some evaluators, particularly those for whom the highest expectations are held, have even a chance to become sources. According to this formulation, those who cannot become sources are disregarded by p.

A second alternative might argue that if the situation has multiple evaluators for whom differential expectations are held, the comparison between the two evaluators would enable the evaluator for whom lower expectations are held to become a negative source (see Chapter 5). Although previous research indicates that the negative source phenomenon did not operate in a single-source situation, perhaps the comparison between the two evaluators would activate a negative source.

It is possible to make ordering predictions for the conditions tested in the multiple-source experiment on the basis of the possible alternative formulations.

The first alternative mentioned—the single-source selection formulation—would hold subjects to be likely to ignore the low evaluator and to form expectations *only* in accordance with the evaluations of the high evaluator. In this case, the $P(s)$ overall for subjects in the H $(+-)$ L $(+-)$ and H $(+-)$ L $(-+)$ conditions should be the same, and the overall $P(s)$ for subjects in the H $(-+)$ L $(+-)$ and H $(-+)$ L $(-+)$ conditions should be the same. The ordering in terms of $P(s)$ would therefore be

$$[\text{H } (+-) \text{ L } (+-) = \text{H } (+-) \text{ L } (-+)] > [\text{H } (-+) \text{ L } (+-)$$
$$= \text{H } (-+) \text{ L } (-+)].$$

If the second alternative—the negative source formulation—is appropriate, subjects will be likely to reverse the evaluations made by the low evaluator. Therefore, more subjects in the H $(+-)$ L $(-+)$ condition will form $(+-)$ expectation states than those in the H $(+-)$ L $(+-)$ condition, and more subjects in the H $(-+)$ L $(+-)$ condition will form $(-+)$ expectation states than subjects in the H $(-+)$ L $(-+)$ condition. The overall ordering prediction, in terms of rejecting influence, would be

$$\text{H } (+-) \text{ L } (-+) > \text{H } (+-) \text{ L } (+-)$$
$$> \text{H } (-+) \text{ L } (-+) > \text{H } (-+) \text{ L } (+-).$$

Referring to Table 7.1 [giving the $P(s)$ by conditions for the multiple-source experiment] and to Figure 7.4 [giving the $P(s)$ by conditions for each quarter], we see that neither alternative formulation receives strong support. The formulation presented in the theory is the only formulation to account fully for the observed orderings of conditions, and the $P(s)$ figures through time provide the strongest support. This does not mean, of course, that these alternative source selection processes were not used by some individuals in each condition. It does mean that only the formulation presented in the theory accounts well for the *overall* behavior of subjects in all conditions.

Summary and Discussion.   The data support primary derivations of the theory concerning ordering of pairs of conditions and overall ordering of conditions. Differences between all pairs of conditions are in the predicted directions, and tests for significance of the magnitudes of the differences are significant beyond the .05 level for four of the five predictions made. Although the difference between the H $(+-)$ L $(+-)$ condition and the H $(+-)$ L $(-+)$ condition is not as large as could be desired ($p = .288$, Table 7.2), there is reason to believe that the influence measure used may not be sufficiently sensitive to reflect larger differences. Previous research using this influence measure suggests that because of decision-making properties of the situation, there may be a ceiling on the number of self responses subjects will make. Camilleri et al. (1972) report that when $(+-)$ expectations are manipulated by the experimenter, with objective evaluative information, subjects show a $P(s)$ of .76. Data from the basic source experiment show a $P(s)$ of .80 with a single high evaluator.

Examination of data on rejection of influence through time shows no consistent effects of the interaction situation on the influence measure. Subjects overall hold differentiated expectations in accordance with the predictions of the theory at the onset of interaction, maintaining these expectations throughout the interaction.

Comparisons of data from the multiple-source experiment with those of the basic source experiment (Table 7.3) show general agreement with secondary derivations of the theory. Six pair-wise inequalities were derived as constituting independent tests of the theory. The data in Table 7.3a, which include person-oriented subjects, supported five of the six inequalities. The comparison between H $(+-)$ L $(+-)$ and HE $(+-)$ was not as predicted; both $P(s)$ figures were .80. There is no apparent theoretical explanation for this lack of difference, although the ceiling effect just mentioned might account for it. When the same comparisons are made with person-oriented subjects excluded, all the predicted inequalities obtain.

Considering the directions and magnitudes of the differences found in the tests of the primary derivations, as well as the orderings obtained in both primary and secondary derivations, we note that only one predicted inequality failed to achieve the customary .05 level; thus we conclude that the data on rejection of influence provide strong support for the theory.

Examining variances of the conditions, overall and through time, showed no conclusive evidence of systematic differences between conditions nor of trends through time. We noted that the highest variance obtained was in the H $(-+)$ L $(-+)$ condition, remarking that the theory makes no prediction regarding this finding.

In considering data from the basic source experiment, we argued that the $(-+)$ expectation state may be inherently imbalanced. Subjects induced to form $(-+)$ expectations may accept them, may try to ignore them, or may vacillate between the two alternatives. The $(-+)$ state produced in this condition of the multiple-source experiment probably is more stressful than that produced in the basic source experiment. In the basic source experiment, only one evaluator is attempting to produce the $(-+)$ state, while in the multiple-source experiment, two evaluators are producing the state. This tension was not evident in the proportion of alternation responses overall or by blocks, but the distributions of responses yielded some evidence of bimodality in the condition, indicating support of the argument.

Variances examined through time showed consistent (although not significant) increases for three of the four conditions, suggesting the possibility of subgroup formation in the populations. Distributions of responses support this possibility for the H $(+-)$ L $(-+)$ and H $(-+)$ L $(-+)$ conditions, with some support also for the H $(-+)$ L $(+-)$ condition, and no support for bimodality in the H $(+-)$ L $(+-)$ condition.

Overall, it does not appear that the interaction situation itself changes the expectation states held by the subjects on the basis of the evaluations of sources. Perhaps the strongest support for the theoretical formulation lies in its clear support over alternative theoretical formulations. In that sense, the experiment can be considered to be a critical test between alternatives, shedding much light on the theory and allowing confidence in the selection of formulations.

This rather useful theoretical formulation enables prediction not only to the four cases tested but to other cases as well. Yet the theory as stated leaves open the precise specification of Assumption 1c. Faced with conflicting evaluations from two sources, the theory holds that p will withhold evaluation. We selected this alternative as the simplest of several possibilities. In the next chapter we further refine the theory by describing these possibilities in detail and presenting an experiment that resolves this gap.

CHAPTER EIGHT

THE TWO–SOURCE EXPERIMENT
AND THE NO–SOURCE EXPERIMENT

Design. We found in extending the theory to cover the case of two evaluators that Assumption 1c leads to the prediction that p will not evaluate any unit performance on which his two sources disagree. Assumption 1c was chosen as the simplest of several alternative ways of dealing with the case of disagreeing sources. The fewest substantive changes in the structure of the theory are required by the assertion that in case of disagreement between two individuals whom p has accepted as sources, p will withhold judgment for that particular performance output. Moreover, the predictions made by this assertion are the same as those from several more complicated formulations for the previous two-evaluator experiment. Thus, as a first statement, the simplest formulation was desirable. However there are two major alternative formulations possible for such a situation, and we examine them in this chapter, presenting two experiments designed to discriminate between them.

To simplify our presentation, the original formulation of Assumption 1c is called the "first alternative." The second alternative says that if p has accepted both evaluators as sources and then finds that they are disagreeing on their unit evaluation, p will pick one of them and will agree with all future unit evaluations attributed to this e. That is, when p is faced with the confusing situation of disagreement between two individuals, both of whom he considers to have more ability at the task than himself, it is now hypothesized that he will choose one of them and will stay with that person's evaluations as a way of reducing the ambiguity of the situation. The way he decides which source to follow could reasonably be considered to be a function of his relative expectations for the two of them: if his expectations for source #1 are slightly higher than his expectations for source #2, the probability that p will choose to stick with #1 should be slightly higher than the probability that p will choose to stick with #2.

If the expectations held for the two sources are equal, p might select one of them randomly and agree with him from then on. Or perhaps p will select the

source he is going to agree with on some other basis, such as similarity of judgment—he might pick the source who evaluates performances in the way p does.
However, exact specification of the process of choosing which evaluator to keep
as the source can be worked out as a later problem, if this alternative formulation
is adopted. For the present, we confront the simpler task of deciding whether p
selects one and only one source, and then stays with him.

The third alternative asserts that when p notices that the sources are disagreeing, he will distribute agreements between the two, sometimes agreeing
with source #1, sometimes with source #2. In other words, p has accepted
both sources, and he will agree with unit evaluations made by both of them.
Since it is obviously impossible to agree with both sources when they disagree
with each other, however, p will pick one of the sources to agree with on every
disagreeing trial. By contrast with the alternative just discussed, this alternative
does not make the decision to agree with one particular source a once-and-for-all
phenomenon. The decision is made anew each time the sources disagree. The
basis on which p decides whom to agree with in this alternative could be the
same as for the previous alternative: the higher the expectations held for a given
source, the greater the likelihood that p will agree with that source's unit evaluation on any given performance.

Thus we have three alternative formulations of Assumption 1c. The first
alternative holds that when p has accepted two individuals as sources because
he thinks both have higher ability than he has, p will refuse to make his own unit
evaluation of a performance output on which the sources produce disagreeing
unit evaluations; he will withhold judgment when his sources disagree. The
second possibility is that when the disagreement between two sources becomes
a problem, p will make a once-and-for-all decision to rely on one of them. The
third possibility holds that at each step of a series of unit evaluations on which
sources disagree, p will decide independently which one to rely on.

The manner in which p treats the case of disagreeing sources will have implications for the expectations that p forms, and consequently, will have effects on
the future interaction patterns of p. However, on theoretical grounds alone there
does not appear to be any simple way to choose between these alternatives. The
first alternative was adopted for the first version of the multiple-source theory
because it is the simplest and because it requires the fewest changes in other
parts of the theory. However the first statement may not always adequately represent the process of acceptance of two disagreeing sources. Thus, to help decide
between the alternatives, it became desirable to design an experiment whose
results could aid in deciding how to formulate this assumption. The three alternatives specify different processes that are believed to occur when the sources
disagree, and the different processes would produce different outcomes in terms
of the expectations that p could come to hold as the result of the evaluations.

Suppose that there are two sources, and p holds equal expectations for both.

From the original formulation of Assumption 1c, p will withhold evaluations while the sources disagree on their unit evaluations; consequently, if two individuals who have been accepted as sources disagree frequently, then because p will have made no unit evaluations of performances, he will not hold differentiated expectations for himself and other after such a series of disagreements. In other words, as far as forming performance expectations is concerned, having two sources who disagree on unit evaluations is useless to the individual. They provide no useful information for him to use in evaluating the performances. From the second possible formulation, p will accept the evaluations made by *one* of the disagreeing sources; thus his expectations will be completely determined by that source. He will form expectations in a manner equivalent to that in the case of a single source, for he has decided to ignore one of the sources, should the two disagree. (For the present we defer the question of which source p will choose.) From the third alternative, p will form expectations, but the states formed will be somewhere between those that would be formed if he were to follow either one of the sources. For example, if one of the sources gives p evaluations that would lead him to form high expectations for his own performance and the other gives evaluations that would lead him to form low expectations for his own performance, p will form "moderate" or "intermediate" expectations for his own performance.

Experimental Procedures.   Two experiments were conducted to help to choose between these alternatives. In the two-source experiment, subjects were faced in the first phase with two extremely high ability evaluators, who were therefore very likely to be accepted as sources; these individuals disagreed consistently on the performance evaluations they made. In the other experiment subjects were told that their phase I performances were to be evaluated, but they never saw the evaluations. Thus they began the critical disagreement trials in phase II without having received *any* evaluations of their previous performances. The second experiment was essentially a no-source condition. The evaluations phase could have been completely eliminated, as far as theoretical considerations go, for no theoretical variables were operative in phase I. We included the judging of slides in phase I to make the entire experimental situation identical to that of other source experiments; in this way, whatever unintended effects were produced by the situation itself would be constant across experiments. Thus we could feel more confident about making direct comparisons of data.

All details of both experiments were the same as those of the previous experiments, with changes necessitated by theoretical considerations. For the no-source experiment, subjects were told that their phase I performances were to be evaluated by person #3; subjects would not see the evaluations, however, nor would they learn of them until after the completion of the second phase. They were not told an ability level for person #3. For the two-source experiment, both person #3 and person #4, were described as having achieved a score of 18 out of 20 on their first tests, thus making it extremely likely that both would be accepted as sources. During phase I, person #3 gave one of the subjects 17 positive evaluations and the other 9 positive evaluations, and person #4 gave the two subjects, respectively, 9 and 17 positive evaluations. In other words, each subject was given both a $(+-)$ and a $(-+)$ evaluation pattern from equally competent sources.

These considerations suggest that if the first alternative (the original formulation) were to receive support from these experiments, data from the two-source experiment should closely resemble data from the no-source experiment. Because of the large proportion of disagreements between the evaluators, subjects in the two-source condition would be expected to withhold unit evaluations in phase I, thus beginning phase II with (0 0) expectations.

If the second alternative were to be supported, data from the two-source experiment should show two populations of subjects: those who had decided to agree with the unit evaluations of person #3, and those who had decided to agree with the unit evaluations of person #4. Of course we could not predict exactly which individual subjects would agree with which evaluator, but about half might be expected to have chosen each of the evaluators. Thus we would anticipate a bimodal distribution of some $(+-)$ and some $(-+)$ subjects.

If the third alternative were to be supported, data from the two-source experiment should show a single population of subjects, and they should have neither a high nor a low expectation for their own performance (since each subject received both a high evaluation and a low evaluation from the respective evaluators). This might be called an "average-average" expectation state.

Subjects were females between the ages of 17 and 24, drawn from the same subject pool that had been used for the two-evaluator experiments and, except for sex, the subject pool that had been used for the first source experiment and the negative source experiment.

Results.   Data from both experiments are considered together, for in some cases—especially the case of the first alternative—relevant evidence comes from comparison of the results of the two experiments. In addition, occasional references are made to data from earlier experiments.

Rejection of influence.   First, we examine the overall mean likelihood of rejecting influence as an indicator of the relative expectations held by subjects in both experiments. Table 8.1 presents the overall mean $P(s)$ figures for both experiments.

TABLE 8.1   OVERALL MEAN $P(s)$ FOR
NO-SOURCE AND TWO-SOURCE
EXPERIMENTS

Condition	n	$P(s)$
0-source	30	.64
2-source	27	.67

For the no-source (0-S) experiment, the mean is .64; for the two-source (2-S) experiment, it is .67. The data of Table 8.1 could be consistent with any of the three formulations of Assumption 1c. From the first alternative formulation, we would expect that subjects in the 2-S group would not have formed expectations because of the disagreement between evaluators in phase I, consequently, their overall mean $P(s)$ should not differ appreciably from that observed in the 0-S condition. From the second formulation, it would be expected that equal numbers of subjects in the 2-S condition would form $(+-)$ and $(-+)$ expectations, and the observed $P(s)$ figure could result from the combining of these two populations. Finally, the third formulation would lead us to predict that all subjects in the 2-S condition would form "average" expectations for self and other; thus it could be said that the observed $P(s)$ figure is the value for these "average" expectations.

Figure 8.1 shows that the overall mean $P(s)$ figure is reflected also in all quarters of both experiments. The separation between conditions is slight in every quarter, and the curves cross once. Table 8.1 and Figure 8.1 indicate that it would be

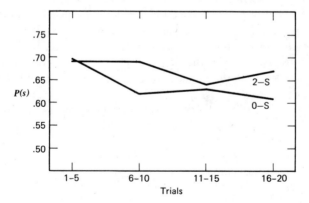

Figure 8.1 $P(s)$ by blocks of five trials for the 0-S and 2-S experiments.

difficult to differentiate between the results of these two experiments in terms of the overall $P(s)$ figures.

Application of a statistical test of whether these two experiments produced different populations also indicates that in terms of overall likelihood of rejecting influence, one could not reject the null hypothesis that they produced equal effect (Mann-Whitney $U = 341.0$, $Z = 1.03$, $p = .30$).

Another comparison can be drawn between data from these two experiments and a previous set of experiments in which subjects' expectations were manipulated by evaluations from the experimenter. These studies, referred to in Chapter 4, could be considered to be a "baseline" against which data from other experiments might be examined. Presumably evaluations from the experimenter *will* be accepted (with probability = 1.0) by subjects in this experimental situation, for the experimenter is known to have access to objective evaluative information. Therefore, so long as a comparable subject population is used for later experiments, we can get an approximate idea of $P(s)$ values to be expected as the result of different expectation states.

In this case, the relevant conditions from the earlier experiment are the experimenter-manipulated $(++)$ and $(--)$ conditions. In these conditions, both subjects were told they had achieved the *same* score in phase I, and this score was described as being either extremely high or extremely low. Thus the subjects receiving the $(++)$ and the $(--)$ conditions were given evaluations to produce self–other expectations that could give no useful information in resolving the phase II disagreements. If subjects believe that they both are extremely good at the task, *or* if they believe that they both are extremely poor at it, they have no way of using this information to resolve a disagreement when it arises later.

Importantly, the overall mean $P(s)$ for the two equal ability manipulation conditions reported by Camilleri et al. (1972) (Table 8.2) differ only negligibly. The equal ability manipulation conditions produced equal likelihood of subjects' accepting influence, whether the expectations they held for self and for other were both high, or both low. This finding, of course, is also consistent with the theory's assertion that the *relative* level of self and other expectations— not the absolute level—is the important determinant of observable behavior.

TABLE 8.2   OVERALL MEAN $P(s)$ FOR
THE EQUAL ABILITY MANIPULATION
CONDITIONS

Condition	n	$P(s)$
$(++)$	31	.67
$(--)$	32	.65

In terms of the 0-S and the 2-S experiments, the striking characteristic of these comparisons is the extreme closeness of $P(s)$ figures for both the manipulated $(++)$ and $(--)$ conditions to figures observed in both the later experiments. Interpreting data from the 0-S and the 2-S experiments in a fashion similar to the interpretation of data from the manipulated experiments, we might conclude that by the measure of overall $P(s)$, neither of the later experiments provided expectations that were useful to subjects in resolving the phase II disagreements.

For the 0-S experiment, phase I clearly produced no useful information, for subjects did not receive performance evaluations in the first phase. For the 2-S experiment, on the other hand, an interpretation of no useful information would be most consistent with the first and third alternative formulations. The first alternative asserts that subjects will not form expectations, and the third alternative asserts that they will form expectations, but of a type that will not help them to resolve disagreements. On the other hand, the second alternative predicts that all subjects in the 2-S experiment will form differentiated expectations (i.e., expectations useful in resolving disagreements), but some subjects will form $(+-)$ expectations and some will form $(-+)$. Because we cannot yet assess whether this occurred, we do not want to state flatly that the results of the 2-S experiment produced expectations that give no useful information in this situation. On the basis of the mean $P(s)$ figures, we cannot reject such an interpretation, which would be consistent with results of the $(++)$ and $(--)$ conditions from the previous experiment.

To summarize the results of examination of $P(s)$ figures, we note three general conclusions. First, it is not possible on the basis of this measure of likelihood of rejecting influence to distinguish between the 0-S and the 2-S experiments. Second, overall $P(s)$ data from both experiments were quite close to those produced using a comparable subject pool and manipulating subjects into the $(++)$ or the $(--)$ expectation states. We interpret these two states as conditions of essentially no useful information to the subject in terms of resolving disagreements, and this interpretation also may be justified for both the 0-S and the 2-S experiments. Third, all preceding results could be consistent with any of the three alternative formulations of Assumption 1c. Because of the importance that has been attached to prediction of overall $P(s)$ in the development of the theory, this suggests strongly an important conclusion; namely, that it is not a question of accepting or rejecting all these assumptions, but rather, a question of accepting *one* from among this set. In other words, all alternatives seem to be "close" to the desired ideal statement. We now begin to examine our data further in the attempt to distinguish between the alternative formulations.

Distribution of Subjects. Although alternative forms of the assumption would not necessarily lead us to expect the 0-S experiment to be distinguishable from the 2-S experiment in terms of rejection of influence, at least some of the alternatives suggest that the distribution of subjects should differ in the two experiments. First let us consider the theoretical implications of the 0-S experiment. Here the subject is faced with phase II disagreements before he has been given any information about the relative abilities of himself and his partner. Thus we assume that subjects begin phase II either with undifferentiated expectations for self and other or with expectations based on their prior experiences independent of the experiment, which vary widely across individuals. In other words, at the outset of the critical trials of the 0-S experiment, we expect to find large variance across subjects in their likelihood of rejecting influence, and we expect to find that the distribution is unimodal. (There is no justification, nor need, for the stronger assumption that the distribution will be normal as well.)

The expected distribution of subjects for the 2-S experiment depends on which alternative formulation of Assumption 1c is adopted. From the original formulation, we would expect the 2-S experiment to produce a population equivalent to the 0-S population (i.e., one with considerable variance across subjects) and a unimodal distribution. From the second alternative formulation of Assumption 1c, we would expect the 2-S experiment to produce two populations of subjects: those who accepted source #3, and those who accepted source #4. Thus variance across subjects would be high, and the distribution of subjects should be bimodal. From the third alternative, we would expect all or nearly all subjects in the 2-S condition to form "average" expectations. Thus variance would be low, and the distribution of subjects should be unimodal.

In examining the amounts of variance obtained in the two experiments, it will be desirable to compare the figures with a "baseline," as well as to make comparison across the two experiments. Therefore, we also present the *expected* variance for each condition, as we did in Chapter 7. The comparison with expected variances introduces an additional complication; calculation of expected variances in these data imposes on them the requirement that the trials be independent. If trials are independent, the self or other resolution on any given disagreement trial is unaffected by the self or other resolution on the preceding trial. We test this assumption by examining chi-square values for one-step response matrices. In so doing, we find that the assumption of independent trials can be made for the 0-S experiment ($\chi^2 = .005$, $p < .95$), but not for the 2-S experiment ($\chi^2 = 4.05$, $.02 < p < .05$). Information from comparisons of expected and observed variances for the 2-S experiment must be interpreted with caution, bearing in mind that the data do not adequately meet one of the assumptions for this test.

Table 8.3 presents variance about the mean number of stay responses per subject, by blocks of five trials and overall. Two comparisons are possible from the data. First, for every block of trials (and for the entire series of 20 trials), variance is lower for the 2-S subjects than for the 0-S subjects. This comparison does not require the independent trials assumption. From this comparison it is possible to conclude that the 2-S experiment produced more uniform effects across subjects than did the 0-S experiment, as measured by these variance data. This conclusion is strengthened by the second type of comparison; namely, expected and observed variances in the two experiments, which shows that for every quarter of the 2-S experiment except the third, the observed variance is *less* than expected, whereas for every quarter of the 0-S experiment, the observed variance is *greater* than expected. As previously noted, however, this finding must be accepted cautiously, for data from the 2-S study do not meet the independent trials assumption.

TABLE 8.3   OBSERVED AND EXPECTED VARIANCES BY QUARTERS AND OVERALL VARIANCES ABOUT MEAN NUMBER OF STAY RESPONSES[a]

Condition	Trials				
	1–5	6–10	11–15	16–20	1–20
0-S	1.22	1.54	1.52	1.20	13.56
	(1.07)	(1.18)	(1.17)	(1.19)	
2-S	.87	.87	1.31	1.09	6.41
	(1.07)	(1.07)	(1.05)	(1.10)	

[a] Expected variances are in parentheses.
[b] Independent trials assumption does not hold for this condition.

Results accord with the interpretation that the 2-S experiment produced more uniform effects across subjects, as measured by variance data. For every block of trials, variance is lower for the 2-S subjects than for the 0-S subjects; although in some cases the difference between the two experiments is not large, it is consistent throughout the series of trials.

The finding of less variance in the 2-S experiment than in the 0-S experiment is consistent only with the third alternative formulation of Assumption 1c; that is, that subjects will accept both sources and will form average expectations as the result of the conflicting evaluations. Undifferentiated expectations, which the first formulation predicts, might be expected to produce approximately equal expected and observed variances; and in accordance with the second formulation, the existence of two populations would be expected to show *greater* variance in the 2-S experiment than in the 0-S experiment.

The first alternative formulation would lead to the expectation that variance in the 2-S experiment would not differ importantly from variance in the 0-S experiment. The number of trials within any block is too small for confidence in such a comparison, but it is possible to compare overall variances of these two experiments for further verification of the conclusion that the conditions did differ. Table 8.4 presents the results of F-tests on the variance ratio of the two conditions.

Table 8.4 appears to indicate that the two conditions produced differences in the amount of variance in subjects' responses. The two-tailed probability of finding a variance ratio of 2.12 by chance was less than .10, if in fact there were no differences produced by the two experiments. This result is inconsistent with the original formulation of Assumption 1c, for this alternative predicts approximately equal variance in the 0-S and the 2-S experiments. In other words, if the first alternative were to be supported by these data, it should not be possible to reject the null hypothesis of no difference in variance between the experiments. But Table 8.4 indicates that the null hypothesis can be rejected at the .10 level of confidence. Although the .10 level is slightly less stringent than the .05 level usually applied, in view of the consistency of variance differences through time, we feel fairly safe in rejecting the null hypothesis here. Thus the first conclusion from the variance ratio test is that the original formulation is not adequate to explain the observed finding from these two experiments.

TABLE 8.4   VARIANCE RATIO TESTING DIFFERENCE BETWEEN THE 0-S AND THE 2-S EXPERIMENTS

σ^2 0-S	σ^2 2-S	df	F	p (two-tailed)	p (one-tailed)
13.56	6.41	29, 26	2.12	$.05 < p < .10$	$.01 < p < .05$

Let us examine the one-tailed probability of occurrence of this variance ratio, under the prediction that variance in the 2-S experiment will be smaller than variance in the 0-S experiment. Such a prediction is made partly *ad hoc*: we already know that variance in the 2-S experiment was smaller than in the 0-S. In applying the one-tailed test, we ask, Suppose we had adopted the third formulation; do the data support it? The one-tailed probability of the observed variance ratio, given the prediction that variance will be less in the 2-S than in the 0-S experiment, is less than .05. This finding would support the third formulation. It would be inconsistent with both the first and the second alternatives. To summarize: data in Table 8.4 are clearly inconsistent with the first formulation, are probably inconsistent with the second formulation, and are clearly consistent with the third formulation. On the basis of overall variance, we can conclude that the empirical evidence so far presented favors the third formulation.

Another differentiation between the three formulations appears when we scrutinize the actual distributions of subjects in the two experiments, by blocks of trials. Such comparisons are generally difficult in experiments of this kind, for the number of subjects and the number of trials are too small for confidence in the results of the comparisons. Recall that we usually have 20 subjects in each condition; this number is sufficient for confidence in the overall differences for all trials between conditions, but not for confidence in differences between blocks of trials nor for differences in the shape of distributions of subjects. However, since the three formulations would predict different shapes of distributions, both experiments were run with 30 subjects—a number we consider to be a minimum for making comparisons on shapes of distributions—by blocks of trials.

Before examining the distributions of subjects, we make explicit the kinds of results that would be expected from each of the three formulations. Because subjects in the 0-S experiment have received no evaluations in phase I of the study, we would expect them to show a broad distribution, with a single mode, at the beginning of the critical trials. Through the course of phase II disagreement resolution, however, we would expect the interaction process itself to produce some differentiation of subjects. To resolve any given disagreement, a subject must decide either that he is correct or that the other is correct. Assumption 2 of the theory predicts that the result of a series of these decisions is likely to lead to the formation of a differentiated expectation state. [The high proportion of disagreements makes formation of equal expectations, $(++)$ or $(--)$, very unlikely.] Therefore, with time, we would expect subjects in the 0-S experiment to begin to differentiate into two types, those with $(+-)$ expectations, and consequently a higher $P(s)$, and those with $(-+)$ expectations, and consequently a lower $P(s)$. The distribution, in other words, should tend to become bimodal as the result of the disagreement interaction phase II of the 0-S experiment. We ought to note one qualification for this differentiation prediction: it is possible that there will not be enough critical trials in phase II to permit this differentiation process to be fully realized. If this is the case, we might not be able to see the two modes, even at the end of the experiment.

The three formulations make quite different predictions for the 2-S experiment. The first formulation asserts that subjects will ignore most of the evaluations in phase I, thus will be equivalent to subjects in the 0-S experiment: the distribution will be unimodal and broad at the beginning and will resolve into a bimodal distribution as the result of the interaction process.

The second formulation asserts that each subject will accept one of the disagreeing sources and will form expectations based on his evaluations. Since the design of the 2-S experiment does not favor either of the sources (because their abilities are equal), we would expect from this formulation that the 2-S experiment at the outset would contain two populations of approximately the same size: those who have formed $(+-)$ expectations and those who have formed $(-+)$ expectations. Furthermore, this bimodality should be maintained throughout phase II, since we know from much previous research that once expectations are formed, in the absence of new information, they tend to be stable.

The third formulation asserts that subjects will accept evaluations from both sources, thus will form intermediate level expectations. At the outset of inter-action, the distribution of subjects in the 2-S experiment should be narrower than the distribution in the 0-S experiment, and it should be unimodal. Further-more, this distribution ought to be maintained throughout the series of trials, for reasons similar to those just given: there is no information that will produce change in expectations.

The distributions of subjects by total number of stay responses for each quarter of the trials for the 0-S and the 2-S experiments appear in Figure 8.2 and Figure 8.3, respectively.

The distributions of subjects in Figure 8.2 conform quite well to those expected on theoretical grounds. In the first block of five trials, subjects are broadly dis-

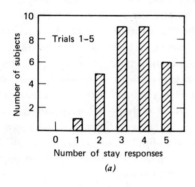

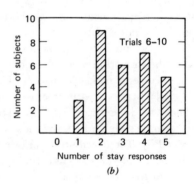

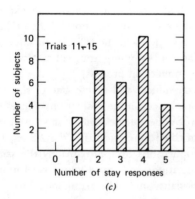

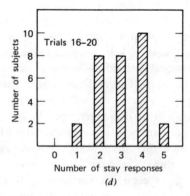

Figure 8.2   Distribution of subjects, 0-S. (a) $\bar{x} = 3.47$, $\sigma^2 = 1.22$; (b) $\bar{x} = 3.10$, $\sigma^2 = 1.54$; (c) $\bar{x} = 3.17$, $\sigma^2 = 1.52$; (d) $x = 3.03$, $\sigma^2 = 1.21$.

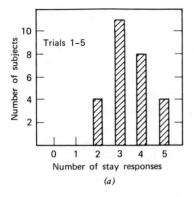

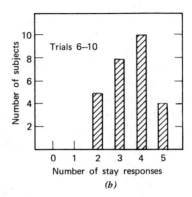

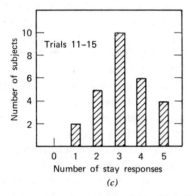

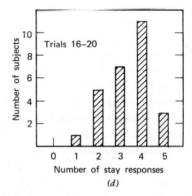

Figure 8.3   Distribution of subjects, 2-S. (a) $\bar{x} = 3.44$, $\sigma^2 = .87$; (b) $\bar{x} = 3.44$, $\sigma^2 = .87$; (c) $\bar{x} = 3.19$, $\sigma^2 = 1.31$; (d) $\bar{x} = 3.37$, $\sigma^2 = 1.09$.

tributed, with a modal number of stay responses of 3.5 and a mean of 3.47. Variance about the mean number is 1.22. Through time, Figures 8.2b to 8.2d show the shape of the distribution changing to become bimodal. The distribution for the final block of trials (Figure 8.2d) seems to be made up of two populations, one with a mode of 2 stay responses and one with a mode of 4 stay responses. The *mean* number of stay responses per subject for the final block of trials is 3.03, which is only slightly different from the mean in the first block. It will be recalled that the mean $P(s)$ curves of Figure 8.1 reflect the failure of over-all mean $P(s)$ to change appreciably in the 0-S experiment. However, comparison of Figure 8.2a and Figure 8.2d indicates that simple comparison of means does not give an adequate representation of changes through time. Modal responses are adequately represented by the overall block mean $P(s)$ of .69. However, data indicate that two populations are beginning to appear within this condition, with approximate $P(s)$ values of .40 and .80. These figures are quite different, and they could reasonably be interpreted as representing a $(-+)$ and a $(+-)$ population, respectively.

The distributions of subjects in the 2-S experiment can be examined in two ways. First, they can be compared with the distributions from the 0-S experiment; such a comparison will have especial relevance for the first formulation of the assumption. Second, the distributions can be examined for changes through time within the 2-S experiment; these comparisons are relevant to all three alternative formulations.

By comparison with the first block of the 0-S experiment (Figure 8.2a), block 1 of the 2-S experiment (Figure 8.3a) shows a more narrow distribution of subjects. This result was already indicated in the variance differences for the first block (Table 8.3). Moreover, the distribution in Figure 8.3a is unimodal. This result would be predicted either from the first formulation or from the third; it would not be predicted from the second formulation, which calls for a bimodal distribution. This information may be conjoined with the first formulation's prediction of *equal* variance for the first block of the two experiments, and the third formulation's prediction of greater variance for the 0-S experiment. It has already been shown that this comparison favors the third formulation; inspection of Figures 8.2a and 8.3a confirms this result.

Possible changes in distributions for the 2-S condition through time may be assessed by comparing Figure 8.3a with Figures 8.3b to 8.3d. From the first formulation, we would predict that the unimodal distribution would change to a bimodal distribution, as it had in the 0-S experiment. There is no evidence that this occurred. The only change appears to be a linear transformation of mean and mode; in Figure 8.3a the mode is 3 and the mean is 3.44; in Figure 8.3d the mode is 4 and the mean is 3.37. In addition, let us compare the figures for variance about the mean number of stay responses in Figure 8.3a to 8.3d. They are, respectively, .87, .87, 1.31, and 1.09. These results do not appear to offer sufficient justification to argue for either a simple increase or a simple decrease in variance through time. Such a finding would be consistent with either the second or the third formulation; it would not be consistent with the first. In addition, the second formulation would predict that every block should show the predicted bimodal distribution of subjects. Yet no block shows a bimodal distribution. Thus we conclude that these comparisons also favor the third formulation of Assumption 1c.

Alternations, which we have examined in previous experiments, show no unusual results, nor do they shed light on alternative formulations of the assumption. Therefore, we omit these data.

Summary and Discussion.   We began this chapter by describing three alternative ways of formulating Assumption 1c of the theory, to deal with the case of two disagreeing competent evaluators. The first alternative states that when sources disagree in their evaluations of a performance output, p will simply withhold evaluation of that performance output. The second alternative states that in the case of disagreeing sources, p will select one source and will agree with his evaluations. The third alternative states that in the case of disagreeing sources, p will distribute his agreements between them, agreeing with each source some of the time. Then we described the no-source and the two-source experiments, which were designed to aid in assessing these alternatives and to aid in the possible reformulation of the theory. Data from these two experiments generally support the third alternative formulation, and are generally inconsistent with either the first or second formulations.

The first analyses performed were overall mean $P(s)$ and mean $P(s)$ by blocks of trials from both experiments. These figures were examined primarily to assess "reasonableness" in view of previous results and to compare the behavioral effects of the two different experimental manipulations in terms of likelihood of rejection of influence. The overall mean $P(s)$ for both experiments (Table 8.1) was approximately .66; as expected, the treatments could not be distinguished by this measure. More important, the figure was impressively close to the values for two conditions of a previous experiment in which subjects held manipulated equal expectations, either $(++)$ or $(--)$, for self and other (Table 8.2). If the previous experiment can be interpreted as one in which subjects had no useful expectation information to help them to resolve the phase II disagreements, the same interpretation *might* plausibly be placed on data from the 0-S and the 2-S experiments. Such an interpretation would be consistent with either the first or the third alternative formulation. Examination of the $P(s)$ figures by blocks of five trials (Figure 8.1) showed that the similarity of data over all trials is also reflected at any point in time through the trials. This finding increases confidence in the interpretation based on overall mean $P(s)$. All these findings were consistent with all three alternative formulations of Assumption 1c. Thus it was concluded that any of the formulations is reasonably satisfactory, the next step being to choose the best from among the three, not to formulate a fourth alternative. Finally, the Mann-Whitney U statistic employed through this series of studies shows that one cannot reject the null hypothesis that the two experimental treatments produced identical populations. We concluded that examination of the mean $P(s)$ figures from these experiments alone cannot serve to distinguish between the alternative formulations of the assumption.

The second set of comparisons involved distribution of subjects within each of the two experiments, and especially changes in those distributions through time. The distributions produced by the two experiments did differ, as indicated by overall variance ratio (Table 8.4). Comparisons between the 0-S and the 2-S experiments were made as the important measure of accuracy of prediction from each alternative formulation.

The experimental treatment of the 0-S experiment would be expected to produce a wide unimodal distribution of subjects about the mean number of self resolutions for the first block of trials. Then the disagreement interaction in phase II would be expected to produce a differentiation into a bimodal distribution of subjects. Both these expectations were confirmed by the distributions presented in Figure 8.2.

By comparison, the first alternative would predict that the 2-S distribution would be bimodal at the outset, remaining that way throughout the series of trials, whereas the third alternative predicts that the 2-S distribution will be unimodal with smaller variance at the outset than the 0-S distribution, remaining that way throughout the series. The distributions in Figure 8.3 are consistent only with the third alternative.

Because variance comparisons (as well as alternations comparisons) are usually dependent on independent trials data, and because data from the 2-S experiment do not meet the independent trials assumption, results from all these comparisons must be interpreted cautiously. Given the consistency of results favoring the third formulation, however, and because there was no single strong piece of evidence favoring the first or the second alternative formulation, we conclude that the third is the one that best predicts the observed data. Accordingly, this formulation of Assumption 1c is incorporated into the final version of the theory in Chapter 10.

These two experiments constitute the last steps in the program designed to formulate and to extend the theory of sources of self-evaluation. In the final chapter we summarize the theoretical and empirical work and present the final version of the theory. First, however, we must examine an issue that appears frequently in discussions of self-evaluation; namely, the idea that the individual in some sense "prefers" a high evaluation to a low self-evaluation and will take steps to maximize the level of self-evaluation that he possesses. This intuitively appealing idea appears to be accepted by many of those who have thought about self-evaluation or who have conducted research in that area. Although we performed no direct tests of the idea, in Chapter 9 we consider the results of some of the research reported in earlier chapters to test ideas related to self-maximization.

CHAPTER NINE

THE MAXIMIZATION MYTH

The belief is prevalent in social psychology that individuals seek to maximize their self-evaluations. Positive self-images are said to be pleasing to the individual, and it is frequently assumed that people will consciously direct their activities to obtain the highest possible self-evaluation in a given situation. The so called maximization idea has considerable intuitive appeal, and it is not at all rare to hear versions of it expressed in nonprofessional circles as well as in scholarly writing. The individual who ignores criticism, who "overlooks" his own faults; the individual who is overanxious to please, who will do anything for a compliment—these are easily recognized stereotypes in our culture because they are frequently met. We have all had experiences with such individuals.

When an idea is current in everyday conversation as well as in professional discourse, it is likely that the idea is part of the store of "common knowledge" of the culture, somewhat like the simple ideas on Newtonian physics which are used every day by people in their work and recreation. If the idea has wide currency in both professional and nonprofessional circles, we might also expect that it has diffused from the former to the latter; the idea was first proposed in professional circles, was tested and received a degree of confirmation there, and consequently was transmitted through textbooks to a lay audience, who explored the notion for its practical usefulness. Some ideas in behavioral psychology fit this description; for example, Pavlov's basic reinforcement propositions (usually now called "conditioning" by laymen) were proposed, tested, and confirmed in professional circles, then employed in practical applications by others.

Curiously, in view of the widespread apparent acceptance for the idea of self-maximization, to our knowledge, neither of the above-mentioned circumstances applies to it. That is, the idea may be part of "common knowledge" in the sense that many people believe it to be true, but it is not part of common knowledge insofar as we lack a single accepted statement of the idea. Nor was the idea proposed and rigorously tested in professional circles before becoming adopted there and by nonprofessionals as well. In fact, the idea appears to be most frequently invoked as a *post hoc* explanation of unexpected results of studies; it is never the subject of direct test. Like many other popular propositions about behavior, the idea of self-maximization seems to rest far more on its intuitive appeal than on any empirical data that could be considered supportive. An intuitively appealing, widely accepted idea that has no empirical support may reasonably be termed a "myth."

Yet an idea's failure to acquire rigorous empirical support does not in itself decrease its utility. The idea could well be useful; and if it were tested, it might in fact receive the support now lacking. Self-maximization clearly is a central issue for any theory of self-evaluation such as ours. At present, our theory does not incorporate any idea of self-maximization. But because the idea is prevalent in social psychology, and because it represents several important issues in a theory of self-development, it merits serious consideration.

Before examining empirical tests, we must state the ideas on self-maximization explicitly and in testable form. There appear to be three distinct main ideas contained in what we have called the maximization myth, each with one or more minor variations. The first line of thought holds that individuals engage in a selective perception that somehow makes them more likely to "cognize" information leading to a high self-image. For example, in familiar terms, we hear of the person who overlooks or discounts criticism and negative evaluations of himself, while believing positive evaluations and accepting them uncritically. The second line of thought is behavioral: individuals in a social situation will respond in ways calculated to gain them praise; they do things they think will gain them social approval and positive evaluations from others. The third idea is that individuals will seek to preserve whatever level of self-evaluation they already possess. We examine each of these major themes in the self-maximization idea, both in terms of conceptualization and in the light of data from the various source experiments.

Cognitive Maximization. The most interesting means of maximization of the self-image from the point of view of social psychology is that of cognitive maximization, or, more generally, cognitive distortion. Distortion is "easier" for the individual than other alternatives; he does not need to expend physical energy to distort, and he is free to distort situations in which he could not produce objective change through behavioral means. In addition, processes of cognitive distortion are well documented in other areas and are of central importance in several current theoretical approaches. The family of "consistency theories" frequently make use of the possibility of cognitive distortion as one mechanism available to an individual striving to achieve "balance" (see, e.g., Festinger, 1957; Newcomb, 1953). Moreover, cognitive distortion is almost entirely under the individual's control. Others may intervene to prevent attempts at self-maximization by behavioral means, but their direct control over cognitions of the individual is minimal. Therefore, cognitive distortion could be used in nearly any situation in which the individual desires to improve his self-image.

One of the earlier statements of the self-maximization idea is presented by Heider in a discussion of attribution.

> The tendency to keep the ego level high is an example. Hoppe showed how this tendency can influence attribution. His subjects frequently tried to clear themselves of the responsibility for failures. "Usually the blame is then put on the material. . . . One evades, as far as possible, the effect of the failure by looking for the cause of it not in the own person but in the neutral sphere of objects."
>
> It is obvious that *this tendency to keep the ego level high* must play a role in attribution. Since origins are assimilated to acts attributed to them, an act of low value, when attributed to the ego, will lower the ego level, and an act of high value will raise it. *However, this will happen only when the stimulus conditions are so strong as to enforce the attribution, that is, if there can be no doubt that the own person is the source.* Often, the possibility of different organizations will exist. *Then the tendency to raise the ego level will structure the causal units in such a way that only good acts and not bad ones are attributed to the own person.* (Heider, 1944, pp. 368–369; emphasis supplied)

In the case Heider describes, the individual "denies responsibility" for acts that are likely to be negatively evaluated. This option does not appear to exist for subjects in our source experiments, for it would mean denying that they made the choices that were negatively evaluated in phase I. However, the theoretically related process of selective perception of positive and negative evaluations certainly was available to them. They could "overlook" negative evaluations and concentrate on positive evaluations, or they could believe that those of their negatively evaluated choices in some sense were not "representative" of their own ability, whereas choices that were positively evaluated were representative. On the more general level, individuals who received a poor score in phase I could believe that this score did not accurately reflect their true abilities, and individuals given a high score could accept it as a valid indicator of their abilities. Any of these processes would constitute cognitive distortion of perception, which would have the consequence of maximizing self-evaluation. The effects of the individual types of distortions cannot be distinguished in our data; the consequences would be about the same for all these processes in our experiments. However, data available permit us to confront the more basic question— whether such distortion did in fact occur.

To measure effects of distortion, we need a comparison of conditions in which distortion might have occurred. One basis for such comparison can be seen by asking, Whose evaluations are more likely to be distorted by subjects—those of the high evaluator or those of the low evaluator? The central assumption throughout this work has been that the high evaluator's opinions could not be ignored in these experiments, and data have supported this idea strongly. Therefore, it seems safe to assume that opinions of the low ability evaluator are more likely to be subject to the effects of cognitive distortion, and we make this assumption wherever possible in examining data for effects of such distortion.

If subjects are given the option of ignoring evaluations of the LE, and if they also want to maximize their self-expectations, we might expect them to ignore negative evaluations from the LE but to accept positive evaluations from him. This would mean that subjects in the LE $(+-)$ condition would form $(+-)$ expectations and those in the LE $(-+)$ condition would (a) ignore the LE and retain undifferentiated expectations or (b) base their expectations only on the positive evaluations they received from the LE (9 out of 20), thus also forming $(+-)$ expectations. If this process were followed for the LE conditions, we would expect it to occur in the negative-source (NS) conditions as well. Since we know from considerable past work that the $P(s)$ of subjects holding $(+-)$ expectations is approximately .80 in this experimental situation, we examine the data for this evidence that the $(+-)$ expectation state was formed.

Table 9.1 presents the overall mean $P(s)$ from the two LE conditions of the first experiment, and from the two NS conditions as well. In none of these four conditions is the figure very close to the $(+-)$ figure of .80, which we would expect if most subjects in a condition formed $(+-)$ expectations. Thus, although some subjects, especially in the two $(+-)$ conditions, may have formed $(+-)$ expectations, there is no support for the idea that many subjects in either of the $(-+)$ conditions did so. The $(-+)$ condition of both the LE and the NS experiments shows a lower $P(s)$ than the comparable $(+-)$ condition and thus constitutes additional evidence that subjects were willing to accept the negative evaluations of themselves. Thus these first comparisons do not point to evidence of a tendency to maximize the self-evaluation in the manner described.

A second test of the same idea can be made using data in Table 9.1, if we assume that the NS is more readily ignored than the LE (or if we assume that

TABLE 9.1   OVERALL MEAN $P(s)$ FOR THE FOUR LOW ABILITY EVALUATORS

Condition	n	$P(s)$
LE $(+-)$	19	.65
LE $(-+)$	20	.58
NS $(+-)$	23	.69
NS $(-+)$	23	.63

evaluations of the NS are more easily distorted than those of the LE). From this assumption, the tendency to maximize self would predict a higher $P(s)$ for the NS $(-+)$ condition than for the LE $(-+)$ condition, the figures for the two $(+-)$ conditions being about the same. These comparisons favor the self-maximization hypothesis; that is, NS $(-+)$ > LE $(-+)$, and NS $(+-)$ $\simeq$ LE $(+-)$. But support is weakened because $P(s)$ for each condition of the NS experiment was higher than $P(s)$ for the comparable condition of the LE experiment, a discrepancy ascribed to subject population differences in Chapter 5. However, on the basis of this test alone, we would conclude that there is some slight support for the idea that individuals will distort evaluations to produce the highest possible self-evaluation.

Let us next consider possible support for a variant of the idea of simple self-maximization through distortion. Here we assert that individuals who are given positive evaluations will accept them, but those given negative evaluations will ignore them. In this experiment we would expect individuals in $(+-)$ conditions to accept the evaluations and to form $(+-)$ expectation states, whereas those in $(-+)$ conditions ought to ignore the evaluations (when possible), consequently having undifferentiated expectations. Making the further assumption that evaluations from the LE and the NS can be ignored, whereas those from the HE cannot, we examine only the NS and the LE conditions for evidence of this process.

The effects predicted on the $P(s)$ would be as follows: HE $(+-)$ = LE $(+-)$ = NS $(+-)$; LE $(-+)$ = NS $(-+)$ = 0-S. These data are presented in Table 9.2. The figures give no support for the $P(s)$ relations predicted from this variant. The predicted approximate equalities for the three $(+-)$ conditions are not observed, nor are the predicted approximate equalities for the two $(-+)$ conditions and the 0-S experiment. An exception is the approximate equality of the fifth and sixth conditions, which is explained more satisfactorily by the original theory than by this variant of the maximization myth. Recall that the original theory would predict the observed relations between the NS

TABLE 9.2   OVERALL MEAN $P(s)$ FOR SIX
CONDITIONS OF SOURCE EXPERIMENTS

Condition	n	$P(s)$
1. HE $(+-)$	19	.80
2. LE $(+-)$	19	.65
3. NS $(+-)$	23	.69
4. LE $(-+)$	20	.58
5. NS $(-+)$	23	.63
6. 0-S	30	.64

and the 0-S experiment: the third condition is greater than or equal to the sixth condition, which in turn is greater than or equal to the fifth condition. Thus there is no support in these data for the idea that individuals maximize their self-expectations by a selective acceptance of positive evaluations and rejection of negative evaluations.

Third, we examine the idea that individuals are able to maximize the self only in more complex social situations. It could be argued that in cases examined so far, subjects have been offered only one potential source of evaluations of their performances; they are given, for example, only information from a single LE. In such a highly controlled and limited setting, it could be argued, a subject lacks selectivity options that otherwise would be present. He has to accept the only available information, whether it be from an evaluator of high or low ability, and whether it be positive or negative evaluations of himself. In a more complex situation, with more than one potential source of information, the individual might take advantage of the greater freedom to choose information, to select evaluations that would maximize the self-image.

The two-evaluator experiments provide an additional potential source of information, and results from these experiments may contain evidence of a tendency to maximize the self. Again we assume that a subject does not have the option of ignoring the high ability evaluator, whether his evaluations are high or low. The subject might ignore the LE, however, if there is also a high ability evaluator in the situation. From the self-maximization idea, we would expect individuals to ignore the LE when that person gave them negative evaluations and to accept his evaluations when positive. Then we would expect the following relations between conditions in terms of $P(s)$: H $(+-)$ L $(-+)$ = HE $(+-)$; H $(+-)$ L $(+-)$ > HE $(+-)$; H $(-+)$ L $(+-)$ > HE $(-+)$; HE $(-+)$ = H $(-+)$ L $(-+)$. Table 9.3 presents relevant data for these comparisons. The third prediction from this idea is supported by these data; the first, second, and fourth are not. Although results appear to favor the maximization idea in one instance, the majority of possible comparisons in Table 9.3 do not confirm it. On the other hand, all possible comparisons in Table 9.3

TABLE 9.3   OVERALL MEAN $P(s)$ FOR SIX CONDITIONS

Condition	n	$P(s)$
H $(+-)$ L $(-+)$	20	.76
HE $(+-)$	19	.80
H $(+-)$ L $(+-)$	21	.80
H $(-+)$ L $(+-)$	20	.58
HE $(-+)$	18	.46
H $(-+)$ L $(-+)$	20	.42

can be explained by dropping the maximization idea and using the extended version of the source theory presented in Chapter 7. Evidently, then, overall results of these comparisons do not support the idea that individuals will seek to maximize the self by selecting among two potential alternative sources of evaluations.

A fourth version of the self-maximization idea might assert that although all individuals *tend* to maximize their self-evaluations, there is variability across individuals in the degree to which they do this. Perhaps some people are better able or more inclined to distort information for the purpose of enhancing their self-evaluations than others. Or, certain features of our experimental situation might produce differential amounts of self-maximization in this experiment, thus only some subjects in these conditions may be able to maximize their self-expectations. It might be argued, for example, that the situation is so highly controlled that only an unusual individual can maximize his self-evaluation; most people are constrained by the design of the experiment to adopt a low self-expectation if that is their assigned experimental condition.

A differential across individuals in a tendency or an ability to maximize the self would, of course, produce variability in the effects of each experimental condition: some subjects would maximize their self-expectations, and some would not. This effect might emerge in a bimodal distribution of subjects in the $(-+)$ conditions and a unimodal distribution of subjects in the $(+-)$ conditions. Following assumptions of the theory and of the earlier tests, we might prefer to look for a bimodal distribution among the LE and the NS conditions, for subjects in these areas probably would have the greatest chance of ignoring low evaluations. However, the same prediction of a bimodal distribution would also be made from other grounds; namely, from the formulation of the source theory, which predicts that some individuals will ignore the LE (regardless of the nature of his evaluations) and some will accept him. The first block of trials from both LE conditions were examined for a bimodal distribution in Chapter 4; contrary to the prediction from a self-maximization idea, the LE $(+-)$ condition appeared to show a bimodal distribution and the LE $(-+)$ condition appeared to be unimodal.

However, if we postulate differential susceptibility of individuals to self-maximization, we might reasonably expect some subjects to be able to maximize their self-expectations even in the HE conditions of these experiments. Distortion for the purpose of self-maximization would be necessary only when a subject received negative evaluations; for when evaluations of his performance were positive, an accurate perception of those evaluations would have the effect of maximizing the self. Thus we would expect to find a unimodal distribution of subjects in the HE $(+-)$ and the H$(+-)$ L $(+-)$ conditions, and a bimodal distribution in the HE $(-+)$ and the H $(-+)$ L $(-+)$ conditions. Distributions of subjects for these four conditions are presented in Figure 9.1.

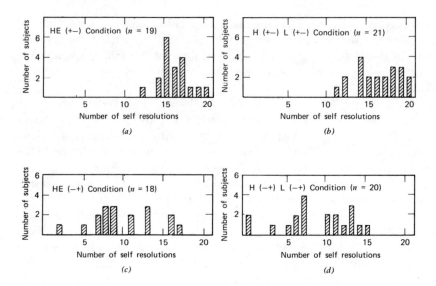

Figure 9.1   Distribution of subjects.

It should be borne in mind that numbers of subjects in all these conditions are small for analysis of the distributions. However, neither (−+) condition (Figures 9.1c and 9.1d) gives clear evidence of a tendency toward bimodality of distribution, as might be expected from a tendency toward self-maximization differing across individuals. All distributions contain some subjects who, by the criterion of overall mean $P(s)$, formed either undifferentiated or (+−) expectations. However, there is no evidence of clustering about a mode of $9[P(s) = .45]$ for one subset and clustering about a mode of $16[P(s) = .80]$ for a second subset in Figures 9.1c and 9.1d. Such a distribution pattern would be necessary to support a claim that in these conditions some subjects form (+−) expectations and a second distinct set of subjects hold either undifferentiated or (−+) expectations. The presence of some subjects with a higher overall number of self resolutions than the mode for each condition is more easily interpretable as the result of normal variance within the condition than as the result of a systematic tendency of some subjects to maximize their self-expectations.

Our final variant on the idea of cognitive attempts to maximize the self emphasizes that self-maximization is a *tendency*; that is, it may lie latent or be unobservable in its effects until forced into view by circumstances. For example, it could be argued that subjects in our experiment are likely to form a high self-expectation if given the opportunity, not solely by selective perception or distortion of the evaluator's opinions, but as the result of being required to behave in accord with their expectations.

In the 0-S experiment, subjects were obliged to form their expectations through interaction, not as the result of evaluations from an evaluator. In this study, it will be recalled, subjects received no performance evaluations from the evaluator in phase I; thus they began phase II either with undifferentiated expectations or with widely varying expectations, which were formed independent of conditions of the experiment. The disagreement interaction was expected to produce the formation of differentiated $(+-)$ and $(-+)$ expectations.

A latent tendency for self-maximization might lead us to predict that all or the majority of subjects in the 0-S experiment would eventually form $(+-)$ expectations; that is, there would be evidence of a tendency to form $(+-)$ rather than $(-+)$ expectations in the 0-S experiment. Such a tendency might be observable in two ways. First, if most subjects were forming $(+-)$ expectations, we might expect that $P(s)$ for this experiment to show a steady rise through the trials. In addition, if only some subjects were forming $(+-)$ expectations, but the tendency to form such expectations were much stronger than the tendency to form $(-+)$ expectations, we might expect to find a bimodal distribution of subjects by the end of the trials, with a noticeably greater number of subjects distributed about the $(+-)$ mode than about the $(-+)$ mode. The latter outcome can be tested by examining Figure 8.2d. There is no clear evidence of bimodality near the end of the trials. Thus the tendency, if it exists, would have to be shown by a rise in $P(s)$ through trials.

Figure 9.2 presents the curve by blocks of five trials, and Figure 9.3 presents data on every even-numbered trial, as well as a cumulative average curve. Because of relatively small numbers of subjects in these experiments, variance across trials makes it difficult to discern trends from a graph of the trial-by-trial $P(s)$. However, the curve can be smoothed by the cumulative averaging procedure, in which $P(s)$ for each trial is averaged in with $P(s)$ for all previous trials. This

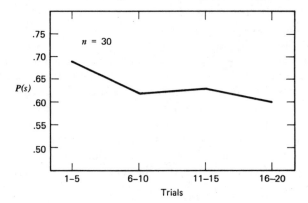

Figure 9.2   Overall mean $P(s)$ for the 0-S experiment by blocks of five trials.

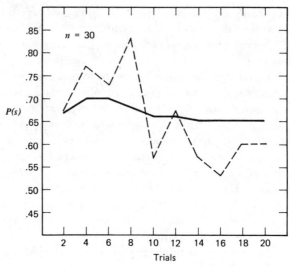

Figure 9.3   Cumulative and raw $P(s)$ curves, 0-S experiment.

procedure serves to diminish any changes in $P(s)$ on final trials of the experiment, but it does not obscure them completely. Any rise in $P(s)$ that occurred through the trials of this experiment would be observable from a cumulative $P(s)$ curve.

None of the curves of the data from the 0-S experiment reveals a tendency for subjects to form $(+-)$ expectations more frequently than $(-+)$ expectations; there is no evidence for a simple rise in the $P(s)$ curve, either by blocks of five trials in Figure 9.2 or by the cumulative average curve in Figure 9.3. In fact, both curves show the opposite tendency: a drop in $P(s)$ through time. The approximate $P(s)$ values for trials 2 and 20 are .67 and .60, respectively.

From results of these comparisons it seems safe to conclude that experimental data contain no strong evidence and little suggestive evidence to indicate a tendency toward what we have called cognitive self-maximization. First, we considered the idea of simple distortion of evaluations from the LE and from the NS; the comparisons showed no evidence that subjects in either of these $(-+)$ conditions could selectively perceive the evaluations and form $(+-)$ expectation states. Second, we considered a variant of the simple distortion argument, which assumed that subjects will accept positive evaluations but will ignore negative evaluations. Comparisons of various conditions of the single-evaluator experiments revealed none of the consequences that might reasonably be expected from this type of selective perception. Third, we examined data to test the idea that only when there is more than one potential source of information available can the individual distort or perceive selectively. One comparison of the one-evaluator and two-evaluator experiments appeared to be consistent with this idea, but three other related comparisons were not. Fourth, we used data from the HE conditions of the experiments to test the idea that the tendency to maximize might be present in variable degrees across individuals. The comparisons yielded no evidence that any subjects were doing this. Finally, we examined data from the 0-S experiment for evidence that self-maximization could be a latent tendency, becoming noticeable only in conjunction with situational factors that require development of differentiated expectations. Again, these data gave no evidence to support such an assertion. As the result of these comparisons, we conclude that data from these experiments contain no persuasive evidence of a tendency to maximize the self-evaluation through cognitive distortion.

Behavioral Motivation.   A second supposed tendency of individuals is to act in ways calculated to evoke approval from others. The seeking of social approval is generally accepted as one basis for explaining the actions of others, and abundant evidence indicates that individuals enjoy receiving approval. However, making a theoretical link between the well-documented observation that individuals enjoy approval to the proposition that much of behavioral motivation can be explained as the seeking of approval is neither a simple nor a straightforward task. Because this linkage often is assumed implicitly to exist, we examine some of its plausible implications with the data of these experiments.

A major theoretical work incorporating the idea of seeking social approval as a motivation is Zetterberg's "Compliant Actions" (1957). In this paper the author states and codifies a set of propositions concerning self-images and motivation, including both the idea of a looking-glass self, which we have adopted, and the idea that individuals will seek to obtain favorable evaluations from others, which we are investigating here. This work was selected because it constitutes an explicit and clear statement of an idea of wide currency in the literature:

> *An actor's actions have a tendency to become dispositions that are related to the occurrence of favorable self-evaluations.* [Postulate of Ego-Needs] (Zetterberg, 1957, p. 184; emphasis in original)

In terms we have been using, the postulate of ego-needs asserts that an actor will tend to display regularly those actions which result in a high self-evaluation. To this, Zetterberg adds the postulate of evaluative compliance, which is a form of the basic assertion of the looking-glass self; namely, that the self-evaluation is determined by the evaluations of others:

> In an action system, any actor has a tendency to develop self-attitudes that are synonymous with uniform evaluations of him that are in the system. [Postulate of Evaluative Compliance] (*Ibid.*, p. 185)

From these two postulates, Zetterberg derives the following:

> THEOREM 1.   An actor's actions have a tendency to become dis-positions that are related to the occurrence of favored uniform evaluations of the actor and-or his actions in his action system. (*Ibid.*, p. 188)

In our terms, we would say that an actor will tend to display regularly (as a "disposition") those actions which are positively ("favorably") evaluated by others in his social environment ("action system"). More simply, the actor will act in ways which (he expects) will gain him positive evaluations from others. This constitutes an explicit statement of the idea that individuals are motivated importantly by a desire for a positive self-image and that each undertakes to enhance his self-image by performing acts that others will evaluate positively. Because an individual might misperceive which acts will in fact gain him positive evaluations, we have included the phrase "he expects"; this does not materially change the intent of the assertion.

If individuals do act in ways which they expect will elicit positive evaluations from others, we must consider next what kinds of acts in our experiments might reasonably be expected to gain approval and positive evaluations from others. Presumably an individual is conscientiously attempting to select the correct answer to the slides in phase I of the study, but whether this will gain him positive evaluations from the evaluator is determined by the $(+-)$ or $(-+)$ condition of the experiment to which he has been assigned. In phase II, the "motivation" assumption would lead us to expect that subjects will make their initial choices with much care, for correct initial choices ought to produce approval and positive evaluations from their partners. However, careful selection of choices in phase I and of initial choices in phase II are already assumed to be motivated by the task-orientation condition of the experiment; thus we cannot assume that choices are evidence of a desire for self-maximization. The self and other resolutions of disagreements in phase II must be considered.

Camilleri et al. (1972) proposed a decision-making model for this experimental situation which postulates three possible sources of "gain" are available to subjects. First, there is gain from self-consistency—what we have called "person orientation," or the desire to make one's own final choices. This gain is assumed to be relatively constant across various experimental and interaction conditions. Second, because of team orientation and team scoring, there is a gain possible from one's partner for making the correct final choice. In other words, it is reasonable to suppose that subjects believe they will gain social approval and positive evaluations from their partners if they make correct final choices to the slides, thereby enhancing the "team score." Third, there is gain of approval and positive evaluation from the experimenter for making correct final choices, since he has communicated to subjects that he "wants" them to perform well at the task. Thus the two external sources of positive evaluation and approval for the subject are his partner and the experimenter, and approval from both will be maximal when he makes the highest possible number of correct final choices.

This analysis directly implies that a subject can maximize approval by sticking with his initial choice every time he thinks it is correct, and by changing his initial choice every time he thinks it is incorrect. What is significant, then, is the possibility that a subject can maximize approval by the behavioral act of changing his initial choice whenever he thinks he is likely to be wrong. Now we determine when subjects are most likely to believe their initial choices are incorrect and scrutinize data from subjects in those conditions for evidence of self-maximization through changing initial choices. At this point, we must assume the source theory under test in this work has received confirmation. Then we can assert that in general, subjects in $(-+)$ evaluation conditions will be those who are most likely to think their initial choices are incorrect, and this will be especially true for subjects who have received negative evaluations from the HE.

If we assume that a behavioral motivation to enhance self-image exists, we might predict that individuals who received mostly negative evaluations will think that most of their initial choices in the disagreement phase were incorrect and will attempt in phase II to maximize approval from their partners and from the experimenter by changing most of their choices. This would mean that the $P(s)$ observed from such conditions as the HE $(-+)$ and the H $(-+)$ L $(-+)$ would be very low. The $P(s)$ for these conditions (Table 7.3a) are .46 and .42, respectively. Whether this is "very low," of course, cannot be determined without some comparison, but since the figures are not very different from .50, we can say that gain from person orientation appears to be nearly as great in this situation as the combined gain from approval of the partner and of the experimenter.

If we consider more closely the inferred intention of subjects in changing initial choices, an additional consequence becomes probable. If the perceived effect of changing initial choices in these conditions is to gain positive evaluations, we might expect that after a series of changes and consequent perceived positive evaluations, subjects would tend to become "satiated"; that is, their desire for additional positive evaluations would diminish, consequently reducing the likelihood of future changes. Thus it might be expected that $P(s)$ obtained when subjects believed their initial choices were likely to be wrong would begin quite low and would rise as desire became satiated. Data for such a trend appear in the cumulative $P(s)$ curves.

Of the conditions from these experiments, those which seem most likely to contain large proportions of subjects holding $(-+)$ expectations are: HE $(-+)$, H $(-+)$ L $(-+)$, and H $(-+)$ L $(+-)$. Figures 9.4a to 9.4c present the cumulative $P(s)$ curves from these three conditions. Two statements apply to all three graphs. First, as has already been noted, they do not start particularly low, as might be expected if the tendency to seek positive evaluation through changing initial choices were rather strong. Second, and more significant, there is no important rise apparent in any of the three curves. If these curves exhibit any simple trend, it is a slight decline. Thus it appears that data from these conditions do not support the idea that subjects are attempting to maximize their self-evaluations by changing their initial choices in the manner described.

Next let us consider a variant of the idea of maximizing positive evaluations of self through compliant behavior. It has frequently been asserted that one consequence of a concern with obtaining a favorable self-image is an increased sensitivity to criticism, or in our terms, to negative evaluations. If this were the case, then by comparison to subjects who had received *no* negative evaluations, we would expect those who had received some negative evaluations to be especially sensitive to further criticism and to be particularly interested in behaving in ways that would elicit positive evaluation in the future. In other words, it might be argued that the effect of previous negative evaluation is to arouse perception of a threat to a high self-evaluation, consequently making an individual more eager to avoid negative evaluations in the future. In a sense, this reasoning also presupposes the reverse of the satiation-type process described in the preceding test; that is, individuals why have previously "lost" some self-esteem through criticism are believed to become more concerned by future threats to their self-evaluation than individuals who have not sustained the loss. This line of reasoning does not require us to assume that only subjects who have accepted a low self-evaluation will be highly concerned with future evaluations. Rather, it applies to all subjects whose existing self-evaluation has been threatened by negative evaluations.

We can examine the idea of increased susceptibility to future evaluations by comparisons of $P(s)$ data from the 0-S and the 2-S experiments. It will be recalled that subjects in the 2-S experiment received negative evaluations from one of the high ability evaluators, whereas in the 0-S experiment, there were no performance evaluations. From the preceding reasoning, we might therefore expect subjects in the 2-S experiment to be more sensitive to future evaluation, consequently more likely to seek approval through changing initial choices.

This idea can be tested by comparing $P(s)$ figures from the two experiments

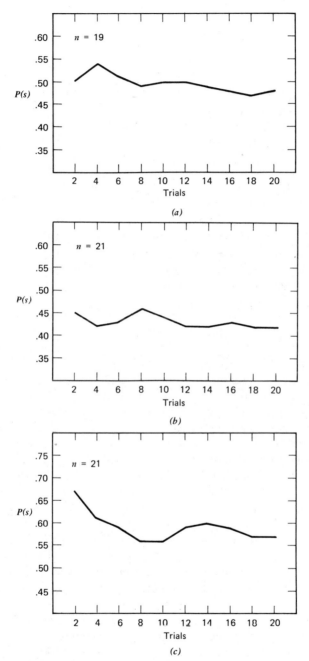

Figure 9.4 Cumulative $P(s)$ curves: (a) HE($-+$) condition, (b) H($-+$) L($-+$) condition, (c) H($-+$) L($+-$) condition.

to see whether subjects in the 2-S experiment were more concerned with maximizing approval from others in this manner; that is, whether data from the two experiments show the relation 0-S > 2-S. Table 8.1 gave $P(s)$ figures from these two experiments. For the 0-S experiment, overall $P(s)$ was .64; for the 2-S, the figure was .67. The data are not consistent with this variant on the idea of self-maximization through compliance; contrary to the prediction, the overall mean $P(s)$ figure for the 2-S experiment is slightly higher than that for the 0-S experiment, although the .03 difference is within the range of chance variation in these experiments.

By the U test, one could not reject the null hypothesis of no difference in overall likelihood of changing initial choices. Two comments are in order regarding interpretation of the U-test results. First, as noted in Chapter 8, we do not want to claim statistical confirmation of no difference; we merely say that the prediction from the self-maximization process described has not been sustained. Second, we note that each of the two cells contains a larger number of subjects than other cells of the source experiments. For a sensitive test such as the Mann-Whitney U, failure to reject the null hypothesis with sample sizes approaching 30 is very likely to be a reliable result.

The third test to be made of self-maximization through behavioral actions involves examination of subjects' reports of their assessment of their own performances in the study. For this, we review the questionnaire administered immediately following the disagreement trials in phase II, in which subjects were asked to estimate how well they did at the slides. If we expect subjects to attempt to maximize approval from their partners and from the experimenter by changing initial choices when they think they were wrong, we should look for the following consequence: among subjects who hold low self-expectations, those who changed their initial choices more frequently should perceive more approval than those who changed initial choices less frequently. This process might affect responses to the questionnaires in two ways, depending on how the "changing behavior" is believed to affect subjects.

First, it might be expected that subjects who had changed more of their initial choices would perceive that they had helped their group to do better at final choices than would subjects who had changed few. That is, if a subject holds $(-+)$ expectations, he might feel that he had done better if he accepted a large proportion of his partner's initial choices than if he accepted only a small proportion, or he might feel that the group members had "worked together" better.

Second, it might be expected that the social approval perceived as the result of changing initial choices would produce a general feeling of satisfaction or pleasure and that this feeling would be more pronounced for $(-+)$ subjects who perceived more social approval; namely, those who had changed more of their initial choices. Since it is not clear exactly which consequence would be expected from the process described, we examine some questionnaire responses for evidence of both results. The cautions regarding interpretation of question-naire data in these experiments should be borne in mind in making the comparisons.

We begin with questionnaires from the HE $(-+)$ condition of the first experiment, since it is reasonable to expect that a large proportion of subjects in this condition hold $(-+)$ expectation states. This is plausible because the overall mean $P(s)$ for this condition was .46, which is close to the value of .42 observed in the earliest manipulated $(-+)$ expectation state experiments.

The independent variable for this test is the greater or lesser proportion of changes of initial choices, as measured by $P(s)$. Subjects in the HE $(-+)$ condition are not distributed normally about the mean $P(s)$ value of .46; the distribution is skewed left. Therefore, the median value of .45 was selected as the cutting point. Subjects making 9 or more self resolutions out of 20 were classified as having made a "high" proportion of self resolutions, and those making 8 or below were said to have made a "low" proportion. Using this cutting point, 10 subjects were classified in the "high" category and 8 in the "low." For subjects' perceptions of their performance and of overall satisfaction, again there is no *a priori* cutting point; thus we have chosen the point on each scale which is closest to the median for subjects' responses.

Specific questions from the questionnaire are the following:

> [perception of group performance] 1. How satisfied are you with what your group accomplished *as a group* on this task?
> (1) extremely satisfied; (2) definitely satisfied; (3) somewhat satisfied; (4) so-so; (5) somewhat dissatisfied; (6) definitely dissatisfied; (7) extremely dissatisfied.

> [overall satisfaction] 4. Taking everything into consideration, how satisfied are you with your participation in today's study?
> (1) extremely satisfied; (2) definitely satisfied; (3) somewhat satisfied; (4) so-so; (5) somewhat dissatisfied; (6) definitely dissatisfied; (7) extremely dissatisfied.

Table 9.4 presents questionnaire responses of subjects from the HE $(-+)$ condition, tabulated according to whether they resolved more or less than the median number of disagreements in favor of self. The data of Table 9.4 do not support the idea that $(-+)$ subjects who changed more of their initial choices perceived greater satisfaction. In fact, the opposite trend is revealed. It could be concluded that these data support the following two assertions:

1. The higher the $P(s)$, the greater the tendency to be satisfied with what the group accomplished.

2. The higher the $P(s)$, the greater the tendency to be satisfied overall with one's participation.

TABLE 9.4   QUESTIONNAIRE RESPONSES FOR SUBJECTS IN
THE HE $(-+)$ CONDITION, ACCORDING TO PROPORTION
OF SELF RESOLUTIONS

	Question 1		Question 4	
$P(s)$	S (1–4)	D (5–7)	S (1–4)	D (5–7)
.45+ (n = 10)	6	4	8	2
.40− (n = 8)	3	5	3	5

If a standard measure of association, Yule's Q, is calculated from these tables, the direct association between $P(s)$ and "group accomplishment" is .43; and the direct association between $P(s)$ and "overall satisfaction" is .74. The most conservative interpretation of these results is that they do not support the idea of self-maximization through behavioral action in the manner described previously.

These three comparisons indeed suggest that data from the source experiments contain no support for the idea that subjects were motivated by seeking approval and positive evaluations. If we assume that subjects in the HE $(-+)$ condition are quite likely to believe that a large proportion of their initial choices are incorrect, and that they believe that they will gain approval and positive evaluations from their partners and from the experimenter by changing many of their initial choices, none of three consequences that might be expected from the "behavioral motivation" version of the maximization myth appears. First, the $P(s)$ figure was not particularly low; and more important, it did not rise through time, as would be expected from subjects' becoming satiated with approval or positive evaluations. Second, we might anticipate that subjects who had already received some negative evaluations would be more concerned with maximizing future positive evaluations through changing initial choices than would subjects who had not received negative evaluations. Comparison of the $P(s)$ values for the 0-S and the 2-S experiments do not support this conclusion. Finally, it might be expected that subjects who had changed relatively more of their initial choices would perceive that their group had performed better, or would perceive more satisfaction with their group participation than would subjects who had changed fewer initial choices. Examination of questionnaire data from the HE $(-+)$ condition disconfirm these predictions; for both questions there was an inverse association of proportion of choices changed and satisfaction.

Reinforcement of Existing Self. Finally, we consider a variant of the idea of self-maximization through seeking positive evaluations from others. This variant argues that everyone possesses some level of self-evaluation (generally, for healthy individuals it is assumed to be a positive self-evaluation) and that much of people's behavior can be interpreted as seeking to *maintain* the level they already possess. That is, the assumed motivation is to preserve the self, not to enhance it. (For one developed version of such a theory, see Secord and Backman, 1961.) In some ways, this third idea combines elements from both the first two. The element of consistency from the first idea clearly is present: individuals seek evaluative information that is consistent with the positive self-evaluations they already possess. They may in addition be more receptive to new confirmatory information, as we would expect from the "cognitive distortion" argument, although this additional assumption is not always made explicit. From the idea of behavioral motivation, we take the elements of assuming that individuals are consciously oriented to gaining certain types of evaluations and that they will in fact act in a way intended to gain those evaluations. This variant is considered separately from the first two, however, because the assumptions that individuals generally possess positive self-images and that consequently they are seeking positive evaluations are often left unstated (though frequently quite clearly implied; see Newcomb, 1956, pp. 581–582 for an explicit statement).

A clear statement of what we have called reinforcement of an existing self appears in a more recent work by Zetterberg, "On Motivation" (1966). By comparison with the earlier essay (Zetterberg, 1957), the author now seems to assume that individuals strive to preserve the existing level of self-evaluation, not to change it in an upward direction. Although no reference is made to the earlier essay in the 1966 work, this change may represent a development in Zetterberg's conceptualization. On the other hand, it could as well be an assumption intended to apply to situations dissimilar to those of the first assumption. In either case, the essay states clearly and explicitly the ideas we intend to convey with the term "reinforcement of an existing self."

> [Identity postulate]: Persons are likely to engage in those actions within their repertoire [sic] of actions which maintain their self evaluation [sic]. (Zetterberg, 1957, p. 125)

Combining this postulate with Cooley's ideas, Zetterberg derives:

> [Theorem of Social Motivation]: Persons are likely to engage in those actions which maintain the evaluations that their associates give to them. (*Ibid.*, p. 127)

We might look for two types of response from subjects in the source experiments attempting to gain self-reinforcing evaluations for themselves. First, focusing on the change in situation between the first and second phases of these experiments, we can ask what behaviors might be expected to gain consistent evaluations in both phases. For all the $(+-)$ conditions, subjects have received positive evaluations in phase I, and for all $(-+)$ conditions, subjects have received negative evaluations for phase I. Since Zetterberg's propositions do not incorporate the notion that the source of evaluations is a crucial variable, we might expect at this point that subjects from all the $(+-)$ conditions would behave alike in phase II, as would subjects from all $(-+)$ conditions. Thus, for example, subjects in the HE $(+-)$ condition would show behavior equivalent to subjects in the LE $(+-)$ condition. All data from previous experiments are inconsistent with this interpretation of the propositions.

However, if we limit ourselves by considering only evaluations from, say, a high evaluator, some more reasonable predictions can be made. Consider subjects in the HE $(+-)$ condition: in phase I they received a high proportion of positive evaluations. To reinforce this state, they would be expected to seek positive evaluations in phase II. By the reasoning used to test the "behavioral motivation" idea, positive evaluations are available in phase II, both from the experimenter and from one's partner, for getting the correct final decision. If we assume that subjects in the HE $(+-)$ condition believe that they have high ability at the task, we ought to be able to expect them to seek positive evaluations in phase II by refusing to change their initial choices, for they are likely to think that their own initial choices are incorrect. Thus Zetterberg's propositions on reinforcement of self would lead us to expect a high $P(s)$ from subjects in $(+-)$ conditions, especially for subjects in the HE $(+-)$ condition. The data confirm this expectation.

But if we examine the self-reinforcement prediction for the $(-+)$ conditions, successful prediction breaks down. Subjects who have received negative evaluations in phase I [e.g., those in the HE $(-+)$ condition] might be expected to seek *negative* evaluations in phase II to maintain their existing low self-images. If they believe that their own initial choices are likely to be incorrect, the way to gain negative evaluations in phase II is to refuse to change their initial choices. This, of course, would lead to a high $P(s)$ for subjects in the HE $(-+)$ condition and in other $(-+)$ conditions, and data do not confirm this. In terms of subjects' seeking to maintain the level of self-evaluation produced in phase I of the source experiments, then, all data from these experiments are disconfirming.

The second type of feasible response is a tendency for subjects to attempt to maintain the levels of self-evaluation they possessed before entering the experiment. We have assumed throughout these studies that for most tasks subjects have a general level of self-evaluation, or a "general expectation state," and that the levels possessed by subjects differ. It might be that subjects in these experiments will respond to the experimental treatment in ways determined partly by the level of expectations they brought with them into the situation. More precisely, we wish to learn whether subjects' responses are determined *to any important extent* by their prior general expectations or whether, as we have assumed, the effects of prior expectations are minimal and are distributed essentially in random fashion across subjects.

In the design of all these experiments, we have taken careful steps to reduce the effects of previous expectations in the situation. For example, the task is described as being a new ability, unrelated to "any of the usual skills, such as mathematical skills or artistic skills." By design, the experiments attempt to produce at the outset a state of undifferentiated or unknown expectations in subjects. Although it is probable that success at this is far from perfect, the experiments nevertheless have been designed with this goal in mind. Thus if we examine data for evidence of a tendency to reinforce the self-evaluations brought to the experiment by subjects, failure to find such evidence cannot be interpreted simply as failure of the self-reinforcement proposition; it could also mean success at this part of the experimental manipulation. However, insofar as we infer that the experimental design did in fact eliminate the effects of prior expectations, we would expect the process already considered to be observable—namely, a tendency to seek in phase II the same kinds of evaluations given subjects in phase I.

If subjects enter the experiment with high or low prior expectations, this fact might reasonably be expected to be observable in the 0-S experiment, where there was no attempt in phase I to manipulate their expectations. Thus, if prior expectations do determine behavior in the disagreement phase, and if subjects enter the experiment already differentiated into $(+-)$ and $(-+)$ states, we might expect to observe a bimodal distribution at the outset of phase II. The distribution of subjects in Figure 8.2*a* is not bimodal.

Second, we might expect that subjects would respond only to evaluations in phase I that were consistent with their previously existing self-evaluations. When evaluations are inconsistent with previous self-expectations, a bimodal distribution of subjects would be produced also: those whose self-expectations were reinforced, and those who ignored the evaluations. Moreover, if subjects responded only to self-reinforcing evaluations in phase I, all conditions of these experiments should show the bimodal distribution of subjects. The reasons for this emerge when we consider an example of a single-evaluator experiment, the LE $(-+)$ condition. Subjects who already hold $(+-)$ expectations will ignore the evaluator, whereas subjects already holding $(-+)$ expectations will accept his evaluations. Thus the distribution again will be bimodal, possibly with the greater number of subjects distributed about the $(-+)$ mode. Similarly, all conditions of the one- and two-evaluator experiments would be expected to display bimodal distributions. The distributions of subjects from many of the conditions of these experiments have been shown in this chapter and in preceding chapters. For them, as well as for conditions not previously covered, there is no good evidence of bimodal distributions of subjects at the outset of the disagreement trials. An especially persuasive argument against such self-reinforcement makes use of data from the 2-S experiment, for in this condition two highly believable evaluators were giving contradictory information. If subjects were responding to them in terms of a previously existing level of self-evaluation, we would expect to see a bimodal distribution in this condition, even if other conditions did not include forces strong enough to produce it. The distributions of subjects in all blocks of the 2-S experiment, which appeared in Figure 8.3, gave no evidence for bimodality.

From these brief comparisons, we conclude that these data contain no evidence of a tendency for subjects to respond to evaluators in terms of a preexisting level of self-evaluation. As noted previously, failure to find such evidence could be due to success at the attempt to minimize the effect of prior expectations in the design of these experiments, or to failure of the self-reinforcement hypothesis. We cannot distinguish between these two interpretations. However, if the lack of evidence of reinforcement of a prior self is attributed to success of experimental design, test of the self-reinforcement hypothesis should be possible from the first type of comparisons: attempts to maintain in phase II the same type of evaluations given in phase I of the experiment. Neither type of comparison yields the kind of data that might reasonably be expected from a self-reinforcement hypothesis.

Summary and Discussion.   We have made several comparisons within data from the source experiments in the attempt to find possible evidence for a tendency to maximize the self-evaluation. The first step, a conceptual analysis of the maximization myth, gave us three versions of the basic idea. The first version postulates a tendency to maximize the self through cognitive distortion of potential evaluative information. The second postulates a tendency to seek positive evaluations through approved behavior. The third suggests that people tend to behave in ways calculated to maintain the existing level of self-evaluation, and it often assumes that the most frequent level is a high one. None of the analyses performed on data from the source experiments produced strong or moderate evidence of effects that might reasonably be expected from one or another version of the maximization myth.

Overall, the results of the examinations of data presented in this chapter seem to confirm our suspicion that ideas about maximization of self or about consistency of self-image and future evaluations are a myth, in the additional sense of being without empirical foundation. That the ideas are prevalent as well as plausible should be evident to anyone familiar with the social psychological literature on the self. That the ideas are theoretically reasonable is demonstrated by the statements of them that are available in the work of such notable writers in the field of self-evaluations as Secord and Backman, Newcomb, Heider, and Zetterberg. However, as with many other generally accepted beliefs, it is desirable to subject the self-maximization myth to empirical test to establish the degree of confidence that ought to be placed in it. We have constructed such tests as are possible from our experimental data, and we have consistently failed to find evidence of any tendency like those described. Although none of the empirical tests was from an experiment designed specifically for test of some version of the maximization myth, the consistency of results of these examinations of data lends confidence to the interpretation. After we had performed these tests on our data, we came to the conclusion stated in the introduction to this chapter: so far as we are aware, there exists no convincing empirical support for the intuitively appealing idea that individuals attempt to maximize their levels of self-evaluations. In fact, some evidence besides ours runs counter the idea, for example, Segal et al. (1970) found that a sample survey of adults gave no evidence for self-maximization in terms of status ranks, and the research reported in Chapter 2 by Jones and his associates indicates that maximization only occurs under certain conditions.

Our conclusions might be objected to on grounds that our conceptualizations of the myth are too narrow or that our experiments do not provide the kinds of social situation in which maximization is thought to occur. To the first objection we reply that we know of no way to test an idea empirically except to state it as clearly as possible and then to compare the predicted outcomes to relevant data. We have tried to formulate the widest possible variety of versions of the maximization idea and to test each version with all applicable data at our disposal. We believe that one reason for persistence of the maximization myth—as well as many other myths about behavior—is that typically they are formulated loosely enough to permit any favorable evidence immediately to be seen as relevant, while grounds are found for dismissing unfavorable evidence.

We have considerably more sympathy with the second type of objection. Our experiments, although intended to produce a situation for studying self-evaluation, do not exhaust the classes of social situations in which self-evaluations function. (We develop this idea a bit further later.) However, if the processes of maximization were as strong and as pervasive as the prevalence of the myth suggests, surely *some* evidence of them should be observable anywhere—even in our experiments and in Segal's surveys!

One possible reason for the prevalence of the myth, as well as for its intuitive plausibility, may be that it derives from confusion of two ideas that are conceptually and empirically separable. The first idea is what we have termed the myth; namely, that individuals in some fashion seek positive evaluations. For this, as we have already argued, it is difficult to find rigorous empirical support or theoretical derivation.

The second idea is that possession of a high self is psychologically pleasing, while possession of a low self is accompanied by psychological tension. This assertion can be separated from the more complex notion that possession of a low self is unpleasant *and* that individuals are aware of this *and* that they will seek to gain for themselves a high self. More importantly, the assertion of pleasure from a high self and tension from a low self can be derived theoretically.

Recall that in Chapter 4 we developed a balance interpretation of consequences of holding the $(-+)$ expectation state. Briefly, this analysis argues that the $(-+)$ state is inherently imbalanced, since an individual perceives both a negative evaluation to himself and a unit relation such as "similarity" with himself. The unit relation is unchangeable; such cognitive dissociation does not seem likely with most individuals. However, the imbalance produced by the negative affect relation (evaluation) might be subject to change—by denial, for example, or by "escaping" from the $(-+)$ state. At the least, while imbalance persists, we would expect an individual to feel psychological tension and perhaps to display alternating behavior and other manifestations of discomfort. All these consequences are plausible in terms of the usual assumptions of balance theory, and some of them have been observed in $(-+)$ conditions of these experiments. By comparison, the condition of high self is balanced, and consequently, should be pleasant and stable.

Crucial in this kind of analysis is the observation that balance theories do not enable simple predictions of the specific way in which a given imbalance will be resolved. We might predict that the imbalanced low self state described would tend to become balanced, but we would not predict that it would become balanced in any specific fashion, such as through the seeking of positive evaluations. Most likely, individuals displaying such imbalance engage in a variety of behaviors; some of these will reduce the imbalance and some will produce new imbalances, thus increasing total imbalance in the system. In addition, individuals may well differ in their abilities to tolerate imbalance, thus in the extent to which they will act to produce the "maximal" state of $(+-)$ expectations. The wide variety of responses to imbalance would produce great variability in data from $(-+)$ conditions, especially through time, and these results have been well documented. However there is no simple way, either in these experiments or in "real life," for subjects to resolve an imbalanced state created by the low self. That this state is unpleasant is intuitively plausible, and the notion can be supported theoretically. That it leads to a simple or a consistent behavior, although intuitively plausible, cannot be supported either theoretically or empirically.

Although results of the analyses in this chapter convince us that maximization does not occur as an invariant process observable in all social situations at all times, our analyses do not rule out the possibility that maximization occurs sometimes, under certain circumstances. Nor would we want to eliminate such a possibility. It seems entirely plausible to us that maximization may occur in certain settings; the relevant question is, What general *types* of situations are likely to produce maximization?

On intuitive grounds, it seems likely that evaluative situations in which the particular task ability is not highly relevant may give an individual an opportunity to maximize his self-image cognitively if he wishes. For example, when people discuss an activity in which none of them has engaged—such as sky diving, or being President of the United States—perhaps certain types of people believe they would be good at the task without much evidence of this. A related type of situation that may lead to maximization involves an individual who is not called on to perform and prove his claimed ability. People who claim to be good at driving a car, or at making love, almost never are asked to demonstrate their abilities; perhaps there is a tendency to magnify one's self-esteem at tasks when the threat of a test is low. Similar ideas are present in the work of Jones and his associates, reviewed in Chapter 2.

Behaviorally, we think that a wide variety of situations is likely to lead individuals to seek approval and positive evaluation from others in the manner posited by Zetterberg (1966). The problem, again, is in specifying types of situations in which such behavior occurs, for clearly it is not universal. Situations defined as apprenticeship cases seem to be a class of social setting in which the learners are likely to be motivated to seek and obtain the teacher's approval by maximizing the self. Perhaps they also act in this way when confidence is felt to be essential to good performance in their situation. Playing football, walking on burning coals, and the child's game of breaking a pencil with the finger are cases in which individuals know they must try to increase their confidence in successful performance before beginning the activity.

It is crucially important to ask *when, under what circumstances*, and *for what types of people* is self-maximization most likely? We know of no direct empirical tests of the variables we mentioned; these are intended to indicate intuitively plausible places to begin a search for such tendencies. We emphasize, however, that neither a blanket statement of the maximization myth as a basic human tendency, nor the more specific versions we formulated and tested in this chapter, deserves the present status of unquestioned acceptance.

The source theories and empirical tests point to at least one critical flaw in the kind of maximization idea prevalent in the literature. Our data show that "who" gives the evaluations to an individual is more critical than "what" the evaluation is; the maximization ideas only consider the evaluator as a source of positive evaluations.

CHAPTER TEN

SUMMARY AND CONCLUSIONS

In this chapter, we conclude the theoretical and experimental work that grew out of our interest in the development of self-evaluation. We present the final version of the source theory, summarize the work of the preceding chapters, discuss implications of our results for a more complete theory of self-evaluation, and attempt to indicate the place of this work in terms of the looking-glass self tradition of self-concept.

What we have just referred to as "the final version of the theory" means, of course, the final version to date. Throughout this work we have noted instances of "finality" of the theory that turned out to be only temporary. This pattern, we feel, best characterizes a growing field. Our theory is final now in the sense that the work reported here completes our program. It is incomplete, we hope, in at least two other senses. First, future empirical and theoretical work may well reveal inadequacies of empirical prediction or logical gaps or errors. Indeterminacies, or cases of prediction that cannot be made as accurately or as unambiguously as would be desired, are apparent even in this "final version." If flaws in our theory are clearly visible, we consider this fact itself to indicate an advantage of the strategy of explicit theory construction. Future work can correct some weaknesses in the present version of the theory, thus producing a more adequate, but still temporary, "final version." Second, we hope that the "final version" of our theory is incomplete in the sense that its scope will be extended further. Scope limitations may be extended—we did this, for example, in Chapter 6, when we removed the scope limitation of known abilities of the evaluators—or additional assumptions may be added to include a larger set of antecedent conditions, such as determinants of self-evaluation other than a source's opinions. From our point of view, a completed theory is an impossibility: no theory ever perfectly encompasses what it purports to explain, and the range of cases it attempts to explain can always be extended. Although we are pleased that our theoretical work has received empirical confirmation and has been systematically extended through integration of additional assumptions to existing ones, we hope that others, finding the present scope too narrow for their interests, will be motivated to extend it.

The first version of the theory, presented in Chapter 4, was intended to apply to simple situations of one evaluator of known ability. The basic prediction was that opinions of an evaluator of high ability were very likely to be "accepted" by the individual and to be used by him in forming conceptions of his own and others' abilities. The first version of the theory was an attempt to state rigorously, and in a way that would permit determinate empirical testing, the ideas of the looking-glass self, and the "significant other." Results from 80 subjects, reported in Chapter 4, support the major predictions. A possible need for reformulation to incorporate the idea of a "negative source" was considered next. Results of an experiment with 50 subjects, reported in Chapter 5, indicated that the theory did not need to be reformulated to include the negative source.

The first extension of the theory was an attempt to widen its scope to include cases in which the ability of the evaluator was unknown but his status was known. The major prediction of the status characteristics version was that in such cases, individuals would attach ability conceptions to evaluators in accord with their status: high status evaluators would be treated like high ability evaluators, and low status evaluators, like low ability evaluators. Results of an experiment with 100 subjects, reported in Chapter 6, supported the major predictions.

The second extension widened the scope considerably, by generalizing assumptions to include more than one potential source of evaluations. In the case of one evaluator, the generalized theory makes the same predictions as the original version of the theory. In the case of two evaluators differentiated by ability, the generalized theory predicts that the individual may accept either one, as a probabilistic function of the expectations held for each. Results of an experiment with 84 subjects, reported in Chapter 7, were in accord with major predictions from the generalized version of the theory.

Finally, we conducted two additional experiments, the no-source and the two-source experiments, to aid in the formulation of Assumption 1c, which makes predictions for the case of two evaluators of equal ability who disagree in their evaluations of the individual. Results from these experiments, in which 60 subjects participated, were in accord with a formulation of the assumption predicting that both evaluators will be accepted and that evaluations from both will be used in forming expectations.

The final version of the source theory thus is a combination of Assumptions 2, 3, and 4 from the first version; Assumptions 5 and 6 from the status characteristics extension; Assumptions 1a and 1b from the multiple-sources generalization; and Assumption 1c from the 0-S and 2-S experiments.

DEFINITION 1.   An interaction situation is *task situation S* if and only if:
                a. There are at least two actors, p and o, performing a task.

b. There are at least two actors, e_1 and e_2, who have the right to evaluate task performances of p and o.

c. p and o have no prior expectations for their own or each other's performance at the task.

d. All actors are task oriented.

e. All actors are collectively oriented.

DEFINITION 2.   e is a source for p if and only if p believes that e is more capable of evaluating performances than p is himself.

ASSUMPTION 1a.   In S, if *only one* actor e is a source for p, then the unit evaluaations made by p of any actor's performances will be the same as those made by e.

ASSUMPTION 1b.   In S, if both e_1 and e_2 are sources for p and both e_1 and e_2 make the *same* unit evaluations of any actor's performance, p will make the same unit evaluations of that performance as e_1 and e_2.

ASSUMPTION 1c.   In S, if e_1 and e_2 are sources for p and e_1 and e_2 make *different* unit evaluations of any actor's performance, p will distribute agreements on unit evaluations between e_1 and e_2.

ASSUMPTION 2.   In S, if p makes unit evaluations of the performances of any actor, p will come to assign to that actor an expectation state that is consistent with the unit evaluations made.

ASSUMPTION 3.   In S, if p holds higher expectations for an actor o_1 than for another actor o_2, then:

a. p will be more likely to give o_1 an action opportunity than o_2.

b. p will be more likely to evaluate positively o_1's future performance outputs than o_2's.

c. p will be more likely to agree with o_1's performance outputs than with o_2's.

d. The probability that p will accept o_1 as a source is greater than the probability that p will accept o_2 as a source, and these probabilities are independent.

ASSUMPTION 4.   In S, the higher the expectations an actor p holds for himself relative to the expectations he holds for an other:

a. The more likely p is to accept a given action opportunity and make a performance output.

b. In case of disagreement with o, the more likely p is to reject influence.

DEFINITION 3.   A characteristic D is a diffuse status characteristic if and only if the states of D are differentially evaluated in the same way by all the actors in S.

ASSUMPTION 5.   In S, D will become a *salient* factor to p for assigning performance expectations to himself and o if and only if he and o possess different states of D.

ASSUMPTION 6.   In S, p will assign expectation states to any actor on the basis of a salient D if and only if p does not believe that D is irrelevant to the task.

As we have indicated, various versions of the theory received empirical confirmation from experiments including nearly 400 subjects. To indicate the degree of empirical support obtainable for the final version of the theory, we use some of those data (reported in previous chapters) to test the predicted ordering of conditions from the several experiments by the final version of the theory. This test involves comparison of slightly different subject pools; recall that some of the experiments used males and some used females, and the experiments were conducted over a two-year period. However, all subjects were regular students at the same junior college, and in all other "demographic" characteristics besides sex—age, socioeconomic status, academic ability, and so on—they are equivalent.

The predicted ordering we test does not include subjects from the status characteristics experiment (Chapter 6), which had a very different subject pool. More important, at this point the theory does not indicate clearly where in the expected ordering of conditions these conditions ought to fall. As discussed in Chapter 6, this is because there is no clear way to determine the precise degree of effect of the status variable.

The predicted ordering also omits results of the negative source and the no-source experiments. In principle, we probably could have included these conditions, for Assumption 3d would lead to the prediction that subjects in the NS experiment would be very unlikely to accept the evaluator's opinions but would show a slight tendency to accept them. Thus we might predict the following: NS $(+-) > 0$-S $>$ NS $(-+)$. The overall mean $P(s)$ figures for these conditions are .69, .64, and .63, respectively; thus the prediction would be sustained. However, it might be objected that Assumption 3d does not clearly apply when expectations held for the evaluator are virtually as low as possible; nor does it explicitly make a prediction for the 0-S experiment. Thus we omitted these cases.

Finally, the two LE conditions from the first experiment are omitted. Again, we might "infer" from Assumption 3d that these cases ought to be placed in the predicted ordering, but we have no precise way to determine how they compare with the H $(+-)$ L $(-+)$ and the H $(-+)$ L $(+-)$ conditions. To derive this relationship, we would need to know a parameter value for acceptance of an evaluator, given his known ability level. Although we could estimate such a parameter from data of these experiments, we would not be completely justified in using the data to test a further prediction employing that parameter.

The seven conditions selected for test are the following: H (+−) L (+−), HE (+−), H (+−) L (−+), H (−+) L (+−), H (−+) L (−+), HE (−+), and H (+−) H (−+) (or 2-S). In Table 10.1 we present the results of the Jonckheere test of the following predicted ordering of these seven conditions:

DERIVATION.   In case of disagreement with o, the likelihood of p's rejecting influence will be in the following order:

H (+−) L (+−) > HE (+−) > H (+−) L (−+) >
H (+−) H (−+) > H (−+) L (+−) > HE (−+) >
H (−+) L (−+).

Results in Table 10.1 support the ordering prediction from the final version of the theory. The differences between median values of the conditions and the ordering of conditions observed would be extremely unlikely to occur by chance if the experimental treatments did not in fact produce the predicted differences in likelihood of rejecting influence.

TABLE 10.1   JONCKHEERE TEST OF PREDICTED ORDERING OF $P(s)$ FROM SEVEN CONDITIONS

Conditions	Mean $P(s)$	n
H (+−) L (+−)	.80	21
HE (+−)	.80	19
H (+−) L (−+)	.76	20
H (+−) H (−+)	.67	27
H (−+) L (+−)	.58	20
HE (−+)	.46	18
H (−+) L (−+)	.42	20
Predicted ordering	$Z = 8.13, p < .05$	

Back Through the Looking Glass.   In translating results of our theory testing program back to the less highly controlled settings in which the looking-glass self ideas originally developed, let us first discuss how self-evaluation develops in settings that are increasingly structured.

In an unfamiliar situation, or when the individual must perform a new task, if there are *no* evaluations made of his performance by any other actor, the individual will come to hold conceptions of his own and others' abilities as the result of the interaction process. One such situation, our 0-S experiment, demonstrated that having to resolve disagreements causes subjects to form differentiated expectations for self and other. About half the subjects decided that they had high ability and their partners had low, and about half decided the opposite. In this situation, the result of constant or near-constant *agreement* between individuals would be formation of high expectations for both self and other: the $(++)$ state. How an individual resolves disagreements, particularly during early phases of interaction, thus has long-lasting effects on his self-evaluation and subsequent behaviors. If he begins by backing down in the face of disagreements *for whatever reason*—because of such structural constraints as status or authority relations, responsibility, or "personality" variables—the likelihood is good that he will form $(-+)$ expectations for himself and the other. If he begins by refusing to accept influence, chances are good that he will form $(+-)$ expectations: a striking feature of this analysis is the strong effect of what may initially look like unimportant interaction accidents (agreement or disagreement) and early behavior choices (accepting or rejecting influence).

When a single actor evaluates others' performances, our results indicate that he may or may not be accepted as a source—roughly equivalent to Sullivan's significant other. If the evaluator is perceived as having high task ability, or if he is known to have access to objective standards, his opinions are likely to be significant; if he is thought to have low ability, he is likely to be ignored. Moreover, the relation between evaluator's ability and his degree of influence appears to be a simple one; the intuitively appealing phenomenon of a negative source does not seem to occur empirically. It is relatively easy to think of training and teaching situations in which children do not have confidence in their instructors precisely because they know the instructors themselves cannot perform well. Our analysis indicates that conceptions of ability can be affected only when the evaluating individual has been accepted as a source, which in turn depends on how his own ability is regarded.

In the more natural setting containing a single evaluator whose ability is unknown, but for whom differentiating status information is available, the status information has approximately the same effect as comparable ability information. High status evaluators are thought to have high ability, and low status evaluators are thought to have low ability; and their respective likelihood of acceptance as sources is affected accordingly. This result indicates, for instance, that teachers who possess the low states of minority status characteristics—including women and blacks—are likely to be less effective sources for children's self-conceptions than teachers of high status, *unless* the children know that the low status teachers possess high demonstrated ability or access to objective evaluating standards. Because much classroom interaction involves the distribution of evaluations, and because children's level of self-evaluation is generally recognized as an important influence on their actual learning, this result implies the need for conscious choice of teachers for classrooms, as well as awareness of possible status and ability effects that can mitigate teachers' influence as sources.

If more than one actor evaluates performances, the individual will accept or reject him on the same bases that would serve if there were only one, and accepting one evaluator does not preclude accepting a second. High ability evaluators are likely to be accepted, and low ability evaluators are less likely to be accepted. Both could be accepted, however, and if they are, they will both affect the individual's self-evaluation. This assertion is in accord with, and can be used to explain, many of the findings of "cross-pressure" effects of parents, teachers, and peer groups on adolescents' self-conceptions.

The interesting case of two disagreeing high ability evaluators, which has sometimes been given the name "conflicting significant others," seems to follow the same principles as the case just discussed. Both evaluators may be accepted, and in fact are very likely to be accepted; the self-image formed then is a product of opinions from both sources. A situation of conflicting sources is psychologically stressful to an individual, and we might expect this stress to produce a distaste for whatever activity is subjected to conflicting evaluations: administrators in businesses and universities often complain about the "double bind," or the "damned if you do, damned if you don't" nature of their jobs. However, insofar as they are concerned strictly with evaluating, it seems that the relative competence of evaluators and the nature of their evaluations are the major determining factors in these cases.

We do not expect that our work will satisfy everyone interested in the social self, nor have we provided answers to all the questions that interest contemporary investigators. Some students of the social self tradition, especially those calling themselves "symbolic interactionists," explicitly reject the efficacy (and even the morality) of experimental studies of behavior. Self-concept, to them, functions in such pervasive and subtle ways that controlled observation is capable of producing only a small part of the picture. To these colleagues we acknowledge the limited scope of our inquiries; indeed, we have intentionally stated our findings in conditional, limited, form. We perform our experiments, not to remove subjects from "reality" nor to produce highly limited findings of limited generalizability; rather, we experiment because this is the way to observe the sometimes subtle effects of variables that occur irregularly or where observation is difficult in more natural settings. The experiments are designed first of all to test a theory, and the experimental situation is one instance of the abstract concepts in the theory. Where the tests are successful, they lend confidence to the more general assertions of the entire theory, and others may wish to verify the theory in settings different from the one we developed.

Because we began by progressively narrowing and focusing ideas from the social self literature, we were able to construct an explicit theory and design determinate tests. As a result of this program, we know more about the social self than we did before; at the same time, the limitations on our knowledge claims should be clear to anyone who wishes to develop knowledge further. It was by stating versions of the maximization myth explicitly, for example, that we were able to compare the ideas to empirical data and to show that the myth should not be accepted uncritically. Similarly, the explicit assumptions of the source theory and the basic source experimental design allowed us to conclude that the negative source does not occur under conditions of interest to us. And because of the explicit theory formulation, it should be clear just which social situations can be explained by our theory and which cannot.

We mentioned earlier that self-evaluation is generally used as if it were an enduring trait of an individual, one that accompanies him from one social situation to another. Our term "expectation state" is limited and relative: relative to a specific task and to a specific other person. In Chapter 3 we detailed some of the theoretical objections to a nonrelative conception of the self, and we have repeatedly stressed the crucial importance of this relative conceptualization. Many social situations in which self-evaluation significantly figures could be clarified by adopting a relative view of the self in interaction.

Black people, especially black school children, are often said to have low self-images, as if they carried this image around with them in all circumstances. From our point of view, such a claim is meaningless. Blacks may well have low expectations for their performance at certain tasks such as school work, and they may have low self-expectations by comparison with white school children; but until the task and the referent others are specified, the claim has neither meaning nor empirical support. There is a good deal of evidence that black children change their "self-image" considerably depending on which others they think they are being compared with, and there is at least a small amount of evidence that they have quite positive self-expectations for certain kinds of tasks. This is, of course, just what we would expect from a theory of expectation states; it is not explainable from a theory of a transsituational "self-image." What is surprising to us is that social psychologists would have to be reminded to "rediscover the primary group."

Moreover, the intervention techniques prescribed from the two approaches differ considerably. If one adopts the view that self-evaluation is absolute and transsituational, the children's self-image may be raised in one context and may be expected to carry over to all contexts. This simply does not occur. Any meaningful change in self-expectation requires explicitly taking account of both the task and the comparison others. (Instances of failure of intervention attempts that overlook task specificity and referent others, as well as success from intervention techniques that do account for these factors, are documented in Cohen and Roper, 1973.)

Satisfactions and Inadequacies.   Finally, we wish to draw explicit attention to what we regard as the major positive contributions of this work, and to some remaining problems. Our intention in this section is to indicate what we regard as the most significant results of our research program and to encourage responses and reactions from others.

The greatest satisfaction comes from the programmatic nature of the theory extension and empirical testing. By this we mean that it has been possible to pursue our interest in issues of the social self by proceeding from established findings to further issues that grow out of, or are related to, this knowledge. Throughout, our strategy has been to move from confirmed propositions to testing of theoretical generalizations. The process by which the single-source theory was generalized to the status-based source theory and then to the multiple-source theory illustrates the strategy. We have been concerned with introducing into the theory the minimum changes that will increase its scope, to take advantage of parts of the theory that previously have been confirmed. Development and use of a standard experimental setting has also been part of the strategy, and many times this has permitted direct comparisons of data from various experiments to answer questions that arose in data analysis. Despite its considerable advantages, programmatic work in this sense is still fairly unusual in behavioral sciences.

Second, we are gratified by the empirical success of the theory building tasks. In most cases, successive versions of the theory predicted outcomes of the experiments quite well; in most cases statistical tests support a high degree of confidence in these results.

Third, we believe that we have had some success at adapting and explicating ideas in the social self literature and at extending the propositions of expectation states theory into a new substantive area of interest. Since understanding of phenomena is based on theories of those phenomena, we point to our theory as contributing to understanding of a major area of social psychology.

Finally, we are pleased with the incidental result that several processes that we and others had assumed to be rather complex can in fact be accounted for quite simply. For example, incorporating the idea of a negative source, or of self-maximization, would have required complex theoretical formulations. Yet results of experiments to evaluate these ideas do not indicate any necessity for this work. Apparently the looking glass functions in a fairly straightforward manner—an encouraging result to us and to other theorists in this area.

We also wish to draw attention to existing gaps in the theory, hoping that this will hasten the time when another investigator can establish ideas beyond our own.

First, we would like to be able to specify more precisely and more completely the process by which evaluations become incorporated into expectation states held by individuals. Support for the idea that the process depends on ability of the evaluator is adequate, and an assertion that the process is independent of whether evaluations are positive or negative also seems to be adequate. However, it would be useful to understand in more detail just how an evaluation, or a series of evaluations, comes to affect cognitions. In a general way, Assumption 2 claims that the process depends on the series of evaluations; but whether the process is a Markov process, a simple accretion, or a probabilistic function of each independent evaluation is not known.

Second, during the course of this research, Professor I. Richard Savage of Florida State University took an interest in the theory and performed a probability theory formalization of the single-source version. His analysis indicates a logical weakness; namely, unless we *explicitly* assume that the following $P(s)$ relations hold between expectation states:

$$(+-) > (0\ 0) > (-+),$$

none of the derivations of the theory can be directly translated into predictions in our experiments. There is no simple way to incorporate this assumption into the English-language version of the theory used in this work, and because we have empirical evidence that the foregoing relations do obtain in the experiment, we have omitted the change in this book. Professor Savage also constructed one simple probability model of the process of accepting evaluations. Results of this analysis, and the model, are in Savage and Webster (1971).

Third, we would like to know whether the conceptualization of acceptance of a source in the final version of the theory is adequate, or whether an independent trials model would be preferable. In the assumptions, it is argued that an evaluator is either accepted or not, and *if* a subject has accepted the evaluator, he will accept all future evaluations. An alternative conceptualization of the process might state that on every trial—that is, with every performance evaluation—the individual decides anew whether to accept the evaluation from an other. Such a conceptualization would eliminate the idea of the source; any other could influence the individual's evaluation of any given performance, and perhaps an other of high ability would be more likely to do so than one of low ability.

Fourth, it would be desirable to be able to explain in more detail how consistent or inconsistent evaluations are incorporated into the overall expectation state: whether the process is best represented by simply adding up all evaluations, by averaging them, or by a more complex process. A branch of psychology dealing with information processing models and person perception has developed some models of similar processes, but no single type of model has received consistently good empirical support. Berger and Fisek (1970) have attempted to describe the general form of the information utilization process for this situation, and Webster, Roberts, and Sobieszek (1972) proposed and tested several specific models of the process. After further empirical confirmation, it would be desirable to extend the source theory in such a way that an information processing model could be rigorously derived from the propositions.

Finally, there are a multitude of substantively interesting areas for which the relation of our theory and data is unclear. For instance, we might reasonably ask what happens when an individual is evaluated by one person of high ability and one of high status; can we in some way predict which of them will be most influential in particular types of cases? We note that in some cases (e.g., athletics coaches or piano teachers), individuals who have neither high task ability nor access to objective standards become accepted sources of evaluation; what implications does this have for a theory such as ours? Are there bases of "source-hood" beyond the three we have identified—for example, formal authority in certain cases? What kinds of relation obtain between our theory and theories in other fields; for example, what are the effects of placing someone who cannot become a source in a formal institutional position to distribute evaluations and sanctions?

We leave our "final version" of the theory at this point, with the hope that future "final versions" will abound.

APPENDIX ONE

THE BASIC EXPECTATION EXPERIMENT

We describe below the "basic expectation experiment," the outline of the experimental design set up by Berger to develop and test expectation states theory.

The physical setting of the basic expectation experiment is a soundproofed room that is visually isolated from other rooms and from adjacent hallways. Since our concern is with the attention and the cognitive states of subjects, the researcher's command of the cognitive inputs available to subjects should be as complete as possible.

Any number of subjects up to four are admitted to the laboratory and are seated at tables separated from each other by movable screens and curtains. Figure A1.1 shows the laboratory facilities at Stanford University arranged for two subjects; the arrangement at Johns Hopkins is similar, though smaller. The experiment requires two adjacent rooms—one for subjects (the activity room), and one for control and observation of the group (the observation room). At the front of the room, visible to subjects, are the two experimenters who conduct the study. A one-way mirror along the wall between the activity room and the observation room permits visual monitoring of the study, and the proceedings are tape recorded through microphones located in the ceiling of the activity room.

The task for the group is to make binary choices about a series of slides projected on the screen. To minimize the effect of previous experience on subjects' performance expectations, the task is described as being, and in fact is, quite unlike any of the usual skill measures, such as vocabulary words or mathematical problems.

The slides contain either one or two patterns, and each pattern is composed of black and white rectangles. The one-pattern set of slides consists of 100 rectangles, arranged more or less randomly. Subjects are instructed to decide, for each slide, whether the pattern contains a greater area of black or of white. Each slide in the two-pattern set is composed of two of the one-pattern slides, one

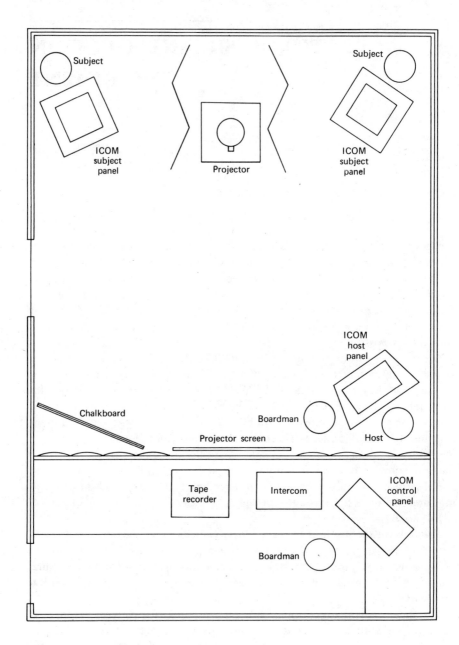

Figure A1.1 Laboratory activity room.

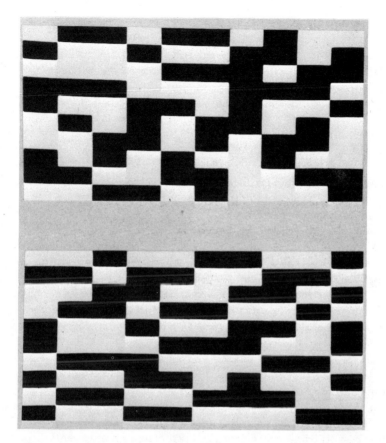

Figure A1.2   Two-pattern Contrast Sensitivity task.

above the other (see Figure A1.2). For the two-pattern slides, the task is to decide which pattern, top or bottom, contains the greater area of white.

The usual period of study allowed before subjects are asked to indicate their
choices is 5 seconds—obviously not nearly enough time to count the rectangles.
Because of the short study time permitted, it is impossible to be certain of a
chosen answer, or to ascertain that there is no correct answer. Patterns are so
varied and complex that the same pattern may be presented to subjects more
than once during an experiment without being recognized as a repeat. Also, any
slide may be turned upside down, or reversed left to right, and be perceived as
unlike its appearance in the original position.

Slides are of two types, *ambiguous* and *near-veridical*. Ambiguous slides are
those for which pretesting in the absence of social influences has established

that the probability of choosing either alternative is .50 ± .02. This property is theoretically significant in that there is nothing inherent in the slides that predisposes either the choices or the evaluation of a person's choices. That is, the probabilities of positively or negatively evaluating another person's choice may also be assumed to be equal.

Near-veridical slides are those for which pretesting has established that the probability of choosing a specific one of the alternatives is between .50 and 1.00. When these are used, the subject has, with probability less than 1, the ability to evaluate on objective criteria the choices made by himself and others. Currently there is a set of one-pattern slides for which the probability of getting the correct answer is .95 ± .03, and there is also a set of two-pattern slides with a probability of .70 ± .08 for getting the correct answer.

For all experiments to be reported here, the set of ambiguous, two-pattern slides was used. (The near-veridical slides are mentioned to indicate experimental possibilities beyond those undertaken in this series of studies; they are not referred to again here.) Using ambiguous slides is theoretically significant because subjects will have no objective criteria, as opposed to social criteria, to aid in evaluating their own and each other's choices. Any effects of influence between individuals in the experiments will be most clearly visible in this setting, for the choice behaviors observed cannot be attributed to properties of the task itself.

Communication between subjects and all other interaction are highly controlled and restricted in the basic expectation experiment. Uniform instructions are read to all subjects, and the subjects are not allowed to talk during the study.

Each subject has on his table a response panel containing buttons for indicating his choices for the slides and lights to show choices made by all members of the group. The host experimenter has before him a master panel showing the lights for all the subjects and containing a relay release button for clearing all panels of lights between trials. In addition, there is a master control panel that is never seen by subjects in the observation room. It is used for two purposes: to record data and to control communication between subjects.

Two features of the circuitry of the interaction control machine (ICOM) deserve special mention. First, the relays are so wired that feedback, either veridical or controlled, is given a subject only after both he and the other have actually made their initial choices. Normal variation in time delay assures that no subject will be given instantaneous disagreement feedback every time. Rather, when the partner actually does hesitate before making a choice, the feedback will also be delayed. Thus we reduce the likelihood of a subject's becoming suspicious of the situation.

Second, each subject's choice relays are interlocked, such that if one choice is activated, the other is rendered inoperative. This means that a subject can make one choice only on each trial, and his choice cannot be changed. This is the logical equivalent of "A or B" but not "A and B," and it has the effect of preventing subjects from changing a given performance output or unit evaluation.

Using ICOM, the following variations in experimental conditions can be manipulated:

1. The subjects may find themselves in initial agreement or disagreement with each other at any stage of the decision-making process. More generally, it is possible to fix and control the probability that subjects are in initial agreement on any given trial.

2. Subject A may find that his partner accepts or rejects subject A's final decision at any given stage. More generally, it is possible to fix and control the probability at any given stage that a subject believes that his partner has made a particular final decision. The probability that a subject's partner accepts or rejects a particular final choice may be made *independent* of the final choice of the subject, or it may be probabilistically *contingent* on the final choice of subject.

3. The machine can be adjusted so that the initial exchange of information is controlled and the final exchange of information is veridical.

4. At any given decision stage the subject may be actually informed of the initial and final decisions of his partner. More generally, the communication of both initial and final decisions between the two subjects may be made veridical.

Figure A1.3 shows the ICOM subject panel set up for the basic source experiment. For most basic expectation experiments, the bottom row of lights, representing final choice feedback *or* a third person's evaluations, is removed. The first and third rows are choice modules; the second (and fourth) are feedback modules. They reveal to the subject the choices that have been made by other group members.

All communication from other subjects is through the feedback modules and is under complete control through the ICOM master panel. Since the feedback can be controlled, subjects can be told that their initial choices on slides are in complete disagreement, in complete agreement, or in any pattern of agreements and disagreements. When subjects are told that their initial choices are in disagreement, acceptance of influence can be measured directly as the proportion of times a subject makes a final choice that is different from his initial choice. The acceptance of influence measure has been extremely important in expectation theory research, and because of this history, it is adopted for these studies. At present, it is important to note that use of the ICOM permits the researcher freedom to choose any pattern of agreements or disagreements for each subject, depending on the conditions called for by the version of the theory under test.

Beyond simple control of feedback, the ICOM offers an extremely powerful advantage to the researcher: it renders operational and permits control over all the relevant interaction variables in expectation theory. In uncontrolled inter-

Figure A1.3   ICOM subject panels.

action situations, the components of interaction are not independent; thus study of any one or two of them must also take into consideration the effects of the others. For example, using the number of performance outputs made by a subject as a dependent variable must also take into account the number of action opportunities he has been given, for actors are unlikely to make performance outputs when not given action opportunities by others. Similarly, using acceptance of influence as the dependent variable in open interaction situations is difficult, for this component is visible only when disagreements occur. But through use of the ICOM, any of the theoretically relevant components of interaction can be studied, as either the dependent or the independent variable, while holding constant the rest of the components. For example, telling the subjects to push a button indicating a choice on the slide corresponds to the giving of an action opportunity; thus the distribution of action opportunities can be controlled while varying the number and type of performance evaluations.

In an expectation theory experiment, subjects enter the laboratory and are seated at desks separated by dividers concealing each from view of the others. Instructions are read by one of the experimenters, and crucial points are repeated and amplified by the second experimenter. The entire experiment may consist of one or more phases, depending on the nature and extent of the manipulations required. A set of slides is presented in each phase, and subjects are asked to register their judgments on the ICOM. The final phase is generally the data collection phase. At the end of the final phase, each subject is interviewed extensively by one of the experimenters to learn whether experimental conditions for test of the theory are met. Following this he is asked not to discuss the study in detail with friends, the entire study is explained to him, all false information given him is corrected, and he is thanked and paid for his time.

Any experimentation, especially that involving some deception, is likely to be stressful to individuals participating in it. Therefore, every attempt is made to minimize the tension-producing aspects of the experience, and interviewers are trained to become skillful at detecting and alleviating whatever tensions are produced by the experiment. Considerable time and attention are devoted to making certain that no subject leaves the experience with tensions or hostilities directed either toward himself or toward someone else. Explaining the experiment to the subjects is a crucial part of this effort: it is essential that a subject leave the experiment without misconceptions about his experience. Subjects have generally reported after the explanation that they felt the experience was worthwhile for them and that they enjoyed it. In spite of the complete explanations given to subjects, there has been little difficulty with their telling others about it. We feel that this is probably the result of the cooperative orientation of students who have participated in these studies, as well as a reflection of the interviewers' success at explaining the significance of the work.

APPENDIX TWO

THE BASIC SOURCE EXPERIMENT

Each group consisted of two subjects, previously unacquainted with each other. As they arrived at the laboratory, they were greeted by a secretary or by one of the two experimenters and led into the activity room. Subjects were seated at tables with numbers 1 and 2 on them, separated from each other by a curtain that allowed both subjects to see the two experimenters and the slide projection screen, but not each other.

The host experimenter introduced herself as "Dr. Gordon" and read the experimental procedures to the subjects. The experiment was described as a two-part study in individual and group problem solving. In the first part, each of the subjects in the activity room was to make choices about a series of 20 Contrast Sensitivity slides. As each judgment was made, it would be communicated to a third student in another room who would evaluate it and would tell each subject whether he thought the answer was correct. It was emphasized that "Person #3 does *not* have an answer key to these slides. However, before he makes his choice for each slide, he will see your choices, and he will evaluate them according to his ability to judge. When he makes his choice, it will be communicated to you on the bottom row of your panels."

The evaluator was described as another student at the same college as the subjects. They were told that he had been scheduled to arrive half an hour before them to permit experimenters to measure his ability at the task. Actually, he existed only as a tape-recorded voice, supposedly coming from a person in another room in the laboratory. This procedure was quite believable for subjects, and use of the tape recording meant that neither subject actually saw the evaluator; hence they could not form any impressions (or expectations) of him on the basis of visual cues. Previous work in expectation theory has shown that in the simplified environment of the laboratory, subjects sometimes form performance expectations for each other based on very slight distinguishing characteristics, or even on inferences from misperceptions of appearance and manner.

Subjects were then shown a sample of the two-pattern Contrast Sensitivity slides and were told that their judgments would reflect the level of ability they

174

possessed at a task called Contrast Sensitivity. The task was described as "the ability to distinguish contrasts between figures or objects," and subjects were advised that people vary widely on the levels of their ability to make accurate judgments on the slides. The intent of this instruction was to define a new task and an associated ability with which all subjects would be unfamiliar; therefore, they would be unlikely to have any expectations for their own performances on this task. Postexperimental interviews confirm that this manipulation was successful.

After the task was described and the method of indicating choices on the ICOM was explained, the second experimenter described a set of "national standards" for the task. A score of 11 to 15 correct out of 20 was described as being a "usual, or average score"; 16 to 20 correct was "rare, and clearly indicates a superior individual performance"; and 0 to 10 correct was "also rare, but indicates a poor individual performance."

After making certain that subjects understood the task and the standards, the second experimenter left the room, ostensibly to determine whether the evaluator had finished having his ability measured. A few minutes later, this tape recording of the second experimenter's voice was played through the intercom into the activity room:

EXPERIMENTER: Pardon me, Dr. Gordon. (Pause.) Person #3 has finished the first set of slides. Out of the 20 slides, he got a total of (8 or 17) correct, and (12 or 3) incorrect. (Pause.) This is an unusual score and would fall into the (*lower* or *upper*) category for an individual performance.

This constituted the LE–HE manipulation. Then the host experimenter presented subjects with the first set of slides. After viewing a slide for 5 seconds, each subject indicated his choice by pressing the appropriate button on the "final choice" row of his panel. This act gave each subject an action opportunity which he had to accept and induced him to make a performance output. After another 5-second delay during which time person #3 was presumably studying the slide along with both subjects' answers, a light appeared on each subject's panel beside the words "#3's choice." This indicated that the evaluator had made a unit evaluation of each subject's performance output. Person #3 sent one of the subjects 17 out of 20 positive unit evaluations; he sent the other subject 9 out of 20 positive evaluations.

After the series of slides the second tape recording was played over the intercom:

EXPERIMENTER: Person #3, how many of the slides did you think person #1 gave the correct answer to?

NUMBER 3:   Number 1? I think he got 17 out of 20.

EXPERIMENTER: And #2?

NUMBER 3:   Uh, 9 out of 20.

This constituted the $(+-)$ or $(-+)$ manipulation. At this point, *if a subject has accepted person #3 as a source*, the theory predicts that he is very likely to hold an expectation state for himself and the other subject that is congruent with #3's evaluations. The theory also predicts that acceptance of #3 as a source will depend on the expectations held for him; that is, on the effect of the LE–HE manipulation.

The recording used for the expectation condition manipulation was the same whether person #3 was described as having low ability or high ability. Therefore, treatment of subjects was uniform across conditions with respect to the words and voice used. That is, the tone and "confidence" of the voice were the same, whether a subject had been told that he possessed high or low ability.

Person #3 was then thanked for his participation and told that the other experimenter would talk with him. This ended #3's role in the experiment. Following this, a short questionnaire was distributed to assess success of the attempted manipulations.

Data for test of the theoretical derivations were gathered in phase II of the experiment. This time, the host experimenter explained, both subjects would work on another series of slides together, "as a team." Each would make an initial choice, would see the other's initial choice, would have 5 more seconds to restudy the slide and to reconsider his initial choice, and would make a private final choice. Initial choices were to be solely for the purpose of exchanging information, to help one's partner to get the best possible final choice. Only final choices were to contribute to the "team score" in the second phase of the study. The intent of this manipulation was to produce the collective-orientation condition required by the theory.

Since initial choice feedback was under control of the experimenter, subjects were told that they disagreed with each other on 20 out of the 23 trials in phase II. Agreements were interspersed after each block of five disagreement trials; that is, on trials 6, 12, and 18. The agreement trials were included to help to alleviate suspicion that the feedback was not veridical and also to help to decrease the tension associated with being forced to resolve continuous disagreements. The proportion of times that subjects in each condition resolved disagreements in favor of themselves on the critical trials, called $P(s)$, was then computed as the measure of *rejecting* influence. This measure constitutes the major dependent variable of the experiment and reflects the abstract theoretical concept "rejection of influence in case of disagreement."

Following the disagreement trials phase, each subject again filled out a simple questionnaire, whereupon he was interviewed alone by one of the experimenters in a two-part session. In the first part, questions are asked to ascertain whether the scope conditions and the antecedent conditions of the theory had been met for that particular subject. For example, if a subject did not accept the definition of the situation as one in which he must consider his partner's initial choice before making his own final choice, the collective-orientation condition was not met. Data from subjects who do not meet the scope conditions required by the theory have no meaning in terms of testing the theory and are excluded from analyses. The second part of the interview is a complete explanation of the study to the subject. The interviewer corrects all false information given during the study—for example, the fact that the disagreements were not real—and explains the reasons for it. Any further questions a subject may have are answered. His cooperation is requested in not discussing the study in detail with friends who might participate in the future, and he is thanked for his help and paid for his time.

APPENDIX THREE

INCLUSION OF SUBJECTS

Not every subject in the sample will meet the conditions required for an adequate test of the theory. Therefore we must exclude from analysis data from subjects who do not meet one or more of the fixed initial conditions of the theory as given in the definition of situation S. For example, since the scope conditions say the theory is intended to apply only to subjects who are task oriented, the theory has no predictions to make for the behavior of a subject who was not task oriented, and his data should be eliminated from the analysis.

The decision to exclude a given subject's data cannot always be made with certainty that the exclusion will not bias results in favor of the theory's predictions. As a guiding principle, the burden of proof lies with showing cause why data from a particular subject should be *excluded* rather than included. This "general error rule" was followed in selection of data for the analyses presented here.

Two more specific rules were also applied to the data from this experiment. (1) Every subject's data were to be included unless a definite reason, decided on before the experiment was begun, could be cited for exclusion. This prevented removing a subject's data on more intuitive grounds, such as his having given an unusual pattern of answers to interview questions. (2) Exclusion required the subject's report of *thoughts* that would remove him from the conditions of the theory, as well as his report of having *come to a definite conclusion* during the course of the experiment *and then acting* in a way congruent with his belief. Thus a subject who reported doubting the existence of the evaluator would not be excluded unless he also reported definitely deciding that the evaluator was an arrangement of the experimenters *and* had thus ignored the unit evaluations in phase I of the experiment. This second rule implied that the several subjects who reported doubts about the arrangements of the experiment—who "thought something was funny" about the disagreements, for example—were to be included.

Specific reasons for exclusion are the following. (1) Clear and definite suspicion about a crucial part of the experiment: disbelief that the evaluator's "score" represented his ability, disbelief that the evaluations in phase I truly represented his opinion of the subjects' answers, or disbelief that the disagree-ments in phase II truly represented the other person's initial choices. (2) Failure of task orientation; that is, absence of motivation to get the correct answer to the slides. (3) Failure of collective orientation; that is, failure to accept the situation as one in which cooperation with one's partner in getting the answers was legitimate and necessary. (4) Gross failure to understand the situation or the experimental instructions. These criteria for exclusion are used for all experiments reported.

It is inappropriate to use experimental data as criteria for exclusion. Hence two sources of information are available to experimenters to use for judging whether a subject did indeed meet the necessary theoretical conditions. The first source is the questionnaires, which were distributed at the end of each phase of the experiment. They contain questions designed to elicit information about whether subjects believed the score assigned to the evaluator, how accurately they thought the evaluator had judged the subjects' answers, and whether subjects were collectively oriented and task oriented during the experiment. Although the questionnaire might at first appear to offer information that is independent of the interviewer's subjective judgment, it seldom proves to be a reliable indicator of subjects' evaluations and beliefs. Individuals are often self-contradictory on parallel questions (those which ask essentially the same thing), and during the interview they occasionally report misunderstanding the questionnaire items. Also, at times it is quite clear that a modesty norm or a degree of annoyance at the experimenter or at the other subject acted to inhibit subjects' making differential ability evaluations in the questionnaire, and these differential evaluations are critical to testing predictions from the theory. Therefore the regular use made of the questionnaire data was to furnish a starting point for questions in the interview, and the interview was to provide the information needed to make the inclusion–exclusion decision.

The interview consists both of standard questions designed to help us ascertain whether the scope conditions of the theory had been met and questions prompted by unusual questionnaire or interview responses. Again, the problem of contradictory answers occasionally arises, but having standardized, previously chosen criterion questions works to prevent this from becoming a major source of uncertainty. Because of the strictness of criteria required to exclude a subject's data from analysis and the small number of exclusions, it is extremely doubtful that subjects whose data would constitute legitimate disconfirmation of the theory were excluded.

Besides those subjects excluded by criteria given above, some are usually classified as being "person oriented." A subject was classified as person oriented if he reported that during the disagreement trials he frequently refused to consider his partner's initial choice in making his final choice.

Person-oriented subjects constitute a failure of collective orientation because they are not willing to consider their partner's initial choice before making their own final choice. Person orientation also may be considered as the failure of the major rule of correspondence in design of these experiments; namely, that observing the proportion of times an individual makes the same final choice as initial choice is a good measure of his willingness to accept influence. We probably would want to conclude that a person-oriented subject had accepted influence on trials in which he thought he was wrong (i.e., his evaluation of the initial choice was influenced), but he refused to make the behavioral acknowledgment by pushing a different button for his final choice.

Person-oriented subjects frequently rationalize their behavior with some version of the statements, "I like to make my own decisions" or "I don't like to let other people influence me." These are both very normative statements in our culture, especially for our subjects' age group and the historical period of these studies. Because statements similar to these are frequently expressed by other subjects who, on the basis of other criteria, are not subsequently classified as person oriented, the classification depends to a certain extent on the interviewer's subjective judgment. Since it is impossible to classify this type of failure of collective orientation with certainty, and because of contradictions of these subjects on exclusion criterion questions, person-oriented subjects were retained in the sample for most analyses of the data.

BIBLIOGRAPHY

Backman, C., P. Secord, and J. Peirce

1963   "Resistance to change in the self-concept as a function of consensus among significant others." *Sociometry* **26** (March): 102–111.

Berger, J., B. P. Cohen, and M. Zelditch, Jr.

1972   "Status characteristics and social interaction." *American Sociological Review* **37** (June): 241–255.

Berger, J., and T. L. Conner

1969   "Performance expectations and behavior in small groups." *Acta Sociologica* **12**: 186–197.

Berger, J., T. L. Conner, and M. H. Fisek, Eds.

1974   *Expectation States Theory: A Theoretical Research Program.* Cambridge. Winthrop Publishers, Inc.

Berger, J., T. L. Conner, and W. L. McKeown

1969   "Evaluations and the formation and maintenance of performance expectations." *Human Relations* **22** (December):481–502.

Berger, J., T. L. Conner, and M. H. Fisek

1973   "A generalization of the status characteristics and expectation states theory." Chapter 6 in Berger, J., T. L. Conner, and M. H. Fisek, Eds. Cambridge: Winthrop Publishers, Inc., 1974:163–207.

Berger, J., and M. H. Fisek

1969   "The structure of the extended theory of status characteristics and expectation states." Paper read at Small Groups Conference, Pacific Sociological Association Meetings.

1970   "Consistent and inconsistent status characteristics and the determination of power and prestige orders." *Sociometry* **33** (September):278–304.

Berger, J., M. Zelditch, B. Anderson, and B. P. Cohen

1970   "Status conditions of self-evaluation." Technical Report No. 27, Laboratory for Social Research, Stanford University, Stanford, Calif.

Camilleri, S. F., and J. Berger

1967   "Decision-making and social influence: A model and experimental test." *Sociometry* **30** (December):365–378.

Camilleri, S. F., J. Berger, and T. L. Conner

1972   "A formal theory of decision-making." Chapter 2, in Berger, J., M. Zelditch, Jr., and B. Anderson, Eds. *Sociological Theories in Progress*, Vol. 2. Boston: Houghton Mifflin Co., pp. 21–37.

Cartwright, D., and F. Harary

    1956   "Structural balance: a generalization of Heider's theory." *Psychological Review*
            63 (September):277–293.

Cohen, B. P., J. Berger, and M. Zelditch, Jr.

    N.D.   "Status conceptions and power and prestige." Unpublished manuscript.
            Stanford, Calif.

Cohen, E. G.

    1972   "Interracial interaction disability." *Human Relations* **25**:9–24.

Cohen, E. G., and S. Roper

    1972   "Modification of interracial interaction disability: An application of status
            characteristics theory." *American Sociological Review* **37**:643–657.

Cooley, C. H.

    1964   *Human Nature and the Social Order*. New York:Schocken Books, Inc. First
            published in 1902 by Scribners. Page references are from 1964 edition.

Coopersmith, S.

    1967   *Antecedents of Self Esteem*. San Francisco:W. H. Freeman.

Couch, C. J.

    1958   "Self attitudes and degree of agreement with immediate others." *American
            Journal of Sociology* **63** (March):491–496.

Freese, L.

    1969   "The generalization of specific performance expectations." Ph.D. dissertation.
            Stanford, Calif.

Freese, L., and B. P. Cohen

    1973   "Eliminating status generalization." *Sociometry* **36** (June):177–193.

Goffman, Erving

    1959   *The Presentation of Self in Everyday Life*. Garden City, N.Y.:Doubleday Co.

Haas, H. I., and M. L. Maehr

    1965   "Two experiments on the concept of self and the reaction of others." *Journal
            of Personality and Social Psychology* **1** (January):100–105.

Hall, C. S., and G. Lindzey

    1957   *Theories of Personality*. New York:John Wiley and Sons, Inc.

Heider, Fritz

    1944   "Social perception and phenomenal causality." *Psychological Review* **51** (No-
            vember):358–374.

Heiss, J., and S. Owens

1972   "Self-evaluation of blacks and whites." *American Journal of Sociology* **78**:360–370.

Israel, J.

1956   *Self-Evaluation and Rejection in Groups*. Stockholm:Almqvist and Wiksell.

James, William

1890   *Principles of Psychology*, Vol. 1. Henry Holt. Reprinted from *Psychology* by William James. New York:Fawcett Publications, Inc., 1963. Page numbers are from 1890 edition.

Jones, S. C.

1966   "Some determinants of interpersonal evaluating behavior." *Journal of Personality and Social Psychology* **3** (April):397–403.

1968   "Some effects of interpersonal evaluations on group process and social perception." *Sociometry* **31** (June):150–161.

Jones, S. C., and H. A. Pines

1968   "Self-revealing events and interpersonal evaluations." *Journal of Personality and Social Psychology* **3** (March).277–281.

Jones, S. C., and C. Ratner

1967   "Commitment to self-appraisal and interpersonal evaluations." *Journal of Personality and Social Psychology* **6** (August):442–447.

Jones, S. C., and D. J. Schneider

1968   "Certainty of self-appraisal and reactions to evaluations from others." *Sociometry* **31** (December):395–403.

Katz, I., E. Epps, and L. Axelson

1964   "Effect upon Negro digit-symbol performance of anticipated comparison with whites and other Negroes." *Journal of Abnormal and Social Psychology* **69**:77–83.

Katz, I., J. Goldston, and L. Benjamin

1958   "Behavior and productivity in biracial work groups." *Human Relations* **11**:123–141.

Kuhn, T.

1962   *The Structure of Scientific Revolutions*. Chicago:University of Chicago Press.

McCarthy, J., and W. Yancey

1971   "Uncle Tom and Mr. Charlie: Metaphysical pathos in the study of racism and personal disorganization." *American Journal of Sociology* **76**:648–672.

Maehr, M. L., J. Mensing, and S. Nafzger

1962   "Concept of self and the reaction of others." *Sociometry* **25** (December):353–357.

Mead, George H.

    1934   *Mind, Self and Society.* Chicago:University of Chicago Press.

Miyamoto, S. F., and S. M. Dornbusch

    1956   "A test of interactionist hypotheses of self-conception." *American Journal of Sociology* **41** (March):399–403.

Moore, J. C.

    1964   "A further test of interactionist hypotheses of self-conception." Technical Report No. 6, Laboratory for Social Research, Stanford University, Stanford, Calif.

    1968   "Status and influence in small groups interactions." *Sociometry* **31** (March): 47–63.

Newcomb, T. M.

    1953   "An approach to the study of communicative acts." *Psychological Review* **60** (November):393–404.

    1956   "The prediction of interpersonal attraction." *American Psychologist* **11** (November):575–586.

Reeder, L. G., G. A. Donohue, and A. Biblarz

    1960   "Conceptions of self and others." *American Journal of Sociology* **66** (September): 153–159.

Rogers, Carl

    1951   *Studies in Client-Centered Psychotherapy.* Washington, D.C.:Psychological Service Center Press.

Rosenberg, M.

    1965   *Society and the Adolescent Self-Image.* Princeton, N.J.:Princeton University Press.

Savage, I. R., and M. Webster

    1971   "Source of evaluations reformulated and analyzed." *Proceedings of the Sixth Berkeley Symposium on Mathematical Statistics and Probability* Vol. 4. Berkeley: University of California Press, pp. 137–141.

Secord, P. F., and C. W. Backman

    1961   "Personality theory and the problem of stability and change in individual behavior: An interpersonal approach." *Psychological Review* **68** (January):21–32.

Segal, David, M. Segal, and D. Knoke

    1970   "Status inconsistency and self-evaluation." *Sociometry* **33** (September):347–357.

Siegel, S.

    1956   *Nonparametric Statistics.* New York:McGraw-Hill Book Company, Inc.

Skinner, B. F.

    1971   *Beyond Freedom and Dignity.* New York:Alfred A. Knopf.

Sullivan, H. S.

1947   *Conceptions of Modern Psychiatry.* Washington, D.C.: W. H. White Psychiatric Foundation.

Videbeck, R.

1960   "Self-conceptions and the reactions of others." *Sociometry* **23** (December): 351–359.

Webster, M., L. Roberts, and B. Sobieszek

1972   "Accepting significant others: Six models." *American Journal of Sociology* **78** (November):576–598.

Yancey, W., L. Rigsby, and J. McCarthy

1972   "Social position and self-evaluation: The relative importance of race." *American Journal of Sociology* **78**:338–359.

Zetterberg, H. I.

1957   "Compliant actions." *Acta Sociologica* **2**(No. 4):179–201.
1966   "On motivation." Reprinted in Berger, J., M. Zelditch, Jr., and B. Anderson, Eds., *Sociological Theories in Progress*, Vol. 1. Boston: Houghton Mifflin Co., pp. 124–141. From Hans L. Zetterberg, *Sociology in a New Key*, Totowa, N.J.: Bedminster Press.

INDEX

A

Action opportunity, definition
   of, 32
Anderson, B., xv
Attribution, 133

B

Backman, C.P., 22, 44-45, 149,
   153
Balance diagrams, description
   of, 45
Bales group, 31
Behaviorism, 2, 9-11, 131
Berger, J., ix-x, xv, 30-31,
   80, 82, 87, 94, 165
Bobrow, S.B., xv
Burden of proof, 80-81

C

Camilleri, S.F., x, 38, 54,
   85-86, 112, 142
Cartwright, D., 45
Cohen, B.P., 81
Cohen, E.G., viii, 165
Collective orientation, def-
   inition of, 31, 34
Conner, T.L., x
Contrast Sensitivity, 167-170,
   174-175
Cooley, C.H., ix-x, 2-3, 8-9,
   13, 15
Coopersmith, S., viii-ix, xii
Couch, C.J., 21-22

D

Deception experimentation,
   173
Dornbusch, S.M., x-xi, 15-18,
   22

E

Entwisle, D., xv
Expectation states, 30-37
 and self-evaluation, 39-42
 formation of, 39-40
 basic experiement, 37, 167-
   173

F

Festinger, L., 132
Fisek, M.H., xv, 82, 87, 165
Freese, L., 81, 87
Freud, S., 1

G

Game, 10
Goffman, E., viii, 2
Grafstein, D., xv

H

Haas, H.I., 23-24

187